Hannah Arendt and the Limits of Philosophy

Dear Karyn & Eric!
I am happy to think
of this book on your
distinguished bookshelf.
Thank you for a beautiful
weekend in New York.
Love, Liz
Dec 1996

Hannah Arendt and the Limits of Philosophy

∎

With a New Preface

Lisa Jane Disch

Cornell University Press

Ithaca and London

First published 1994 by Cornell University Press.
First printing, Cornell Paperbacks, 1996.

⊛ The paper in this book meets the minimum requirements of the American National Standard for Information Sciences—Permanence of Paper for Printed Library Materials, ANSI Z39.48-1984.

Library of Congress Cataloging-in-Publication Data

Disch, Lisa Jane.
    Hannah Arendt and the limits of philosophy / Lisa Jane Disch.
        p.   cm.
    Includes bibliographical references and index.
    ISBN 0-8014-3013-5 (cloth : alk. paper).—ISBN 0-8014-8378-6 (pbk : alk. paper)
    1. Arendt, Hannah—Contributions in political science.
    2. Political science—Philosophy.   3.   Democracy.   4. Feminist
    theory.   I. Title.
    JC251.A744D57   1996   96-16196
    320.5′092—dc20

For my mother's friend, Betty Brackett

Contents

I∎

Preface to the Paperback Edition

▮

In 1994, one year before the fiftieth anniversary of the Allied victory in World War II, the curators of the Smithsonian Institution announced plans for an exhibit at the National Air and Space Museum. Though their proposal was neither behind the times nor too late, it must nonetheless be deemed untimely. It would have installed the newly restored fuselage of the Enola Gay, the plane that dropped the first atomic bomb on the Japanese city of Hiroshima, in time to commemorate the Pacific Victory. Understanding that relics of the past speak neither for themselves nor unambiguously, the curators planned to display the artifact with an interpretive script that would distill current academic debates into text-bites for easy assimilation by the itinerant museum reader.

The script placed the Enola Gay at the focal point of two irreconcilable but simultaneously valid historical narratives: at once the crowning achievement of applied nuclear physics and the inciting moment of Cold War uncertainty regarding the technologies of warfare. The restored relic would mark a disjuncture, an instant that brought an age of confidence in progress to a close and initiated an age of skepticism. In effect, the proposed exhibit broke faith with the typically modern consciousness of time as what Jürgen Habermas calls "a scarce resource for the mastery of problems,"[1] as well as with its optimistic narrative of history as the unfolding of progress toward peace.

---

1. Jürgen Habermas, *The Philosophical Discourse of Modernity,* trans. Frederick Lawrence (Cambridge: MIT Press, 1990), 6.

It is not surprising that World War II veterans protested the exhibit as an insult to their achievement and a betrayal of the American spirit. Nonetheless, by insisting that, as the principal actors, it was their prerogative to tell the story of that event, they abrogated the very debt to the past that they professed to honor. As Hannah Arendt writes: "Action reveals itself fully only to the storyteller, that is, to the backward glance of the historian, who indeed always knows better what it was all about than the participants. All accounts told by the actors themselves, though they may in rare cases give an entirely trustworthy statement of intentions, aims, and motives, become mere useful source material in the historian's hands and can never match his story in significance and truthfulness" (HC, 192). Such claims cast doubt on the widely held belief that "intentions, aims, and motives" are the original sources of action and the means by which it is judged; these claims have put Arendt at the center of contemporary academic controversies about agency and responsibility. Like the Enola Gay proposal with its juxtaposition of discontinuous narratives, Hannah Arendt's work also challenges the time-consciousness of modernity together with the regimen of action as problem solving that it implies.

It is as serious for a political theorist to question these tenets as it is for a museum curator to tarnish the memory of a revered relic. Many scholars regard political theory as a commemorative inquiry that is, like a national museum, deeply implicated in redeeming the emancipatory promise of modernity. Of the charges that Arendt's impieties typically evoke, one interests me especially because of the company to which it assigns her. This is the judgment that Arendt was a "political existentialist" who propounded an "aesthetic" or "theatrical" ideal of politics, unfettered by purpose and indifferent to ethical considerations, an ideal that is inimical to democracy. The claim marks Arendt as German in a particularly deprecating way, implying that, despite her emigration to the United States, she failed to emancipate herself from the conservative populist heritage of German romanticism and from her teacher, Martin Heidegger.

In their own way, such scholarly insinuations about Arendt's allegiances are no less vulgar than the gossiping that was stimulated by the revelation, in 1982, of the prewar affair. Implicitly accusing Arendt of collaborating with the enemy, these interpretations insidiously recapitulate the essentialist designations that German Nazis used to disown and disenfranchise the German-Jewish population. In effect, they decide the question of an identity that was conditioned by the traditions of German humanism, secular Judaism, totalitarian terror, and American democracy just as unimaginatively as do those who would sum up her life story in a single demand: How could the Jewish philosopher have fallen in love with the *Rektor-Führer*?

The charge that Arendt reduces politics to spectacular display is all the more curious in that it takes its bearings from a line of argument that other scholars have interpreted as a distinctive critique of liberal democracy. Contrary to the privatist axiom that democratic political order is founded on private self-interest, Arendt asserted that the self is an exclusively public phenomenon that only action can disclose. She regarded self-disclosure as a lost legacy of a distinctly American political freedom and, inspired by the civil rights, free speech, and anti-war movements that erupted in her lifetime, tried to revive that legacy in the present. The passion for self-disclosure that some scholars interpret as Arendt's nostalgia for her lost homeland, others regard as a pariah's praise for the country in which she so happily spent her exile.

In this book, I contend that scholars who charge Arendt with reducing politics to a spectacle staged for its own sake have not taken seriously her reluctance to endorse the time-consciousness of modernity or its narrative of progress. Expecting her to conceive politics as collective activity oriented toward problem solving, they interpret her concern to emphasize the "revelatory character" of action as an obsession with self-aggrandizement (HC, 178). Expecting her to practice political theory as a timely enterprise that pushes the emancipatory movement of modernity forward, these critics also dismiss the centrality of storytelling to Arendt's work.

Arendt held that storytelling, not explanation, is the work of the political theorist. This follows from her insistence on the uniquely public character of action and of the self that action discloses. Arendt argued that actions cannot be explained because they are not reducible to the motives, goals, and intents of those who carry them out. Whereas action discloses "who" we are, that "who" bears no necessary correspondence to the one who I think I am, who I intend, aspire, or even *agree* to be. As Arendt puts it, "nobody is the author or producer of his own life story" (HC, 184). In the contractual idiom of liberalism, individuals may initiate action but they cannot authorize it.

Although they would likely refuse the parallel, scholars who take this conception of action to aestheticize politics are like the veterans and others who supported the censorship of the proposed Enola Gay exhibit. So urgent is the desire to possess time as a resource for solving problems, that all resist Arendt's insight that actors forever initiate events that they cannot and would not author. Although it is unlikely that the Smithsonian curators consulted the works of Hannah Arendt in planning the Enola Gay exhibit, she identified their working premise. They produced a text that no American actor would or could author. They also configured the exhibit to frustrate the reconciliatory power of narrative, using the gallery space to put discontinuous and competing stories into play and leave them unreconciled.

The title of the exhibit announces its purpose from the start, "The Crossroads: The End of World War II, the Atomic Bomb, and the Origins of the Cold War." The curators put the "crossroads" theme into effect by proposing to display the fuselage at the junction of abruptly discontinuous hallways. The exhibition in the first, leading up to the fuselage, was to begin with a meticulously even-handed account of Japanese and United States aggressions, and to culminate with the bombings of Hiroshima and Nagasaki. Despite all efforts at dispassionate narration, the text of this section slipped into an adventure screenplay. It featured scientists figuring out how to harness the power of the universe, military strategists figuring out how to deploy it, and recruits, initially reluctant and bewildered, training to be the daredevils of the "first ordnance squadron" without knowing what they were doing.

Whereas the narrative of the first galleries would have concluded with the successful completion of the bombings, the second was to begin out of sync. Mementos on loan from the peace museums of Hiroshima and Nagasaki would retell the moment of the first impact from "Ground Zero." Visitors would proceed at a turn from the restored fuselage to encounter the shattered faces of two wristwatches, a clock frozen on the moment of impact in Hiroshima, stills and videos of the disfigured survivors of the blast, and the lunch box of the Hiroshima high school girl whose remains were never found but whose repast was eerily preserved. Installed at the meeting place of these discontinuous chronologies, the Enola Gay would have been a bright and shiny reminder that America could not reach this pinnacle of modern know-how, the telos of history, without stopping time for the vanquished.

In light of the celebratory tenor of most of the officially sponsored commemorations, it is not so surprising that World War II veterans, members of Congress, and even the putatively liberal press received the proposed exhibit as an affront to what its head curator would later call an "article of national faith," the conviction that dropping the bomb had saved millions of lives.[2] Although questioning this tenet had become commonplace among academics, intellectuals, and even the general public, the Smithsonian proposal went beyond questioning to commit what many regarded as secular blasphemy.

It was one thing for the American public to entertain its doubts about the bombing on the fiftieth anniversary of the war. Seeing these doubts exhibited at the National Air and Space Museum, the most popular of the Smithsonian's sixteen federally funded attractions, was a different matter altogether. Traditionally understood, museum space is monumental space. It produces national identity seamlessly and palpably by displaying images and artifacts from the past in such a way as to settle the uncertainties that victory inevitably engenders about the privileges of membership. Tranquil space, it affords its visitors a self-assurance born of recognizing oneself in what Henri Lefebvre calls "a collective mirror more faithful than any personal one."[3] Smithsonian Secretary Dr. Michael Heyman acceded to this view when he announced that the proposed script would be withdrawn in favor of "one every American can be proud of."[4]

2. Tom Crouch, testifying in May 1995 to the Senate Committee on Rules and Administration, as quoted in Philip Nobile, ed., *Judgment at the Smithsonian* (New York: Marlowe, 1995), xv.

3. Henri Lefebvre, *The Production of Space,* trans. Donald Nicholson Smith (Cambridge: Basil Blackwell, 1991), 220.

4. Quoted in Paul Goldberger, "Historical Shows on Trial: Who Judges?" *New York Times,* February 11, 1996, sec. 2, pp. 1, 26. See also Tom Engelhardt, "Fifty Years under a Cloud: The Uneasy Search for Our Atomic History," *Harper's Magazine* 292 (Jan. 1996).

In the end, the curators mounted the exhibit that the veterans claimed to have wanted. Ground Zero was expunged from the text. The fuselage became its own point of reference, displayed with an entourage of its own spare parts and interpreted by a new script that detailed its restoration process. A single placard represented the war's end in the most reassuring terms, explaining that "the use of the bombs led to the immediate surrender of Japan and made unnecessary the planned invasion of the Japanese home lands . . . [that] would have led to very heavy casualties among American and Allied troops and Japanese civilians and military."[5]

Hannah Arendt was, like the curators of the Smithsonian, a storyteller of World War II. The artifact charged to her care, however, was not a machine with an ambivalent legacy of destruction and victory but an emancipatory narrative whose legacy she regarded as no less ambiguous. This story promised that the cultivation of reason would advance critical self-consciousness and democratic self-determination. Like many post–World War II intellectuals, Arendt believed the promise of reason to be horribly betrayed by the organized barbarism of the concentration camps. Thus, her responsibility, as she understood it, was to hand that legacy down in such a way as to question the debt that the contemporary world owes to its emancipatory project. Whereas the Smithsonian curators failed in their attempt to put forward competing stories about modernity, Arendt succeeded. Her work prompts readers to suspect the ideal coupling of time and progress and to question the role that political theorists and public intellectuals have in underwriting that partnership.

Arendt took up storytelling to practice political theory as an untimely pursuit. Following Walter Benjamin, she regarded storytelling as a way for the theorist to deal with events and their consequences during an age when the canons of historiography, discursive argument, and political thought had lost their capacity to put "the past in order" (MDT, 198). In contrast to these more conventional narrative modes, Arendt wrote that storytelling "reveals meaning without committing the error of defining it" (MDT, 105). This is not to say that a story is an immediate and, therefore, authentic account of events but, to the contrary, that the integrity of a

---

5. David E. Sanger, "Enola Gay and Little Boy Exactly Fifty Years Later," *New York Times*, August 6, 1996, sec. 5, p. 3.

story does not stand or fall on whether it succeeds in conveying a message to an audience. As Benjamin put it, in contrast to information, which delivers events "shot through with explanation, . . . it is half the art of storytelling to keep a story free from explanation as one reproduces it."[6] A storyteller leaves it to the audience to assign meaning and thereby to endow the account with an "amplitude" that information lacks for surrendering its value to the current moment. Whereas Benjamin lamented that storytelling had all but ceded its place to information in an age of exigencies, Arendt contended that storytelling would have its place in public life so long as one respected the proper distinctions between acting, which "almost never achieves its purpose" (HC, 184), and "doing" (MDT, 147) or "making," which is evaluated according to its success (HC, 220).

By this distinction between acting and making, Arendt denounced sovereignty as a metaphysical fallacy whose imposition on politics could only reduce action to instrumental calculation. She argued that sovereignty, the ideal of one man who "remains master of his doings from beginning to end," encouraged actors to mistake strength for power (HC, 220). Whereas strength is a "reliable" and calculable entity, power is an immaterial and unquantifiable effect of relationships that are contingent and transitory. It exists, she writes, wherever people agree to be "mutually bound by promises" to a precisely specified, short-term purpose (HC, 245). Promises, in turn, are not founded on universal truth, shared faith, or common identity, but actuated only in concerted speech and action.

By this recourse to promise making, Arendt's work eludes categorization as either modernist or postmodernist. She neither joins in the radical skepticism about collective agreement that is a hallmark of postmodern political thinking nor subscribes to the ideal of discursive rationality that is characteristic of neo-humanist theorists of legitimacy. Instead, Arendt affirms that action, with its "inherent tendency to force open all limitations and cut across all boundaries," necessarily exceeds prior constraint (HC, 190). Because of the unpredictability of action, agreement can neither secure accountability nor ground the distinction between the legitimate exercise of power and the illegitimate imposition of force.

6. Walter Benjamin, *Illuminations,* ed. Hannah Arendt, trans. Harry Zohn (New York: Schocken Books, 1985), 89.

Critics who repudiate Arendt for turning politics into a performing art take their accusation to be justified on this point: Has Arendt not renounced all basis for differentiating between principled democratic action and mob rule? Does she not even go so far as to celebrate illegitimacy as the inevitable price that must be paid for revelatory public spectacles? There is a response to these objections in Arendt's insight that action is initiating events that one cannot author and may even wish to disown.

Despite her contention that action "almost never achieves its purpose," Arendt does not pretend that it is inconsequential. Rather, "it 'produces' stories with or without intention as naturally as fabrication produces tangible things" (HC, 184). Stories are the effects of action; they disclose its principles, but only after the event and never definitively. Principles, then, are not limiting conditions to be warranted in advance of actions and invoked later as measures of legitimacy. Instead, the two are simultaneous: principles are at once "in" action but not comprehended by it and "without" action but not external to it (BPF, 152).

Must principles be anchored in problems? Must actions solve them? Is judgment simply a matter of certifying that an action conformed to decisions taken beforehand? Not for Hannah Arendt, who regards action as purposive but not problem-oriented, and judging, in turn, as repetition without the necessity of reconciliation.

The failed Smithsonian proposal is an exemplar of Arendtian storytelling which acquits her of the charge that by writing against time she fostered skepticism and indifference toward the present. The exhibit would have made Arendt's point that action exceeds all subjective motive and intent by displaying the Enola Gay as the focal point of stories that no single narrator could tell. The curators' initial refusal to display the fuselage as a trophy from the mission that ended the war gave life to Arendt's claim that action cannot be judged by the measure of success. Although they would not embed the relic in a chronology of problem solving, they did not glorify its flight as a risk undertaken for its own sake. Finally, by configuring the exhibit to set irreconcilable narratives into play, they did not arrest judgment but precipitated it.

Acknowledgments

∎

When I was about eight, a teacher at Foster Elementary School in Evanston, Illinois, told me that if you wanted someone to live forever you should make him or her a character in a book. The disappointing thing about writing an academic book is that many of the people who have been important to it do not appear in it as characters. Even so, this book has its cast of characters quite in addition to its central figure, Hannah Arendt. This project did not begin from a disciplinary interest in the limits of philosophy but from the experience of reading Hannah Arendt's writing, to which I was drawn by tastes and commitments I acquired long before graduate school.

Thanks go first to my mom and dad, Elaine and Edward Disch. They raised me with great care and attention to my education, in the broadest sense, which has proven to be an incalculable privilege. This book is dedicated to Betty Brackett because I think her presence in my parents' life had a great deal to do with the place they wanted me to have in this world; this was the best way I could think of to share a piece of this work with them, as they have supported so much of its labor.

For ten years, Benjamin Barber has mentored my intellectual interests and writing. He has also taken care to help me into this profession, beginning with the day he allotted me fifteen minutes in front of a lecture hall full of Rutgers undergraduates to refute what I thought was his outrageously sexist interpretation of *Othello*. Thanks are due also to Carol Gilligan, who convinced me not to write my dissertation on Rous-

seau, and to Gordon Schochet and Susan Carroll, who read my disser-
tation and assured me it would be worth rewriting. This project would
not have taken the direction it did without the two years I spent at the
University of Chicago teaching in the Social Science core or without the
three years I have been affiliated with the Center for Advanced Feminist
Studies at the University of Minnesota. Finally, I thank the professors at
Kenyon College who first taught me to read political theory: Pamela
Jensen, Patrick Coby, Harry Clor, and the late Robert Horwitz.

Composing this book as an assistant professor, enjoying a well-
financed institutional public space for my work, has made a difference.
I consider myself fortunate to have held a tenure-track job during the
writing of this book and to have done so at a university where my
teaching coincides almost perfectly with my research interests and my
course load leaves me time to write. The Graduate School of the University of Minnesota supported this work both with summer research
grants and with a single quarter release from teaching. The Department
of Political Science funded a work-study student to help with the details
of its final production and subsidized the costs of printing and copying
various drafts. A summer stipend from the National Endowment for the
Humanities also supported its composition. I thank the Faculty Research
Office of the Graduate School at University of Minnesota for their advice
on preparing the NEH application. My colleague Ellen Messer-Davidow
was exceptionally generous in helping me to write the proposal.

The graduate seminar room is another space that this job has opened
for me, and the graduate students with whom I have worked at Minnesota have contributed to my intellectual development. I have also ben-
efited greatly by working on *Signs*, collaborating with Mary Jo Kane,
conversing with Naomi Scheman, and attending the semi-regular meetings of the Wednesday evening reading group with Thomas Atchison,
Susan Heineman, Kathleen Fluegel, Jeremy Iggers, Rhonda Leibel, and
Ronald Salzberger. For reading and responding to various pieces of this
project, I thank Evelyn Davidheiser, Raymond Duvall, James Farr,
Lawrence Jacobs, Daniel Kelliher, W. Phillips Shively, Kathryn Sikkink,
Tracy Strong, David Sylvan, and Robert Taylor. Richard Flathman and
Joan Cocks were the first people to read this work cover to cover, and
their comments improved the final version. I thank Roger Haydon for

asking them to read it and for being a kind and constructive editor. For assistance in the production stages of this book, I thank James Smith, Marie Schorp, and, at Cornell University Press, Joanne Hindman, Carol Betsch, and Mary Lash. For their work on the preface, I am grateful to Roger Haydon and the invincible women's writing group: Jean O'Brien, Jennifer Pierce, and Kathleen Fluegel.

Parts of Chapters 4 and 5 have already appeared as "More Truth than Fact: Storytelling as Critical Understanding in the Writings of Hannah Arendt," *Political Theory* 21 (1993), 665–694, copyright © 1993 by Sage Publications, Inc., and reprinted by permission.

The last word rightfully belongs to the friends who have helped me be at home in this world, one of the themes in Arendt's work that made me want to write about her. I thank Siobhan Moroney and Francis Greene for our ongoing conversations about political theory, the profession, and the latest films. Thanks to Greg McAvoy for homemade bread and pasta and to Susan Bickford for extending her friendship to me and for reading parts of this work as its friend. And to Steven Gerencser, whose confidence, patience, and optimism have made it easy for me to find both solitude and companionship: this must be the place!

L. J. D.

Abbreviations

∎

Hannah Arendt

"A"   "Action and the Pursuit of Happiness," lecture delivered at the American Political Science Association, 1960, Library of Congress, MSS Box 61, 1.

BPF   *Between Past and Future.* Enlarged ed. New York: Penguin, 1977.

HC   *The Human Condition.* Chicago: University of Chicago Press, 1958.

"IH"   "The Image of Hell," *Commentary* 2 (1946): 291–295.

JP   *The Jew as Pariah: Jewish Identity and Politics in the Modern Age.* Ed. Ron H. Feldman. New York: Random House, 1978.

"JP"   "The Jew as Pariah: A Hidden Tradition," *Jewish Social Studies* 6 (1944): 99–122.

LKPP   *Lectures on Kant's Political Philosophy.* Ed. Ronald Beiner. Chicago: University of Chicago Press, 1982.

LM   *The Life of the Mind.* 1 vol. Ed. Mary McCarthy. New York: Harcourt Brace Jovanovich, 1978.

MDT   *Men in Dark Times.* New York: Harcourt Brace Jovanovich, 1968.

OT   *The Origins of Totalitarianism.* 1 vol. New York: Harcourt Brace Jovanovich, 1979.

OV   *On Violence.* New York: Harcourt Brace Jovanovich, 1969.

"R"   "A Reply [to Eric Voegelin's Review of *The Origins of Totalitarianism*]," *Review of Politics* 15 (1953): 76–84.

RV   *Rahel Varnhagen: The Life of a Jewish Woman.* Trans. Richard Winston and Clara Winston. New York: Harcourt Brace Jovanovich, 1974.

"SST" "Social Science Techniques and the Study of Concentration Camps," *Jewish Social Studies* 12 (1950): 49–64.

Hannah Arendt/Karl Jaspers

C   *Correspondence: 1926–1969.* Ed. Lotte Kohler and Hans Saner. Trans. Robert Kimber and Rita Kimber. New York: Harcourt Brace Jovanovich, 1992.

Immanuel Kant

CJ   *Critique of Judgement.* Trans. J. H. Bernard. New York: Hafner Press, 1951.

1 Introduction:
Storytelling and the Archimedean Ideal

I∎

Since the mid-1980s, it has become increasingly common to claim to do
theory by telling stories. References to narrative and storytelling have become an almost obligatory gesture for theorists who defy the academic
norm of detached writing and refuse the privileged position of impartiality to which such writing implicitly lays claim. References to storytelling are an admission that any theorist writes not from an Archimedean
standpoint but from a specific location that affords only a partial perspective on his or her society. Roughly thirty years before it became fash-
ionable to do so, Hannah Arendt told an audience at the American
Political Science Association that "no matter how abstract our theories
may sound or how consistent our arguments may appear, there are incidents and stories behind them which, at least for ourselves, contain as
in a nutshell the full meaning of whatever we have to say" ("A," 1). What
does it mean to assign "full meaning" to stories? By making such a claim,
does Arendt depict critical understanding as a kind of intuition, celebrating the immediacy of experience over abstract theory? If, instead, she
understands a story to be a reconstruction of experience, then what justifies the claim that stories offer critical insight?

   In this book I use the political thought of Hannah Arendt to break
out of an impasse that exists among contemporary theorists regarding
the possibility of critical understanding and its relationship to experience. Storytelling marks this impasse: it is heralded with equal confidence by humanist critics of modernity who claim to speak from the

experience of marginality and by poststructuralist critics of humanism who claim to discredit experience as a ground for critical understanding. Arendt's conception of storytelling makes an innovative contribution to this debate because she identifies it neither as a vehicle for the authentic critical voice of the oppressed nor as a means by which endlessly to postpone the authoritative moment that is necessary to criticism and to action. Rather, she calls storytelling the way one trains the imagination to "go visiting"(LKPP, 43). The visiting metaphor casts critical understanding as a process, not a designated location, and advances a conception of judgment that is situated but not standpoint-bound.

By stories, Arendt meant everything from the casual anecdotes told by friends over dinner or by parents to children, to novels and short stories, to the narratives and essays she herself wrote for the *New Yorker* and *Commentary*. Storytelling was an integral part of her political philosophy in that it was a method she employed and a way she described what she was doing. Though Arendt's habit of telling stories is often mentioned, only a few scholars pay serious attention to the remarks she made about it in early essays and in unpublished research outlines and memos where she worked out her analysis of totalitarianism. Storytelling is thus one of the less exploited riches of Arendt's work.[1] It demands serious attention because it is the closest she comes to explaining the relationship between her innovative approach to political theory and the experiences that moved her to adopt it.

Arendt's assertion that all abstract theories began as particular experiences, that they only "sound" abstract and "appear" consistent when couched in abstract arguments, expresses her skepticism about any claim

---

1. Until 1974 there was only one book-length study of Arendt's political thought. Since then, her work has been the subject of fourteen monographs, several edited volumes, and over fifty articles in scholarly journals. Unlike the academic industries that have sprung up around interpretation and application of the theories of John Rawls, Jürgen Habermas, or Michel Foucault, the attention to Arendt's work has been significant without generating anything of the consistency of a school of political thinking or an approach to politics. Some of the scholars who have written about storytelling include Seyla Benhabib, "Hannah Arendt and the Redemptive Power of Narrative," *Social Research* 57 (1990); David Luban, "Explaining Dark Times: Hannah Arendt's Theory of Theory," *Social Research* 50 (1983); Elisabeth Young-Bruehl, "Hannah Arendt's Storytelling," *Social Research* 44 (1977); and Ernst Vollrath, "Hannah Arendt and the Method of Political Thinking," *Social Research* 44 (1977).

to abstract universal validity in the human sciences. Her remark implies that she took objectivity, which purports to be an achievement of method, to be no more than an effect of the rhetorical convention of speaking from nowhere. She also suggests that consistency, though touted as an inherent property of rationality, is merely an appearance created by discursive narrative. Finally, she acknowledges the impropriety of telling stories to a learned audience:

> It is neither customary nor wise to tell an audience, and least of all a learned audience, about the incidents and stories around which the thinking process describes its circles. It is much safer to take listener and reader along the train of thought itself, trusting to the persuasiveness inherent in the succession of connected things, even though this succession hides as well as it preserves the original source out of which the thought process arose and from which it flew. ("A," 2)

Though Arendt typically presented her "old fashioned storytelling" apologetically, as if it were insufficiently scholarly or professional, this passage makes a far more provocative suggestion by contrasting the activity of thinking against the structure of scholarly argumentation. She describes thinking as a circling process, the "mapping survey of the region which some incident had completely illuminated for a fleeting moment" ("A," 11) and argumentation as a linear "train of thought" that carries its listeners and readers along an apparently purposive succession of ideas. If one should not tell stories to fellow scholars it is not because stories are beneath them; rather, it is because to do so is to make one's arguments vulnerable to challenge (1–2). As she puts it, "To begin with telling the anecdote of a real incident is against all the rules of the game; but these rules are not absolute, they are rules of caution rather than laws of thought and hence can be broken" (3). Caution is advisable because storytelling discloses the arbitrariness of the appearance of consistency, opens one's thought-musings to rival orderings, and invites contrary interpretations of the incidents that inspired them.[2]

2. Elizabeth Minnich remembers Arendt telling stories in graduate seminars to spark her

I suggest that Arendt's apologies for her storytelling were disingenuous. She regarded it not as an anachronistic or traditional way of speaking but as "the only way for gaining at least a minimum of plausibility for statements which can neither be demonstrated in conclusive argument nor hope to be accepted as self-evident truths" (A, 3) Storytelling is, then, a kind of judging. As Dagmar Barnouw has argued, it "is a serious matter for Arendt because the meanings of stories are meant to be judgments of reality, of experience."[3] But as Arendt's remarks suggest, the unique advantage of putting forth a judgment in a story is that it is not secured against questioning. To tell a story is to break the usual "rules of caution" and refrain from the rhetorical moves that would give one's position the appearance of unquestionability.

Given that Alasdair MacIntyre associates storytelling with traditional ways of situating the self in society, it may seem odd to talk about it as a mode of critical understanding. In *After Virtue*, MacIntyre denounces the fragmentation of society and of the self that is wrought by modern individualism. He invokes storytelling as a means by which to reestablish the "pre-modern" ideal of moral character as the virtuous self "whose unity resides in the unity of a narrative which links birth to life to death as narrative beginning to middle to end."[4] Storytelling consolidates that self by restoring to it the context of beliefs about duty, responsibility, and honor in which it is traditionally embedded.

In a traditional context, storytelling is a vehicle for the transmission of legendary tales that prescribe a people's identity, usually in opposition to an excluded other or others.[5] Jean-François Lyotard argues that such

---

students to critical thinking. She recalls that these "stories freed, and invited, an effort to understand their internal meaning and an equal effort to understand what they meant to us." "Hannah Arendt: Thinking as We Are," in *Between Women*, ed. Carol Ascher, Louise De Salvo, and Sara Ruddick (Boston: Beacon Press, 1984), 173–174.

3. Dagmar Barnouw, *Visible Spaces: Hannah Arendt and the German-Jewish Experience* (Baltimore: Johns Hopkins University Press, 1990), 15. The first chapter of this perceptive study also interprets Arendt's storytelling as a radical critical response to Kantian humanism.

4. Alasdair MacIntyre, *After Virtue* (Notre Dame: University of Notre Dame Press, 1981), 191.

5. In Paul Smith's terms, storytelling conventionally functions to "cern" a collective subject. *Discerning the Subject* (Minneapolis: University of Minnesota Press, 1988), xxx–xxxiii.

tales are self-legitimating. They allow "the society in which they are told, on the one hand, to define its criteria of competence and, on the other, to evaluate according to those criteria what is performed or can be performed within it. . . . They thus define *what has the right to be said and done in the culture in question,* and since they are themselves a part of that culture, they are legitimated by the simple fact that they do what they do."[6] In other words, exemplary tales have a disciplinary effect in that they set forth and celebrate communal norms in a way that insulates them from questioning. There is no way to resist a heroic example in a tradition-bound society that will not be assimilated to it and taken as proof that the would-be critic is really a misfit, a deviant, a disrupter, or a failure in some other sense.[7]

If from this perspective storytelling is both unreflective and quintessentially old-fashioned, how do contemporary theorists justify its use as critical understanding? It is in answer to this question that storytelling becomes a contested concept among contemporary critical theorists. Humanist critics of modernity argue that storytelling becomes a vehicle for resistance when marginals tell stories. Marginal voice is frequently defended as a means to constitute a consensual standpoint from which to criticize systematic relations of oppression.[8] But storytelling is also claimed by poststructuralist critics of humanism, who are radically skeptical toward any claim to knowledge that is defended with reference to a privileged standpoint, whether that standpoint be described as embedded in social relations of power or suspended above them.[9] In this view,

6. Jean-François Lyotard, *The Postmodern Condition: A Report on Knowledge* (Minneapolis: University of Minnesota Press, 1984), 20, 23; emphasis added.
7. On the irresistibility of disciplinary norms, see Michel Foucault, *Discipline and Punish,* trans. Alan Sheridan (New York: Vintage, 1979), esp. 293–308.
8. See, for example, Catharine MacKinnon's account of feminist consciousness-raising in "Feminism, Marxism, Method, and the State: An Agenda for Theory," *Signs* 7 (1982): 515–543.
9. It may be appropriate that there is little consensus on the distinction between postmodernism and poststructuralism. Following Jameson, I use "postmodern" to refer to the economic and cultural conditions associated with postindustrial, technologically mediated, multinational, capitalist societies. I use "poststructuralism" to refer to the various antifoundationalist theories that not only attempt to explain the phenomena of postmodernism but are also constitutive of those phenomena. See Fredric Jameson, *Postmodernism, or the Cultural Logic of Late Capitalism* (Durham: Duke University Press, 1990).

storytelling is not a means to build consensus but to dispute it by pre-senting the assumptions a society takes to be natural or necessary as social constructs whose universality is open to question. Before situating the work of Hannah Arendt in this debate, I will explicate these two positions in greater detail.

Proponents of storytelling as marginal voice claim that stories of mar-ginals work to challenge the *content* of the "official story" and to prob-lematize the implicit rules that construct official narratives—*by the way they sound*—as more persuasive than marginal narratives. Marginality is frequently defended as a potential source of emancipatory knowledge on the grounds that experiences from this location, when informed by "in-tellectual and political struggle," constitute a perspective that is truer than the partial, self-serving knowledge of the privileged.[10] This com-mitment to an experiential base "helps to erect and maintain a sense of authenticity, without which our work will probably fail to connect sig-nificantly with our community's agenda of social action."[11] Marginal narrative may be most effective as a strategy of critique in rule-governed, bureaucratic societies where authority is highly rationalized and the le-gitimacy of the official discourse rests on its abstract generality and the purportedly universal rectitude of its standards. Marginal stories, both oral and written, are particularist. They challenge the official claim to universality, document resistance against official norms, and, most im-portant, show that the official claim to hold standards that are abstract, universal, and hence neutral with respect to power is false. The stories of marginal critics show the very pretense of an Archimedean vantage point to be an exercise of unquestionable force. In turn, they suggest that disciplinary norms that accord greater credibility to abstract argu-ment than to storytelling perpetuate marginality by defining knowledge

---

10. Sandra Harding, "Conclusion: Epistemological Questions," in *Feminism and Method-ology*, ed. Sandra Harding (Bloomington: Indiana University Press, 1987), 185. See also Alison Jaggar, *Feminist Politics and Human Nature* (Totowa, N.J.: Rowman and Allan-held, 1983), 377–389; Nancy Hartsock, *Money, Sex, and Power* (Boston: Northeastern University Press, 1985), chap. 10.

11. John O. Calmore, "Critical Race Theory, Archie Shepp, and Fire Music: Securing an Authentic Intellectual Life in a Multicultural World," *Southern California Law Review* 65 (1991): 2168.

in terms of an authoritative style of voice that is at odds with the socially conditioned hesitancy and deference of outsiders.[12]

But a problem with identifying storytelling with marginal criticism is that social critics are not the only ones who tell stories, and there is nothing inherently critical about particularism. In fact, it can be precisely the opposite, as when reassuring anecdotes are used to counter statistics on declining social conditions or powerful cultural stereotypes are deployed to reinforce particularist prejudices. Furthermore, marginal criticism has obvious affinities with traditional humanism in that it claims to give voice to a self-reflective individual on the authority of his or her experience of oppression. To the extent that proponents of marginal voice assert a naive expectation that the stories of the oppressed are inherently truthful and authentic and so can be taken literally, they provide little defense for storytelling in the theoretical climate of postmodernity.

The hallmark of poststructuralism is radical skepticism toward any claim to a privileged critical standpoint or an inclusive consensus such as that which marginal critics hope to build. From a poststructuralist perspective, marginal criticism is no alternative to Archimedean abstraction. It reproduces the foundationalist power move it purports to resist by establishing a subject or subjects who claim to speak legitimately for the cause of universal liberation, albeit not on the grounds of an abstract, rationalist claim to philosophical authority but on a claim to critical understanding conferred by oppression. As in the traditional model, marginal storytelling functions to describe the bounds of a political identity; the only difference is that it does so for a group that is marked as deviant by prevailing norms. For some poststructuralist theorists, then, the oppositional force of storytelling is that it disputes *any* claim to authority. Telling a rival story opens the "evidence of experience" to contestation, challenges the authority of any unitary critical conscious-

12. There is a wealth of knowledge, both cultural and academic, about the authoritative self-presentation of insiders and the socially conditioned hesitancy of outsiders. In feminist scholarship, see Carol Gilligan, *In a Different Voice* (Cambridge: Harvard University Press, 1982); Mary Field Belenky, Blythe McVicker Clinchy, Nancy Rule Goldberger, Jill Mattuck Tarule, *Women's Ways of Knowing* (New York: Basic Books, 1986).

ness, and diffuses the reality—whether marginal or universal—on which it claims to be premised.[13] Storytelling, then, makes visible the fact that experience never just *is*, but is always narrated, thereby directing attention to the discourses by which "experience" is produced, and to the processes of transcription by which it is constituted as evidence.[14]

Poststructuralist theorists conceive of storytelling not as a way to ground theory in experience but to "historicize" the categories that serve to produce a foundational understanding of experience and then serve as a foothold for authority. Joan Scott writes, "The history of these concepts (understood to be contested and contradictory) then becomes the evidence by which 'experience' can be grasped and by which the historian's relationship to the past he or she writes about can be articulated."[15] In contrast to theorists of marginal voice, who seem to claim an unmediated, authentic insight into experience, Scott suggests that storytelling is critical for its capacity to bring to light the indeterminacy of experience. As with marginal voice theory, storytelling here is credited with bringing insidious power relations to the surface; it does so, however, not by "telling how it is" to be oppressed, but by charting the repression that undergirds any claim to "tell how it is," whether advanced from the center or the margin.

The differences between marginal and poststructuralist conceptions of storytelling come into focus with exceptional clarity in the work of Jean-François Lyotard.[16] Lyotard's critique of humanism intersects with mar-

---

13. Joan Scott, "The Evidence of Experience," *Critical Inquiry* 17 (1991): 777.

14. This conception of storytelling is advanced with exceptional clarity in the field of anthropology, where the practice of fieldwork quite literally requires that stories be elicited and then transcribed before the ethnographer can stand on the authority of experience. James Clifford has argued that a conceptual shift has taken place within this discipline, from invoking experience as a ground of ethnographic authority to analyzing the literary and political practices of telling the fieldwork story. He regards the shift toward telling the fieldwork experience as a story as a critical move for its potential to disclose the process by which an ethnography is produced. This disclosure, in turn, demonstrates the "polyvocality" of culture, diffuses the unitary voice of ethnographic authority, and, thereby, demonstrates that the ethnographer's standpoint is not omniscient but partial and limited. James Clifford and George Marcus, eds., *Writing Culture* (Berkeley: University of California Press, 1986), 15.

15. Scott, "Evidence of Experience," 798.

16. There are, as Judith Butler has argued, many disagreements about theory and method

ginal criticism in that he, too, calls into question the technique of legitimation by an appeal to abstract principle and opposes storytelling against the abstraction of scientific and philosophical rationalism. But there is a significant difference between the kinds of stories that follow from the postmodern condition of "incredulity toward metanarratives" and marginal criticism. Where marginal stories build consensus, and so can be allied with Enlightenment humanist "master narratives" that promise universal peace, Lyotard argues that in the postmodern condition it is not in consensus but in fragmentation and discontinuity that emancipatory promise resides. The ideal of consensus gives way to a plurality of local knowledges and, in turn, to the assertion that the incommensurable differences among these knowledges make any pretense to global community inevitably authoritarian. Agonistic storytelling supercedes the master narrative of ultimate reconciliation, and consensus-building critique cedes to "paralogy": the continual provocation of dissent by argumentation whose purpose is to bring to light and provoke contestation over the implicit rules that constrain the production of new ideas and determine the boundaries of political communities.[17]

A more powerful defense of storytelling as marginal criticism begins from the premise that it is precisely because they call for interpretation—that they cannot be taken literally—that stories make a powerful vehicle for marginal critical theory. The claim is that stories are more adequate than arguments to depict the ambiguities of a social reality that is never linear but many-sided and multidimensional. For example, Kimberle Crenshaw has argued that stories are suited to represent "compound discrimination" against those who are marginalized by the intersection of various social factors. Compound discrimination is "theoretically erased" by disciplinary modes of argument in which conventions about relevance and streamlined analysis—the "train of thought"—make it

---

among theorists who are rhetorically grouped under the heading "poststructuralist." I do not suggest that Lyotard is representative of postmodernism, only that his work is especially relevant to mine because he constructs the postmodern critique of humanism in terms of the theme of narrative. See "Contingent Foundations: Feminism and the Question of 'Postmodernism'," in *Feminists Theorize the Political*, ed. Judith Butler and Joan W. Scott (New York: Routledge, 1992), 1–21.

17. Lyotard, *Postmodern Condition*, xxiv, section 14.

difficult to treat more than one factor at a time.[18] Furthermore, because it is interpretive (as opposed to definitive), a story can disclose that what counts as a "real" rendering of a political conflict is not simply a matter of truth but also of rhetoric.[19] That is, defining the "way it is" is not simply a task of fact-gathering but an interpretive contest; in turn, it is power, not dispassionate objectivity (which is itself a pose of power), that settles disputes among rival interpretations.

Proponents of marginal voice use storytelling to shift knowledge from a center that purports to be impartial, uniform, and omniscient, to a margin that acknowledges the heterogeneity and inevitable partiality of any standpoint. Proponents of agonal storytelling protest that such a shift reinstates the authoritarianism of Enlightenment subjectivity and the empiricism of experience-based knowlege claims. Marginal critics counter, in turn, that the use of poststructuralist theory (rather than marginal experience) to diffuse authority and differentiate political collectivities reproduces a version of Archimedean impartiality that substitutes for the ideal of a voice from nowhere "a new postmodern configuration of detachment, a new imagination of disembodiment: a dream of being *everywhere.*"[20] Although the epistemology is different, the effect is to reconfirm the preference for abstract theory over experiential critical understanding.

The conflict between marginal and agonal storytelling is not just an esoteric theoretical puzzle. It is a debate about the limits of mutual

18. Kimberle Crenshaw, "Demarginalizing the Intersection of Race and Sex: A Black Feminist Critique of Antidiscrimination Doctrine, Feminist Theory, and Antiracist Politics," *The University of Chicago Legal Forum* (1989): 148, 139.

19. Many legal scholars have begun to call attention to the fact that discerning the "right" principles in a legal case is a matter not just of argument but of persuasive storytelling. Furthermore they have started to use storytelling to bring to light within the legal system mechanisms of exclusion that insidiously perpetuate the marginalization of outsiders by constructing their stories as different and less persuasive. For an entire issue devoted to narrative, see *Michigan Law Review* 87 (1989) and especially Kim Lane Scheppele, "Foreword: Telling Stories," 2073–2098. See also Derrick Bell, *And We Are Not Saved* (New York: Basic Books, 1987), and *Faces at the Bottom of the Well* (New York: Basic Books, 1992); Patricia Williams, *The Alchemy of Race and Rights* (Cambridge: Harvard University Press, 1991); Kristin Bumiller, *The Civil Rights Society* (Baltimore: Johns Hopkins University Press, 1988).

20. Susan Bordo, "Feminism, Postmodernism, and Gender-Scepticism," in *Feminism/Postmodernism*, ed. Linda J. Nicholson (New York: Routledge, 1990), 143.

understanding that raises political questions about the viability of democratic ideals. Specifically, Are non-coercive relations possible, within and among the various groups in this world, *in light* of its plurality? These questions can be framed in terms of an epistemological dilemma: Is it possible to account for storytelling as a practice of critical understanding without recourse to the kind of Archimedean pronouncement that stories claim to unmask or to essentialist claims about the sincerity and authenticity of the marginal scholar?

Just how can the political thought of Hannah Arendt help to extricate democratic and critical theorists from this tangle? Hannah Arendt saw herself neither as a defender of Western humanism nor as its antagonist; instead, she termed herself a pariah, a critic from within, who wrote "in manifest contradiction" to its bifurcation of philosophy and politics (HC, 17). Nearly twenty years after her death, both humanist critics of modernity and poststructuralist critics of humanism claim her as an ancestor. Although Jürgen Habermas claims to have inherited his ideal of communicative rationality from Arendt,[21] poststructuralist critics of Habermas's work locate Arendt's thought in the tradition of skepticism toward universal reason that begins with Nietzsche and Heidegger.[22] In contrast to both of these, I argue that Arendt's political philosophy and conception of storytelling are unique in being, as she puts it, beyond "dogmatism and skepticism" (LKPP, 32).

Arendt first introduces storytelling as critical understanding in her

21. Jürgen Habermas, "Hannah Arendt's Communications Concept of Power," *Social Research* 44 (1977): 3–24; "On the German-Jewish Heritage," *Telos* 44 (1980): 127–131. Gerard P. Heather and Matthew Stolz are quite critical of Habermas's attempt to appropriate Arendt into his own attempt to reconcile philosophy and politics and reinvigorate the Enlightenment project of critical reason. They write that "Habermas, constrained as he is by the philosophical passions of critical theory, has in fact misread Arendt's evaluation of Aristotle." In "Hannah Arendt and the Problem of Critical Theory," *Journal of Politics* 41 (1979): 2–22. Margaret Canovan is more generous to Habermas, arguing that he misreads Arendt's work "creatively," in working out his own ideas. In "A Case of Distorted Communication: A Note on Habermas and Arendt," *Political Theory* 11 (1983): 105–116.

22. Bonnie Honig, "Toward an Agonistic Feminism: Hannah Arendt and the Politics of Identity," in Butler and Scott, *Feminists*, 215–235; Dana Villa, "Beyond Good and Evil: Arendt, Nietzsche, and the Aestheticization of Political Action," *Political Theory* 20 (1992): 274–308.

writings on totalitarianism. There she argues that totalitarianism is not only a political crisis but also a "problem of understanding" that was precipitated, in part, by Western philosophers who formulated an ideal of detachment toward politics.[23] She claims that this tradition was constrained from the outset by its origin in Plato's abandonment of politics out of disgust and anger at the execution of Socrates. From its inception, she argues, there was an "abyss between philosophy and politics" that left that tradition without the conceptual and ethical resources to understand totalitarianism and resist it.[24] Storytelling is the way Arendt proposes to bridge this abyss and to account for the possibility of principled opposition to totalitarianism. It is, then, her resistance to the abstract impartial model of critical thinking that predominates in the Western political tradition.

Arendt's attack on Archimedean thinking differs from that of poststructuralist and feminist critical theorists in an important way. She argues that the problem with the Archimedean model is not its claim that critique should be impartial but its assumption that impartiality entails an absolute withdrawal from worldly interest. Iris Young, for example, identifies it with disinterest, writing, "Impartial reason aims to adopt a point of view outside concrete situations of action, a transcendental 'view from nowhere' that carries the perspective, attitudes, character, and interests of no particular subject or set of subjects."[25] It is this assumption that constructs the debate between proponents of Archimedean thinking and their critics as an impasse between objectivist pronouncements and subjectivist testimony: if impartiality necessarily entails absolute detachment, then theorists have no choice but to discard the "baby" of critical distance with the disingenuous objectivity in which it has consistently bathed. Arendt objects to this assumption, claiming that Western

23. Hannah Arendt, "Notes for Six Lectures"; "The Great Tradition and the Nature of Totalitarianism," The New School, March 18–April 22, 1953, Library of Congress, typescript.

24. Hannah Arendt, "Philosophy and Politics: The Problem of Action and Thought after the French Revolution," lecture series delivered at Notre Dame University, 1954, Library of Congress, MSS Box 76, 32. One part of these lectures has been reconstructed and published as "Philosophy and Politics," Social Research 57 (1990): 73–103.

25. Iris Young, Justice and the Politics of Difference (Princeton: Princeton University Press, 1990), 100.

thought is so deeply rooted in the Archimedean ideal that its transcendent detachment has come to seem necessarily connected to impartial criticism when it is only contingently so.[26] She counters that impartiality "is not the result of some higher standpoint that would then actually settle [a] dispute by being altogether above the melée"; instead, it "is obtained by taking the viewpoints of others into account" (LKPP, 42). One can have critical detachment without an absolute withdrawal from political commitments by means of a practice Arendt calls "visiting," entertaining stories from the plurality of perspectives that constitute any public realm.[27]

Visiting differs from Archimedean seeing in that where the Archimedean thinker steps outside the world, the visitor ventures into it to regard it from a plurality of unfamiliar perspectives. It also differs from particularist testimony in that the persons who give testimony expect something different from their audience than does the storyteller. A testimonial is self-expressive: it asserts "this is the way *I* see the world." The testifier wants to be heard and to be responded to with empathic affirmation. In contrast, a story exhorts its auditor to "go visiting," asking, "how would *you* see the world if you saw it from *my* position?" The "visitor" is invited not empathically to assimilate the different perspectives he or she finds, but rather, to converse with them to consider how they differ from his or her own.

Although it is clear from Arendt's lectures on Kant's *Third Critique* that she meant "visiting" to be an answer to the problem of political judgment, it is not altogether clear from this metaphor how it manages to be both engaged and critical. Discerning an answer to this problem is one of the principal concerns that animates this book because it is here that I think Hannah Arendt makes her most provocative contribution to contemporary critical debates. This conversation increasingly

26. Arendt's rejection of absolute detachment is quite similar to that of Michael Walzer, who writes that "critical distance is measured in inches." In *Interpretation and Social Criticism* (Cambridge: Harvard University Press, 1987), 61.

27. Renato Rosaldo also argues that there is a connection between marginality and storytelling that gives rise to the possibility of social knowledge that is neither objectivist nor subjectivist. He does not explain this connection, however. See *Culture and Truth: The Remaking of Social Analysis* (Boston: Beacon Press, 1989), esp. chaps. 2, 6, and 7–9.

tends to be a dialogue of dogmatisms, in which humanists are constructed as imperialistic defenders of timeless truths, particularists as simple-minded defenders of truthful testimony, and poststructuralists as an irresponsible elite espousing a radical skepticism that only the very privileged can afford. Arendt came to the questions that fuel this debate before there were labels to describe these positions and, consequently, before there was so great an urgency to identify with one against the others. Perhaps because she does not speak its language, her work is rich in resources to address some of this debate's more difficult problems.

Today to frame questions of identity as a critique of Enlightenment humanism is almost exclusively an academic preoccupation. But for Hannah Arendt, and other secular, assimilated, middle-class German Jews of her time, the discordance between the liberalism of the German Enlightenment and German politics was a matter of lived experience. These were Jews who took their German heritage and German citizenship to be, if not a matter of course, at least relatively unquestionable. At that time, Germany was a place where middle-class Jews and Germans were at home together, even though their society was by no means fully integrated. For example, in Königsberg where Arendt grew up, residential neighborhoods were segregated by both ethnicity and class.[28] And although Jews neither held permanent positions at the university nor were appointed to local or provincial government positions, they nonetheless "contributed schoolteachers and artists to the larger community, in addition to the more prevalent doctors and lawyers."[29] Jews and Germans were at home, then, in the sense that they shared a cultural and intellectual setting, if not equal political power. The Nazi regime dis-

---

28. The Jews of Königsberg were probably more segregated among themselves by class than the Jewish and German middle class were by ethnicity. According to Elisabeth Young-Bruehl, "The Jewish business and professional families lived in a district called the Hufen, near the spacious Tiergarten, in middle-class comfort. Working-class Jews, known to even the descendants of Russian emigrants as *Ostjüden*, Eastern Jews, lived on the south side of the Pregel River near the oldest Orthodox synagogue. . . . Middle-class Jews and lower-class Jews seldom met, and very few of the lower-class Jewish children made their way into the *Gymnasium*, where there were only three or four Jews in each form." See *Hannah Arendt: For Love of the World* (New Haven: Yale University Press, 1982), 10.

29. Ibid.

placed Jews from this home by rendering German-Jewish identity first a suspect, then a "subhuman" category.

For Hannah Arendt, who was raised and educated into the tradition and milieu of the German Enlightenment, Nazi Germany was simultaneously a rupture of the philosophic tradition to which she had been trained and of the web of relationships that secured her place in the world. She had studied first at Marburg with Martin Heidegger and later at Heidelberg with Karl Jaspers, taking up the German philosophical legacy from its two most influential twentieth-century exponents. Her attic apartment at Marburg was a modern-day *salon*; at Heidelberg she was regarded by many as "a modern version of the Jewish Rahel Varnhagen among her highly cultivated and aristocratic Gentile friends."[30] At that time, National Socialism was not yet known to be a serious movement, and its public presence consisted in little more than the occasional anti-Semitic remark.

But the years that followed Arendt's completion of her doctoral thesis coincided with Hitler's rise to power. According to Elisabeth Young-Bruehl, there was a gradual shift in Arendt's thinking from the academic and philosophical to the political and historical. During this time, she became increasingly involved with Kurt Blumenfeld and his Zionist circle, traveling around the country to lecture on Zionism and German anti-Semitism in different cities. By 1933, when Hannah Arendt was twenty-six years old, world events brought her to a turning point. After the burning of the Reichstag and the anticommunist propaganda and arrests that followed it, she began to engage in active resistance against the Nazis. Early that spring, she offered her Berlin apartment as a "way

---

30. Ibid., 68. Rahel Varnhagen (1771–1833), daughter of jewelry dealer Marcus Levin, hosted the most influential *salon* in late-eighteenth-century Berlin. Varnhagen is distinguished for starting the Goethe cult, which celebrated a uniquely introspective and empathic model of friendship. See Liliane Weissberg, "Writing on the Wall: Letters of Rahel Varnhagen," *New German Critique* 36 (1985): 157–173, 159. In addition, her salon attracted leading philosophers such as Schlegel, Schleiermacher, and Hegel. See Joanne Cutting-Gray, "Hannah Arendt's *Rahel Varnhagen,*" *Philosophy and Literature* 15 (1991): 234. Arendt chose Varnhagen to be the subject of her *Habilitationschrift,* a kind of second dissertation that is a prerequisite to obtaining a post in a German university. Hitler's rise to power interrupted her work on this project. Although it was never finished to her satisfaction, Arendt eventually agreed to publish it in 1958.

station" for communist fugitives. At Blumenfeld's urging, she also agreed to do clandestine research at the Prussian State Library, collecting documentation of anti-Semitic activity to be presented at the Eighteenth Zionist Congress in Prague. In the midst of this work, she was arrested and detained for eight days. She fled Germany immediately afterward for Prague, and then eventually traveled to Paris, where she lived and worked for various Zionist causes until her emigration to New York City in May 1941.[31]

In a television interview in 1964, Arendt explained how it was that events in 1933 brought her to the point of political activism. In effect, she told the story of the incidents that contained "as in a nutshell" the meaning of her argument that totalitarianism was not just a political crisis but a problem of understanding. She described that year as a "shock" to her and many other German Jews, but not because of "Hitler's seizing power," because every Jew "who was not a little crazy for at least four years prior to 1933" knew Hitler as an enemy:

> [Hitler's electoral victory] was, of course, terrible. But it was
> political, it wasn't personal. . . . The problem, the personal
> problem, was not what our enemies might be doing, but what
> our friends were doing. This wave of cooperation—which was
> quite voluntary, or at least not compelled in the way it is dur-
> ing a reign of terror, made you feel surrounded by an empty
> space, isolated. I lived in an intellectual milieu, but I also knew
> many people who did not, and I came to the conclusion that
> cooperation was, so to speak, the rule among intellectuals but
> not among others. *And I have never forgotten that.* I left Ger-
> many guided by the resolution—a very exaggerated one—that
> "Never again!" I will never have anything to do with "the
> history of ideas" again.[32]

The fact of uncoerced betrayal was what convinced Arendt of the failure of philosophy and friendship. It was this that left an "empty space"

---

31. Young-Bruehl, *Hannah Arendt*, 92–107.
32. Hannah Arendt, Gaus Interview, 1964, cited in Young-Bruehl, *Hannah Arendt*, 108, emphasis added.

where there had been a public constituted by professors, university colleagues, and the gentile intellectuals of Marburg and Heidelberg.

Despite her "exaggerated" resolution, Arendt forgave her anger against intellectuals in general and turned out to have more than a little "to do" with the history of ideas. But she did not forget the experience, which she took as proof of two distinct but interrelated facts: that philosophy is inadequate to inspire resistance in times of political crisis, and that friendship has political significance in such times. As she puts it, "our great tradition . . . remained so peculiarly silent, so obviously wanting in productive replies, when challenged by the 'moral' and political questions of our time."[33] The metaphor Arendt used to characterize her experience of this "peculiar silence"—being "surrounded by an *empty space*"—is a striking image of abandonment. The emptying of the public is what happens whenever people refuse to speak up in the face of a violation of purportedly common humanist norms. However varied and even divergent our relationships to such an event, it is by speaking up against it and acting in response to it that we make it—and ourselves— real. By their cooperation with the Nazis, or just their simple complacency in the face of Nazi power, the intellectuals of Arendt's generation destroyed her trust that traditional humanist norms were adequate to guarantee the "reality of the public realm" against an unprecedented attack on humanity (HC, 57).

In the Berlin of 1933, Hannah Arendt experienced the "shock" of being made a pariah. She chose to write political theory from this position, not from that of a "professional thinker," even though her training would have permitted her to do so (LM:I, 3). Notwithstanding the claims of those who locate her as a descendant of either Heidegger or Kant, I maintain that Hannah Arendt never did take up the position within the tradition of Western philosophy for which she had been educated. She even refused this position when it was handed to her as a gift, as it was in Copenhagen eight months before her death, where the Danish government awarded her the Sonning Prize for Contributions to European Civilization. This was the last and probably most prestigious of several occasions where the world that had made Hannah Arendt a

33. Hannah Arendt, "Understanding and Politics," *Partisan Review* 20 (1953): 377–392, 385.

pariah attempted to call her back, by recognizing her place in the very civilization in whose name she might have been annihilated.[34]

Arendt did not let the irony of the occasion escape mention, remarking at the outset that it is "no small matter to be recognized for a contribution to European civilization for somebody who left Europe thirty-five years ago—by no means voluntarily—and then became a citizen of the United States, entirely and consciously voluntarily because the Republic was indeed a government of law and not of men."[35] Refusing, as she puts it, to be "changed into a public figure by the undeniable force not of fame but of public recognition," Arendt affirmed her choice to position herself as a pariah thinker. She presented herself to her audience as someone who inhabits many worlds without belonging wholly to any one: "I am, as you know, a Jew, *femini generis* as you can see, born and educated in Germany as, no doubt, you can hear, and formed to a certain extent by eight long and rather happy years in France."[36] I suggest that Arendt took storytelling to be a way of writing that is particularly suited to this way of inhabiting the world. The questions she pursued were not given by the history of ideas but by her experiences as a thinker in dark times. Her remarks about storytelling, however scattered and offhand, explain her decision to write as a pariah and defend, in a uniquely provocative way, the relationship of "living experience" to critical understanding (BPF, 87).

One thing of which I am reminded every time I use Arendt's work in the classroom is that she, like any powerful thinker, created her own vocabulary. Sometimes she did so by introducing new words, and sometimes by rendering familiar terms in unfamiliar contexts. In the next chapter of this book, I lay out the political lexicon that Arendt employs to mount a resistance to the philosophical norm of Archimedean thinking. There are two complementary aspects to this philosophical norm. One is a conception of power as leverage, and the other a conception

---

34. According to Young-Bruehl, Arendt was both "the first American citizen and the first woman to receive an honor that had been bestowed upon Winston Churchill, Albert Schweitzer, Bertrand Russell, Karl Barth, Arthur Koestler, Niels Bohr, and Laurence Olivier," *Hannah Arendt*, (461).

35. Hannah Arendt, untitled address upon receipt of the Sonning Prize, Copenhagen, Denmark, April 18, 1975, Library of Congress, 1.

36. Ibid., 2.

of knowledge as abstract impartiality. In Chapter Two I treat Arendt's response to the first of these and in Chapter Three her critique of the second. In Chapter Four, I make a close analysis of Arendt's comments on storytelling in her early writings and unpublished outlines of *Origins of Totalitarianism*. I argue that in these writings she raises questions about critical understanding to which she does not return until the end of her life. In Chapter Five I interpret the *Lectures on Kant's Political Philosophy* in light of these earlier dilemmas. My reading of this work differs significantly from that of several commentators who take it to be Arendt's return to Kantian rationalism. I argue that Arendt reads Kant against the grain, appropriating his work not to restore the possibility of political universals but to do without them. In Chapter Six I continue to detail Arendt's resistance to Kantian rationalism by moving from her abstract writings on philosophy to the writings in which she puts "visiting" into practice—her essays on literature and the correspondence with Jaspers. In Chapter Seven, I depart from the task of explicating Arendt's writings to explore her possible contributions to contemporary attempts to specify radical democratic practices.

2 The Critique of Power as Leverage

I█

If the mark of a rich and complex work of political theory is to inspire multiple interpretations, then *The Human Condition* must be counted either a great work or a hopelessly ambiguous one. Of the many books considered classics in contemporary political thought, this one may be unique for being better loved by poets than by scholars. W. H. Auden wrote that it is a book "which gives me the impression of having been especially written for me...[in that] it seems to answer precisely those questions which I have been putting to myself."[1] Martin Jay counters that "despite the obvious breadth of her knowledge and the unquestionable ingenuity of her mind, the political thought of Hannah Arendt is...Built on a foundation of arbitrary definitions and questionable, if highly imaginative, interpretations of history and previous political thought."[2] It is also unique as a study of action by a philosopher who, though she was herself no political actor "except by accident and by necessity," set out explicitly to understand politics from an activist's perspective and created a language to give it voice.[3] In fact, this vocabulary did inspire students who participated in the Free Speech Movement and Freedom Summer.[4] In this chapter I lay out the terms of Arendt's

1. W. H. Auden, "Thinking What We Are Doing," *The Griffin* 7 (September 1958): 4.
2. Martin Jay and Leon Botstein, "Hannah Arendt: Opposing Views," *Partisan Review* 45 (1978): 361.
3. Paul Ricoeur, "Action, Story, and History," *Salmagundi* 60 (1983): 63.
4. Jay and Botstein, "Hannah Arendt," 349. During a personal conversation in 1988 Richard

political lexicon, which, I argue, establishes a vocabulary for a conception of political power that anticipates debates in contemporary feminist and democratic theory.

If this seems an implausible project, that is because Arendt's relationship to both democracy and feminism is contested. Where Jürgen Habermas credits her with writing a critique of Western political thought "which articulates the historical experiences and the normative perspectives of what we today call participatory democracy,"[5] Sheldon Wolin accuses Arendt of having a deep antagonism toward democratic equality. Wolin is relentless in his criticism of her vision, which he describes as "a politics of actors rather than citizens, agonistic rather than participatory, encouraging qualities that would enable men to stand out rather than to take part of."[6] On the other hand, Nancy Hartsock argues that Arendt participates in an alternative tradition of "women on power" because she alters "the concept of heroic action . . . shifting it away from an individual competition for dominance and toward action in connection with others with whom one shares a common life and common concerns."[7] An early essay by Hanna Pitkin appears to close Arendt's work to both feminist and democratic readings, as she pronounces that Arendt's inability to escape the confines of the classic ideal of Homeric heroism "undermine[s] her own effort to save public, political life."[8] More recently, Seyla Benhabib has argued that there are both "agonal" and "associative" dimensions to Arendt's work, the former corresponding to the exclusive realm of the *polis*, "a competitive space in which one competes for recognition, precedence and acclaim," and the latter

Bernstein told me of Arendt's influence on the northern activists who participated in Freedom Summer. James Miller uses Arendt's vocabulary to describe the New Left's experimentation with participatory democracy in *Democracy Is in the Streets* (New York: Simon & Schuster, 1987).

5. Jürgen Habermas, "Notes and Commentary: On the German-Jewish Heritage," *Telos* 44 (1980): 128.

6. Sheldon S. Wolin, "Hannah Arendt: Democracy and the Political," *Salmagundi* 60 (1983): 7.

7. Nancy Hartsock, *Money, Sex, and Power* (Boston: Northeastern University Press, 1984), 217.

8. Hanna Fenichel Pitkin, "Justice: On Relating Private and Public," *Political Theory* 9 (1981): 338.

to no particular place or time but, rather, to collective action "coordinated through speech and persuasion" wherever and whenever it occurs.[9]

I think that the debate over the question of Arendt's disposition toward the masculinized, elitist politics of the Homeric age has obscured one of the most exciting aspects of her work: Arendt's critique of the Archimedean norm. This norm consists in conceiving of power as leverage and assuming that abstract impartiality is requisite to knowledge. Arendt counters leverage with "acting in concert," which is a model of solidarity premised not on a common identity or essential sameness but on a limited, principled commitment to respond to a particular problem. She counters abstract impartiality by specifying the political and intellectual position of the pariah. Pariahs are those who are forcibly excluded from power by their persecution as a people and who learn as a consequence a special humanity and solidarity not just with their own but with other persecuted peoples.[10] One of the most innovative aspects of Arendt's political theory is her attempt, over the course of her work, to define the vantage point of the pariah without either reproducing the norm of Archimedean impartiality or lapsing into an uncritical partisanship.[11] Arendt's pariahs are poets, novelists, and essayists who would have nothing to write about if they were not embedded in the web of human experience but whose very commitment to the act of *writing*

---

9. Seyla Benhabib, *Situating the Self* (New York: Routledge, 1992), 93.

10. Jennifer Ring has also called attention to the importance of the pariah to appreciating the differences between Arendt's conception of political action and the agonistic model of the polis, arguing that the pariah is "more quietly central in Arendt's work than the blustering Greek man of action." "The Pariah as Hero: Hannah Arendt's Political Actor," *Political Theory* 19 (1991): 441.

11. Thirty years ago, many readers missed the subtleties of Arendt's arguments that look so innovative in the present context. For example, Daniel Bell interpreted Arendt's refusal of Jewish partisanship in her analysis of the Eichmann controversy as Archimedean arrogance. He charged that she had "cut all ties" to her Jewish identity and found in her reports "the unmoved quality of the Stoic, transcending tribe and nation, seeking only the single standard of universal order." "Alphabet of Justice," *Partisan Review* 30 (Fall 1963): 418. Summing up the polemical readings of many of her contemporaries, Jeffrey Isaac observes that Arendt "was accused of virtual treason against her people, for effacing the line between the guilt of the Nazis and the innocence of the Jews, for having more sympathy with Eichmann than with the six million he had helped to murder." See "At the Margins: Jewish Identity and Politics in the Thought of Hannah Arendt," *Tikkun* 5 (1990): 89.

means that they are not fully at home anywhere in the world. They are marginals in the sense of existing on the fringes of a plurality of intersecting worlds, neither at the "absolute margin" of the Archimedean vantage point nor at the center of a particular tribe.[12]

In *The Human Condition*, Arendt takes up the position of the pariah, or self-consciously marginal critic, by claiming to write in "manifest contradiction to the tradition" of Western political theory (HC, 17). From the start, Arendt positions herself as a critic who works within a tradition while attempting to renegotiate its fundamental assumptions. She considers the first and most important of these to be the belief—that she takes to originate with Plato and to determine the course of the tradition thereafter—that the ideal *polis* "has no aim other than to make possible the philosopher's way of life"(14). To this end, philosophers have attempted to discipline the noisy inconsistencies of politics by turning "action into a mode of making"(229). The success of this project "is easily attested by the whole terminology of political theory and political thought, which indeed makes it almost impossible to discuss these matters without using the category of means and ends and thinking in terms of instrumentality"(229). This argument locates Arendt in a tradition of critics of modernity that includes thinkers on the left—from Marx, to Weber, to the Frankfurt school—and the right—from Nietzsche, to Heidegger, to Allan Bloom—who have chronicled and protested the rise of instrumental rationality.

What makes Arendt's position in this tradition interesting is that her work is not easy to locate on the left-right ideological continuum. She is most often recognized for arguing that action is in danger of disappearing from the modern age because of the rise of the social, which she describes as the infiltration of the public realm, an arena that should be reserved for human excellence in speech and action, by the routine tasks associated with "housekeeping," or the satisfaction of human needs (28). Although this argument allies Arendt with the right by affirming a traditional separation of economics and politics, there is a second aspect of her critique of modernity that is less frequently remarked upon.

---

12. I borrow this phrase from Kristina Rollin, who proposed it in a seminar at the Center for Advanced Feminist Studies, University of Minnesota, 1993.

Arendt argues that action is endangered not only by the bureaucratization of public life but also by the very language of politics and political philosophy. Language is crucial to the possibility of action because the public realm exists only by virtue of the "presence of others who see what we see and hear what we hear"(50). According to Arendt, deeds and the various interpretations they inspire in those who witness them constitute the "reality" of politics. Absent a language that admits of meaningful distinctions between instrumental behavior and principled conduct, *there can be no action at all.* This claim that the language of the Western tradition is inadequate for principled action makes Arendt a pariah to that tradition. Her project in *The Human Condition* is to introduce a new lexicon of political theory that provides for the possibility of acting on principle.[13]

Despite Arendt's claim to write "in manifest contradiction" against the fundamental assumptions of Western political theory, her most important works seem at once to break new ground and retreat from it (HC, 17). Arendt's groundbreaking acts are her critique of Archimedean posturing in philosophy and her creation of a new lexicon of politics that begins with the terms *plurality, natality,* and *publicity.*[14] Her retreat is the distinction she draws between the "public" and the "social," which echoes classic dualisms. These two aspects of her theory are internally inconsistent. Arendt's claim that there is a crisis of freedom in the modern world that is due to the erosion of the boundaries that protect the private and public realms from the pressures of necessity and her narration of this crisis of modernity as a story about the "rise of the social" are nothing short of an Archimedean pronouncement (HC, 38). But it is precisely such pronouncements and such narratives against which she

13. See Gerard P. Heather and Matthew Stolz, "Hannah Arendt and Critical Theory," *The Journal of Politics* 41 (1979): 18.
14. Other scholars have remarked on the significance of Arendt's vocabulary. Sheldon Wolin writes that *The Human Condition* "brought something new into the world. It introduced a distinctive language and with it a new political sensibility which invested politics with a high seriousness and dignity that transcended the dreary and trivial categories of academic political science." In "Hannah Arendt and the Ordinance of Time," *Social Research* 44 (1977): 92. Similarly, Heather and Stolz argue that "*The Human Condition* should remind us of the *Leviathan*, for both are great exercises in the arts of political naming," "Hannah Arendt and Critical Theory," 18.

directs her critique of political philosophy. Thus, the position Arendt takes as a theorist in the Western political tradition who writes against its fundamental assumptions is more radical than the one she takes up as a public intellectual in contemporary debates about the putative crisis of modernity.

No doubt, these inconsistencies are one reason Arendt's work has generated a multiplicity of incompatible readings. I do not aim to reconcile the tensions in Arendt's work or to resolve the confusions her writing has generated. But I will argue that many scholars have read and evaluated her work in light of the very norms and assumptions she calls into question, thereby playing out on its terrain the drama of assimilation that protects established ideas against the challenges of pariahs.[15] I propose to do with her work what she did with the writings of Lessing, Kafka, and others whom she deemed pariahs: to read it through the frame of its most radical insights.

Political theorists who are in search of models of democratic politics adequate to challenges raised by contemporary feminism and other critical theories are mistaken to rule Arendt's work out of consideration. Her work anticipates two distinct but mutually implicating problems in contemporary democratic theory. The first is the problem of solidarity or the "unified public," and the second is that of public judgment.

As Iris Young has argued, contemporary theorists of participatory democracy have tended to make collective action contingent on the achievement of a "unified public that in practice tends to exclude or silence some groups."[16] Even when democrats explicitly acknowledge differences among citizens and recognize the inevitability of conflict, the ideal of the unified public can be smuggled into a theory in two ways.

15. A striking exception to this is Margaret Canovan's recent study. Reading Arendt's work with an eye for the complexity of her thought and a sensibility for her unconventionally poetic "voice," Canovan concludes unequivocally that Arendt's work is rightfully mentioned "in the same breath" as that by Hobbes, Locke, and the rest. Arendt's work, Canovan argues, stands the very test of greatness that she herself proposed: "in the course of her own response to the experiences of her time, Arendt also 'augmented' the world by one word: the word 'plurality'." *Hannah Arendt: A Reinterpretation of Her Political Thought* (New York: Cambridge University Press, 1992), 281.
16. Iris Young, *Justice and the Politics of Difference* (Princeton: Princeton University Press, 1990), 5.

This can happen as a result of cultural imperialism, which is the failure by a dominant group to recognize that it is just one social group among others and that its values and practices are no less particular than those of the various groups it constructs as different. The ideal of the unified public can also insinuate itself into a conception of democracy through what Nancy Fraser calls the "socio-cultural means of interpretation and communication."[17] These might be summed up as the authoritative "voice" through which groups constitute themselves in public and articulate demands for resources and other forms of recognition. The ideal of the unified public emerges whenever a community advances a narrow conception of voice, whether it be defined juridically, as an argument to which any reasonable person would have to assent, or romantically, as the shared intuitions and experiences of a particular alienated group. I argue in this chapter that Arendt's new lexicon of politics offers a conception of solidarity that is not unifying because it appeals to neither a common identity nor a reductionist conception of rationality but, instead, is enacted by means of promising.

The second point at which Arendt's work intersects with contemporary democratic theory is the problem of public judgment. If Benjamin Barber is correct in claiming that democratic politics calls for "public action and thus for reasonable public choice, in the presence of conflict and in the absence of private or independent grounds for judgment," then its possibility depends on there being some way to justify public principles and goals that neither reintroduces an abstract imperative nor plays on parochial prejudice.[18] Like many contemporary theorists, Arendt argued that rationalist moral imperatives and prejudices, however different they may be in theory, have a similar political effect in that

17. Nancy Fraser, "Toward a Discourse Ethic of Solidarity," *Praxis International* 5 (1986): 425. According to Fraser, these include "the officially recognized vocabulary in which one can press claims; the idioms available for interpreting and communicating one's needs; the established narrative conventions available for constructing the individual and collective histories which are constitutive of social identities; the paradigms of argumentation accepted as authoritative in adjudicating conflicting claims; the ways in which various discourses constitute their respective subject matters as specific sorts of objects; the repertory of available rhetorical devices; the bodily and gestural dimensions of speech which are associated in a given society with authority and conviction."

18. Benjamin R. Barber, *Strong Democracy: Participatory Politics for a New Age* (Berkeley: University of California Press, 1984), 120.

both impose a certainty on politics that forecloses debate and relieves citizens of their responsibility to make decisions.[19] In the next chapter and in those that follow it, I argue that Arendt addresses the problem of public judgment through a unique conception of storytelling. She views it neither as a means to hand down tradition nor as a vehicle for personal self-expression but as a practice of situated critical thinking.

In this chapter I lay out Arendt's critique of one aspect of the Archimedean norm, its construction of power as leverage. I argue that the vision of politics she recommends is neither elitist nor stereotypically male. After explicating Arendt's vocabulary in such a way as to highlight its possible connections to contemporary democratic and feminist theory, in the concluding section I identify the ways in which Arendt reproduces aspects of Western political thought that are antagonistic to both of these.

Criticizing Political Philosophy as Archimedean Thinking

Archimedean thinking is characterized by a claim to a vantage point outside of time and place that is, by virtue of its disinterested impartiality, uniquely and exclusively qualified to arbitrate worldly conflicts of interest. This vantage point purports to be detached and disembodied, that is, it ignores particular characteristics such as skin color, gender, and sexual or ethnic identity. In contemporary critical theories, the Archimedean point is frequently invoked as an exemplar of the myth of perfect objectivity, the claim to a position from which to observe and to judge "reality" without participating in it or having an impact on it.[20]

---

19. Jeffrey C. Isaac criticizes Arendt for the extremism of her position on judgment, arguing that her suspicion of "the claims of any theory purporting to speak with epistemic authority about the world of opinion" rules out all possibility of a critical social science. *Arendt, Camus, and Modern Rebellion* (New Haven: Yale University Press, 1992), 238. If democratic political transformation cannot occur without the systematic critical analysis of social inequality that such a science aims to provide, then the work of Arendt and others who make judgment so central to their theories is more visionary than pragmatic.

20. This vision of impartiality corresponds to what Thomas Nagel calls "overobjectification," which he deems the mistake of seeking "a single complete objective account of reality." *The View from Nowhere* (New York: Oxford University Press, 1986), 162.

It is taken to be a classic example of the legitimation of unlimited power by a claim to knowledge that purports to be disconnected from political interests.

Although Arendt is a critic of the Archimedean norm, she describes it somewhat differently. She argues that, far from concealing the knowledge/power relationship, Archimedes quite explicitly sought the position at which knowledge and power intersect. What Archimedes wanted was to move the earth, and what he proposed was a theory of leverage, recognizing that "our power over things grows in proportion to our distance from them."[21] Thus, the Archimedean point is not *beyond* power but, rather, a position from which to exercise a certain kind of power made possible by the claim to a certain kind of knowledge. In contrast to Michel Foucault and to critical theories influenced by his work, Arendt does not claim that truth is always complicit in power relations; rather, she makes a more limited claim only against the Archimedean norm.[22] She argues that its model of objective detachment assimilates *both* knowledge and power to a mechanical model of leverage that, when applied to the realm of human affairs, becomes an exhortation to force. Furthermore, the problem she identifies with the Archimedean model of knowledge is not even that it claims to be impartial but that its version of impartiality takes the thinker too far out of the world. Arendt writes that although "we must always remove ourselves . . . from the object we wish to study . . . the withdrawal needed for cognitive acts is much more limited than what Archimedes . . . had in mind." As she sees it, the problem with the Archimedean vantage point

21. Hannah Arendt, "The Archimedean Point," reprint of a lecture for the University of Michigan College of Engineers, 1968, Library of Congress, MSS Box 61, 6.
22. See, for example, the interview "Truth and Power," where Foucault appears to identify all truth claims with the Archimedean ideal of disembodied objectivity. He claims that "truth isn't the reward of free spirits, the child of protracted solitude, nor the privilege of those who have succeeded in liberating themselves. Truth is a thing of this world: it is produced only by virtue of multiple forms of constraint." Michel Foucault, *Power/Knowledge*, ed. Colin Gordon, trans. Colin Gordon, Leo Marshall, John Mepham, and Kate Soper (New York: Pantheon, 1980), 131. Maybe Foucault recommends the genealogy of "subjugated knowledges" as a way out of the knowledge/power conundrum, but the extensive debates on this question are beyond the scope of this book.

is that it makes *abstraction* a requisite of impartiality and thereby makes possible the exercise of power absent "any attention to human interests."[23] Arendt's claim differs from those of radical critics of humanism in two respects. Not only does she hold open the possibility for ways of knowing that do not involve the subjugation of the self and of others, but she even suggests that it might be possible to have some version of impartiality that would not be detached from "human interests."

Though her critique of knowledge is carefully qualified, Arendt's argument against the tradition of Western political philosophy is quite sweeping. She argues that political philosophers of the tradition are to be faulted for reproducing the knowledge/power relation that is prescribed by the Archimedean norm.[24] The heart of her criticism is that Plato, and those political philosophers who followed him, have written about politics as if from an Archimedean vantage point that assumes not just that the life of the mind is preferable to that of action but also that the latter has to be constrained for the sake of the former. It is this second assumption, that "every kind of activity, even the processes of mere thought, must culminate in the absolute quiet of contemplation," to which Arendt objects because it has produced a tradition of political philosophy that is inimical to action (HC, 15). The problem is that all political philosophers are Archimedean thinkers who have conceived of politics in terms of "the concept of rule," which Arendt defines as "the notion that men can lawfully and politically live together only when

---

23. Arendt, "Archimedean Point," 6, 25.
24. As Bhikhu Parekh and Margaret Canovan have noted, Arendt's monolithic construction of "the" tradition is somewhat mitigated by the distinction she makes between "political 'philosophers' and political 'writers' who 'write out of political experiences and for the sake of politics'." Canovan, *Hannah Arendt*, 202, citing an unpublished essay by Hannah Arendt, "From Machiavelli to Marx," 1965 Library of Congress, MSS Box 39 023453. Parekh, *Hannah Arendt and the Search for a New Political Philosophy* (Atlantic Highlands: Humanities Press, 1981), 2. Nonetheless, in *The Human Condition* she appears to identify the tradition primarily with Plato, as if no subsequent thinkers offered a meaningful alternative to that theoretical framework. However contestable this vision of the tradition may be, it is not my purpose to entertain that debate. It has already been argued effectively and by many scholars that the Western political tradition is not reducible to a single plot but contains multiple stories that can be both oppressive and liberating.

some are entitled to command and the others forced to obey"(222). Arendt rejects this conception of politics by introducing a distinction between rulership and leadership.

Rulership and leadership can be distinguished on the basis of their different constructions of the relationship between knowledge and action. Rulership, Arendt claims, "opens a gulf" between two modes of action that the Greeks prior to Plato considered interconnected(222). These two modes are "the *beginning* made by a single person and the *achievement* in which many join by 'bearing' and 'finishing' the enterprise, by seeing it through (189; emphasis added)." Plato not only separates these modes of action but also casts them hierarchically and in opposition to each other, defining beginning as a function of knowledge and achievement as a function of execution without thought. Thus, rulers exert the power of their expertise over subjects whose task it is to execute commands. If the two modes—beginning and achievement—are understood to be interconnected aspects of action, then there can be no vanguard but the tasks of leaders and followers must be interdependent. The leader, who begins or "set[s] something into motion," is dependent for its achievement on the help of others who "join the enterprise of their own accord, with their own motives and aims,"(177, 222). In turn, those who participate in achieving the action depend upon the leader "for an occasion to act themselves(189). Although Arendt recognizes a distinction between leaders and participants, both are simultaneously knowers and doers; consequently, the relationship between the two is one of collaboration rather than command.

Leaders depend on the spontaneous participation of a plurality of others who are actors in their own right and who, as such, can neither predict nor control the course of events they set into motion. Philosophers have attempted to substitute vanguard rule for leadership "in the hope that the realm of human affairs may escape the haphazardness and moral irresponsibility inherent in a plurality of agents"(220). Consequently, "he who acts never quite knows what he is doing [and so] . . . becomes 'guilty' of consequences he never intended or even foresaw"(233). The advantage of vanguard rule is that it introduces a "division between those who know and do not act and those who act and do not know," thereby assigning full responsibility to the ruler in exchange for absolute sovereignty over the subjects (223). This separation of knowledge from action is the definitive character of sovereignty.

Arendt describes leadership in a letter to Karl Jaspers. She writes that the "most remarkable thing" about the student protests against the Viet Nam War at the University of Chicago was that "there were no leaders before, but then leaders emerged. Primarily responsible for the exemplary order was a very gifted, twenty-year old Jewish girl who led the proceedings and had absolute authority"(C, 641). In contrast to rulers, leaders emerge in the very performance of an action. Their authority rests not on credentials, prior expertise, or an "office," but on the things they do and say at the scene.

Arendt's critique of rulership, then, is a critique of the Archimedean norm. This norm has two aspects, both of which carry perverse consequences for politics. It prescribes a model of power as control over others. This power is legitimated, in turn, by a model of knowledge as that which is prior to the "human interests" of a particular time and place. She counters this norm with a model of collaborative power and situated knowledge.

The New Political Lexicon

Arendt effects her departure from the philosopher's view of politics with a metaphor: that freedom and power are not individual prerogatives but, rather, conditional on "the human ability not just to act but to act in concert" (OV, 44). She takes the premise from which philosophers have tried to escape, that politics begins with "a plurality of agents" in relation to each other, and transforms it from an "intrinsic 'weakness,'" of the human condition to a source of uniquely human power (HC, 234). In opposition to philosophers' claim that freedom is impossible if one must depend on the collaboration of others who are knowers and actors in their own right, Arendt claims that solitary sovereignty is not possible for human beings; human freedom depends, instead, on collective action. To unfold the implications of "acting in concert" as a critique of Archimedean thinking and an alternative to it, it is necessary to first lay out Arendt's new lexicon of politics, beginning with the terms *natality* and *plurality*.

The first and most important word in Arendt's lexicon is "plurality," which she calls "*the* condition—not only the *conditio sine qua non*, but the *conditio per quam*—of all political life"(HC, 7). Plurality is a rich term, with several intertwining meanings. Most simply, it names human multiplicity. It signifies that "men, not Man, live on the earth and inhabit the world"(7). It also names diversity, which she describes paradoxically as *sameness* in *difference*. By this she does not mean that deep down we are all the same in spite of apparent differences, but that "we are all the same, that is, human, in such a way that nobody is ever the same as anyone else who ever lived, lives, or will live"(8). This second aspect of plurality means that the possibility of community is never simply given or essential to human beings but must, rather, be built by speech and action. Finally, plurality names the fact of human interconnection, the "web of human relationships which exists wherever men live together"(184). This web is actualized in speech, the faculty by which human beings communicate what is distinct about themselves and acknowledge others as equals (178). Plurality is *the* condition of political life because if it were destroyed or suppressed, "the world, which can form only in the interspaces between men in all their variety, would vanish altogether"(MDT, 31).

Next to plurality, the most important word in Arendt's lexicon is "natality," "the capacity of beginning something anew, that is, of acting"(HC, 9). Natality is not literally synonymous with birth; rather, it is a "second birth" in which we begin "something new on our own initiative"(176–177). She writes, "Politically speaking, the decisive trait of the human condition is not that men are mortal, but that they are being born; birth, rather than death, is the decisive factor in all political organization which must ever stand ready to receive new beginners into a communal pattern which is more permanent than each of them."[25] To think of natality in terms of biological birth is to lose what makes it distinctive for Arendt, which is that natality is neither the inevitable

---

25. Hannah Arendt, "Philosophy and Politics: The Problem of Action and Thought after the French Revolution," 1954, 15a, Library of Congress, MSS Box 76.

outcome of a biological process nor the equally inevitable consequence of social conditioning. She calls natality "a second birth" in which "With word and deed we insert ourselves into the human world" (HC, 176). Where the first birth is the involuntary outcome of biological and technological processes, this second birth is the outcome of the education we receive after we are born. The task of education is not just socialization, but individuation, to inspire "beginners" with the spirit "of undertaking something new, something unforeseen by us" (BPF, 196). Education culminates in natality—the enactment of something new.

Although it seems more straightforward than the concept of plurality, natality is also a concept in which many themes intersect. One of these might be termed the dilemma of entrance. Emancipated Jews in Europe prior to the Holocaust who were confronted with the task of integration into Christian society faced three possible courses of action. These were to accept the terms of that world as it was and assimilate to it (the course of the *parvenu*), to establish enclaves of Jewish culture even at the cost of material deprivation (the course of the pariah), or to attempt to enter society and change it to acknowledge Jews *as Jews*. The last one, the course of the conscious pariah, is an entrance in the spirit of natality because it means refusing both separatism and assimilation. It may be "stimulated by the presence of others whose company we may wish to join, but . . . never conditioned by them"(HC, 177). Thus, it is original in two distinct senses, as a spontaneous public performance, and as an act of judgment. Dagmar Barnouw brings out this second aspect, describing it as an act of "choosing the company with whom one wants to spend one's life (of the mind)."[26] Natality is an act of individuation that is achieved, paradoxically, by a declaration of connection to those whom one respects enough to want to be joined in friendship with. It is, then, far more complex than it appears, encapsulating themes from Arendt's post-war writings on Jewish identity and anticipating her last writings on judgment.

A deep respect for individuality inheres in the terms natality and plurality that is distinct from competitive individualism. Arendt celebrates

---

26. Dagmar Barnouw, *Visible Spaces: Hannah Arendt and the German-Jewish Experience* (Baltimore: Johns Hopkins University Press, 1990), 19.

initiative but defines it against the grain of the image of the lone hero who succeeds against the odds of the mediocrity that surrounds him. Where the lone hero story sets up an opposition between individualism and community, Arendt transforms both sides of this dichotomy. She argues that individuality, although of course at odds with conformity, depends on being recognized by people one respects and recognizes in turn. This tension Arendt maintains between individuality and community is one of the distinctive aspects of her political theory. She affirms that every person is unique but cautions that this individuality only manifests itself in acting in concert with others.

There is a third concept that is so critical to Arendt's political vision that it is surprising that she does not make it a distinct term in her lexicon. This concept is "publicity," which means everything that "can be seen and heard by everybody" and the "common world" that is both the artifice created by human hands and the "affairs which go on among those who inhabit the man-made world together."[27] The distinctively political connotation of publicity is openness, which exists wherever a question, problem, or event is submitted to argumentation. Publicity depends on natality, which initiates the process of discussion, and on plurality, which gives it a space in which to occur. This space, the public realm, exists by: "the simultaneous presence of innumerable perspectives and aspects in which the common world presents itself and for which no common measurement or denominator can ever be devised. For though the common world is the common meeting ground of all, those who are present have different locations in it, and the location of one can no more coincide with the location of another than the location of two objects." Public realms exist wherever those who gather to discuss an event or a problem "see and hear from a different position"(HC, 57). Their multiple locations guarantee that they will not be fused together, as in the collective will of a totalitarian regime, but arrayed around an open space.[28]

27. HC, 50, 52. Parekh has also noted the peculiarity of Arendt's presentation of publicity, writing that "although the concept of public space is crucial to her ontology, she neither clearly defines it nor articulates its structure," *Hannah Arendt*, 92.

28. Canovan has charted the connections between the main themes of *The Human Condition*, *The Origins of Totalitarianism*, and Arendt's unpublished writings on the total-

Arendt calls this space variously the "interspace"(MDT, 31), "in-between" or "*inter-est*, which lies between people and therefore can re-late and bind them together"(HC, 182). She writes, "This 'between' can be a common ground and it can be a common purpose; it always fulfills the double function of binding men together *and* separating them in an articulate way"(R, 81). With her insistence on commonality and articu-late separation, Arendt makes an observation that bears on the conflict between proponents of "unitary" democracy who envision political com-munity grounded in an essential sympathy, and proponents of "adver-sary" democracy, who argue that given a diversity of identities and interests, abstract procedure is the best protection against tyranny.[29] Al-though these two seem quite different in that the former is premised on unity and cooperation and the latter on competition, Arendt's work suggests that they are alike in leaving individuals' points of connection and points of difference unstated and unarticulated. Where attention to differences jeopardizes unitary democracy, which depends on the myth of a common consciousness that is so deeply felt that it would not be contested and may not even need to be stated, the effort to achieve commonality is simply irrelevant in a liberal democratic society, which is adversarial precisely because it is assumed that contestation is *all* there is and no common interest can come of it. Consequently, the integrity of liberal democracy turns on a tacit consensus with respect to the pro-cedures that guarantee the interests and rights of individuals in the ab-stract. With Arendt, contemporary critical theorists have argued that both unitary identity politics and adversarial liberalism tend toward ho-mogeneity, the former by virtue of assuming that "we" all are particular

itarian elements in Marx. Her investigation of these unpublished writings shows that arguments from the various studies of totalitarianism influence the later work in two ways. Plurality and the public space are, as it is commonly understood, a kind of antidote to totalitarian rule. In addition, however, Canovan argues that the story Arendt tells about modernity in *The Human Condition* is determined by the parallel she saw between totalitarian terror and what she took to be the modern rise to prom-inence of the activities of labor and consumption, together with the values associated with them. Canovan suggests that some of the polemicism of the later work follows from predispositions Arendt carries into it from the earlier study. See *Hannah Arendt*, chaps. 3 and 4.

29. Jane Mansbridge lays out these two categories and compares their conceptions of in-terest in *Beyond Adversary Democracy* (Chicago: University of Chicago Press, 1980).

in the same way (i.e., as blacks, as sisters), and the latter by virtue of abstract categories that purport to be neutral but in fact represent a particular perspective.[30]

Arendt's suggestion of the possibility of a common interest that accomplishes the contradictory task of uniting individuals and separating them in an "articulate way" departs in important ways from both liberal and communitarian understandings of interest. In contrast to the interests of interest group pluralism, Arendt's interests are not private bargaining chips, defined with reference to individual goals and traded competitively on the political "market." In contrast to the communitarian ideal, the *"inter-est"* is not a common cause that in some way expresses the authentic beings of its disparate participants and harmonizes their wills. That she calls it an "in-between" suggests that it is a commonality; at the same time, however, her insistence on argumentation suggests that commonality does not mean concord. As she puts it, the public realm is an "area in which there are many voices and where the announcement of what each 'deems truth' both links and separates men, establishing in fact those distances between men which together comprise the world"(MDT, 30). Arendt defines *"inter-est"* with characteristic perversity. It is not a commonality that unites individuals, such as a competitively achieved bargain or revealed common essence, but one that "links and separates" them: the "between" that sustains Arendtian solidarity is *distance*.

Arendt's description of the public space as an area that is created when people exchange the "announcement of what each 'deems truth,' " suggests that there is a relationship between *"inter-est"* and principle. This relationship is not deterministic, where the common interest would simply follow from shared principles. Rather, the *"inter-est"* is a matter of principle that lies "in-between" in the sense that it affects citizens' relationships with each other sufficiently to move them to argument and

30. There is a vast body of scholarship criticizing the tendency toward false universality in both the essentialism of identity politics and the abstraction of liberalism. Some especially cogent examples of these arguments include Susan Moller Okin, *Women in Western Political Thought* (Princeton: Princeton University Press, 1979), and *Justice, Gender, and the Family* (New York: Basic Books, 1989); Young, *Justice*; Carole Pateman, *The Disorder of Women* (Stanford: Stanford University Press, 1989).

possibly to collective action. It can be defined only as they debate the terms of those relationships and as they learn, over the course of an action, what is compelling enough to sustain a collective commitment.

It is crucial to Arendt's conception of action that "inter-est," which is the catalyst to action, not be defined as a determining force, which would put it at odds with natality. Consequently, she is careful to dif-ferentiate principles from motives and intents. Motives and goals are "determining factors" that necessarily reduce action to behavior; in or-der to conceive of action in terms of natality, as that activity in which freedom is "primarily experienced," there must be a political language for action that can call it to account without deducing it either from a predetermined motive or a projected goal. Arendt's answer to this prob-lem is the "principle" that neither determines nor calculates an action, but "inspire[s], as it were, from without." Because they are not internal to individuals' wills, principles are distinct from motives; they are also "much too general to prescribe particular goals, although every partic-ular aim can be judged in the light of its principle once the act has been started"(BPF, 151–152). As is typical of Arendt, her remarks at this crucial point in her thought are brief and beguiling; she seems at once to invoke and to resist the conventional understanding of principles.

For example, her list of principles includes some customary exam-ples—honor, glory, virtue, distinction, excellence—together, surpris-ingly, with "fear or distrust or hatred." While the first five of these are typically timeless and abstract ideals, the last three are emotional re-sponses that can be principled depending on the context in which they are expressed. Even more contradictory than her list of principles is her discussion of their characteristics. She seems to make timelessness a fea-ture of principles when she asserts that they differ from goals in that they "can be repeated time and time again" and from motives in that their "validity . . . is universal . . . not bound to any particular person or to any particular group." But she retreats from this position when she introduces a second set of distinctions among "the judgment of the intellect which *precedes* action . . . the command of the will which *initi-ates* it, [and] the *inspiring* principle [that] becomes fully manifest only in the performing act itself"(emphasis added; BPF, 152). Here she dif-ferentiates principles from concepts and from imperatives, both of which can be stated in words and apprehended intellectually. Principles have to be enacted. As such, they are embedded in history and their meaning, though not their validity, is tied to the particular stories they inspire. Finally, principles seem to be neither concrete nor abstract; they are not concrete because they can never be fully realized but are subject to "inexhaustible" repetition, and they are not abstract because they have to be seen and heard by everybody.

Although it eludes definition in terms of the usual oppositions between universality and particularity, reason and emotion, and ideal and actuality, this conception of principle makes perfect sense in light of publicity. Principles do not motivate action, they cannot be used to pass judgment on it, nor can they be achieved by it. But they are uniquely public in that it is in action that they come to light. The speeches that people make in the attempt to cast a problem, event, or question as an "*inter-est*" and the actions they make in response to it reveal their principles. This is not to say that principles can be stated by a declaration of purpose or list of accomplishments; this suggests that they can be fully determined and so confuses them with motives and goals. Although a person can be said to "have" motives and goals, a principle cannot be possessed by or attributed to anyone. Principles are revealed indirectly by what we say and do, not defined by what we say about them or claim to do in their name. Principles are the intangible "in-between" that sustains Arendtian solidarity.

Principled solidarity is Arendt's proposed alternative to liberal and communitarian understandings of common good. This alternative is a politics defined neither by an all-encompassing common identity nor by a putatively natural characteristic such as rational self-interest; rather, it is defined by a question or problem that admits of principled disagreement. As she puts it, "The reality of the public realm relies on the simultaneous presence of innumerable perspectives and aspects in which the common world presents itself" (HC, 57). In other words Arendt's concept of publicity redefines solidarity by shifting the locus of the possible common purpose that inspires collective action from the "inner selves" of political actors to an "articulated" common interest in the world.[31] This would be a duplicitous move if Arendt simply instantiated

31. Political theorists Ernesto Laclau and Chantal Mouffe employ the term *articulation* to

a putative "common world" in place of "common sense." Although Arendt maintains that there is a common world "out there" separate from individuals' perceptions of it, she argues that in itself this world is no more than a "meeting ground" that in no way determines or produces a common interest. On the contrary, Arendt writes that "Without being talked about by men and without housing them, the world would not be a human artifice but a heap of unrelated things to which each isolated individual was at liberty to add one more object." (HC 204). The "common world," then, is not present *in itself* in the public realm; instead, it only appears refracted through the perspectives and aspects that "throw light" on an event (MDT, viii). Consequently, the bases for common interests are no more "out there" to be seen than they are "given" by a common identity or consciousness.

Arendt's answer to the problem of collective self-determination in a plural society is this conception of public spaces that exist around common interests that are relative to a particular situation. But the terms of this situation are not given in advance, and neither are its members designated in advance. Rather, it is by means of disagreeing about the meaning of an event or problem that people talk themselves into a common situation. What they have in common is not something inside them. Instead, commonality is potentially "in" a situation, depending on how that situation is defined. This potential is realized if, in exchanging the "innumerable perspectives and aspects" in which the situation appears to each of them, people manage to articulate these aspects into an interpretation that renders it a problem compelling enough to inspire their cooperative action. Even among those who decide to make com-

---

explain the way in which an hegemonic order constitutes a position of dominance and to account for the possibility of democratic opposition that is not grounded in a unitary class, ethnic, or gender identity. As Arendt does, these theorists pose articulation as an alternative to the fragmentation of pluralist liberalism on one hand and to totalizing or essentialist conceptions of community on the other. It displaces both the concept of a plurality of competing interests given prior to and represented through politics and the belief in an underlying essential unity that is expressed in communitarian politics. In contrast, articulation is "the result of political construction and struggle." Its starting point is plurality, and its task is to build connections around various democratic demands by means of a contest in which none of the contestants is privileged by its structural position. *Hegemony and Socialist Strategy* (New York: Verso, 1985), 65.

mon cause, commonality is not discovered by recognizing how "we" are all alike; rather, it is constructed by learning how each of us sees differently. The articulation of a public space involves committing to an action while acknowledging the possibility of ongoing differences among the participants and providing for the possibility of continuing public criticism.[32]

I have argued so far that Arendt's understanding of democracy differs from both the liberal pluralist conception of adversarial interest group competition and the unitary ideal that identity politics often presupposes. A further distinction can be made between Arendt's "plurality" and the radical pluralism that purportedly describes the "postmodern condition." Lyotard characterizes postmodern society as a discontinuous aggregate of incommensurable language games. Using terms that call Arendt's "web" of plurality to mind, he describes a social "fabric formed by the intersection of at least two (and in reality an indeterminate number of) language games, obeying different rules."[33] There is a crucial difference between Arendt and Lyotard, however. Where Lyotard takes "plurality" to denote the presence of incommensurable differences, Arendt claims not the *incommensurability* of differences but their *irreducibility* "to a common measurement or denominator." This distinction is important because irreducibility holds out the possibility of intersubjective dialogue and mutual understanding. At the same time, however, the fact of plurality suggests the likelihood that such dialogue will gen-

32. Ron Feldman's account of Arendt's preference for the *Yishuv* (the Jewish community in Palestine prior to statehood) over the establishment of the majority Jewish state of Israel suggests that it is precisely this conception of an articulated public space that accounts for her position on Israel. Arendt viewed the *Yishuv*, with its construction of a specifically Jewish cultural homeland, as sufficient to the articulation of a public space and opposed the move to establishing Israel as a traditionally sovereign state on the basis of religious identity. "For Arendt, the Jewish homeland is a political space, a human world created by conscious human effort where a Jewish culture can come into being; this the *Yishuv* achieved, without political sovereignty and without being a majority in Palestine. Precisely because a Jewish community had been built where people could appear to each other, where there was an audience for works of literature and art, Jewish cultural genius no longer needed to either abandon its Jewish roots in favor of 'universal' European culture or else be relegated to the category of folklore." Ron H. Feldman, "Introduction," JP, 36.

33. Jean-François Lyotard, *The Postmodern Condition: A Report on Knowledge,* trans. Geoff Bennington and Brian Massumi (Minneapolis: University of Minnesota Press, 1984), 40.

erate not one all-encompassing public but various publics with various inter-ests; in turn, the articulation of inter-est within them will involve dispute and conflict.[34]

Arendt's new lexicon of politics addresses the problem of the unitary public by redefining solidarity from something that is grounded in abstract rationality or common identity to something that is articulated by means of public speech and action. This redefinition of solidarity opens the way for Arendt to propose a new understanding of collective action, one that draws its energy not from unanimity but from plurality. This is what she is getting at with the metaphor "acting in concert." The possibility for acting in concert exists *in potential* wherever people who are otherwise different meet in a common situation and manage to articulate its various aspects into an interpretation that renders it a problem that is compelling enough to inspire their collective action. By the articulation of a common problem, they open a space "in-between" and constitute themselves as a public. The question is, Just what is the process of articulation by which publics are constituted?

It is significant that there is no theoretical account of the processes of collective speech and action in *The Human Condition*. Absent such an account, as Jürgen Habermas has argued, Arendt has no way to differentiate between an ideologically forced consensus and a publicly achieved democratic agreement.[35] The closest Arendt herself comes to such an account is in an unpublished essay, written in 1954, in which

34. There is no small controversy regarding what Arendt's elusive concept of "public space" refers to. Margaret Canovan, for example, equates it with the "common set of worldly institutions" by which all citizens of a particular community are joined together (*Hannah Arendt*, 226). The problem with equating the public with common institutions is that it begins to elide the discontinuity in Arendt's work between government and politics. As Canovan herself notes, the public spaces Arendt cites as exemplary of politics were opened by demonstrations like the civil rights movement and anti-war protests (183). Such actions were certainly not coterminous with the institutions of liberal government and society but protests against them. As Jeffrey C. Isaac has recently argued, far from envisioning a single, all-encompassing public "that might replace the institutions of representative government, Arendt envisions the pluralization of political space." In "Oases in the Desert: Hannah Arendt on Democratic Politics," *American Political Science Review* 88 (1994): 160.

35. Jürgen Habermas, "Hannah Arendt's Communications Concept of Power," *Social Research* 44 (1977): 3–24.

she presents Socratic dialogue as a model of public discourse.[36] In her discussion of the dialogues of the "historical" Socrates, Arendt confirms what is only implicit in *The Human Condition*—that articulating a common interest does not mean resolving all difference and dissent into an all-encompassing communal consensus but means, on the contrary, coming to understand just how different we may be apart from our concern with the specific matter at hand.[37]

Arendt sees in the Socratic dialogue a shift of solidarity from the self to the world that is similar to that which she effects with publicity. According to this model, the possibility for commonality is not in the essential identities of the persons in conversation but in the fact that they exist in the same world. But, even though the sameness of that world is a given, the commonality is not. This distinction between sameness and commonality follows from plurality: that any situation is constituted by a plurality of perspectives means that people can be in a "same" situation without having a common experience. For sameness to take on the quality of a common-ness about which one feels deeply enough to take action in concert, there must be an exchange of perspectives so that each friend comes to understand "More than his friend as a person, [but] . . . how and in which specific articulateness the common world appears to the other who as a person is forever unequal or different."[38] This exchange takes place in the Socratic dialogue, which neither begins from a common consciousness nor proceeds by means of empathic identification. It starts instead from the assumption that "the

---

36. Arendt apparently revised one section of this essay—"Philosophy and Politics"—for publication, even though she never published it. It was published posthumously in *Social Research* 57 (1990): 73–103.

37. LM: 1, 168. It could be objected that Arendt exaggerates the publicity of the Socratic dialogue. It is neither plural, as Plato frequently depicts Socrates' interlocutors as morally and intellectually unworthy of him, nor open, as Socrates knows in advance what he wants to accomplish by it. Arendt's portrait of Socrates rests on a belief that she stipulates but does not defend, that "there exists a sharp dividing line between what is authentically Socratic and the philosophy taught by Plato," 168. The historical, "authentic" Socrates, Arendt argues, was genuinely uncertain, believed he had nothing to teach, engaged in questioning for its own sake, and believed everyone was worth talking to.

38. Arendt, "Philosophy and Politics," 83–84. This reference and subsequent references in this section are to the posthumous version of the text.

world opens up differently to every man, according to his position in it; and that the 'sameness' of the world, its common-ness . . . or 'objectivity' (as we would say from the subjective viewpoint of modern philosophy) resides in the fact that the same world opens up to all and that despite all differences between men and their positions in the world—and consequently their *doxai* (opinions)—'both you and I are human'." What Arendt is describing in this somewhat unwieldy sentence is a process of articulation that begins from plurality, the recognition of equal humanity in light of differences. The condition that makes this articulation possible is friendship, which equalizes the discussants, not economically but politically, by enabling them to "become equal partners in a common world."[39] It is friendship that makes possible the articulation of common interests.

The kind of friendship Arendt has in mind is not intimacy, but public friendship, mediated by individuals' partnership in a common world. It is the common world, and the distance it imposes between friends, that makes room for plurality in the relationship.[40] Intimate friendship values sameness, which is confirmed in personal conversations that proceed by the intuitive recognition of another's point of view with a minimum of explanation. By contrast, in public conversation, the claim to immediate understanding is suspect, because it shuts down communication. Where intimate exchanges begin in mutual recognition, public dialogue might be described as beginning in what Mikhail Bakhtin calls "mutual non-understanding," proceeding in the mode of translation.[41] Conversation

39. Ibid., 80, 83.
40. Fred Dallmayr suggests that this peculiar close-distant quality is common to both public and intimate friendship when he writes, "In cultivating a friendship, I believe, we also become susceptible to a certain uniqueness or unfamiliarity which we do not wish to invade or transgress—a belief congruent with a Heideggerian passage which depicts man basically as a 'creature of distance,' or rather as a creature whose farness emerges precisely under conditions of nearness or close proximity." Whether it is only a quality of public friendship or of both public and intimate friendship, Dallmayr's words are a beautiful rendering of the connection between Arendtian plurality and friendship. See *Polis and Praxis* (Cambridge: MIT Press, 1984), 10.
41. Bakhtin introduces the idea of conversation in the mode of translation in the analogy he draws between novels and conversations. Bakhtin argues that the distinctive character of a novel is that it is a form of narrative that can (though it need not) accommodate multiple speakers, languages, and ideological perspectives. He calls this its

in the mode of translation is the process that makes it possible to understand the "specific articulateness" in which the world appears to the plurality of individuals located in it.

There is an example of public friendship in Arendt's exchange with Gershom Scholem over *Eichmann in Jerusalem*. The comment she writes to Gershom Scholem about their strongly worded and deeply felt differences of opinion over that work illustrates just how much she prizes debate and difference as an aspect of public friendship and how important she took that kind of exchange to be in political life. Urging Scholem to publish his criticisms of her work and her response not in the third person but in their original form as a personal exchange of letters, she tells him that "The value of this controversy consists in its epistolary character, namely in the fact that it is informed by personal friendship" (JP, 251).

Although suggestive, the model of the Socratic dialogue is inadequate to the task of specifying the means by which to articulate a common *inter-est*. First, it prescribes face-to-face, one-on-one communication that is not transferrable to politics. Second, Arendt's stipulations about the "historical" Socrates notwithstanding, his rhetorical skill is a kind of power that it would be disingenuous to deny if he is to be a model of democratic citizenship.[42] Possibly Arendt never developed this line of argument for publication because she recognized its inadequacy. In any case, her failure to specify the communicative practices by which democratic communities can be articulated is an important shortfall in her account of the public space.

"Galilean perception of language." M. M. Bakhtin, *The Dialogic Imagination* (Austin: University of Texas Press, 1981), 366. In contrast to the story of a novel told from the Archimedean position of an omniscient narrator, the story of a Galilean novel is dialogic: it is told from multiple perspectives and in multiple languages. Bakhtin suggests that a Galilean novel exemplifies for its readers the dynamics of a good conversation: its "dialogues . . . push to the limit the mutual nonunderstanding represented by people who *speak in different languages*," 356. If conversations are, indeed, Galilean and "multiple" with respect to language, then communication in a conversational mode cannot be a matter of unmediated understanding but must proceed instead in the mode of translation. See also Donna Haraway, "Situated Knowledges: The Science Question in Feminism and the Privilege of Partial Perspective," *Feminist Studies* 14 (1988): 589–590.

42. For a provocative discussion of this question and defense of Socrates, see Gregory Vlastos, *Socrates: Ironist and Moral Philosopher* (Ithaca: Cornell University Press, 1991).

So far, I have explicated three words that I take to be the most important terms in Arendt's political vocabulary: plurality, natality, and publicity. I have argued that these terms anticipate contemporary critical theorists' attempts to provide a nonfoundationalist account of democratic community. That is, a community grounded neither in common identity nor in universally valid moral principles. Arendt attempts to account for the possibility of solidarity and collective action without either invoking an underlying common identity or appealing to transcendent reason. I think Arendt's account is distinctive for the tension in her concept of plurality, which affirms that the starting place of political theory is simultaneously the irreducible differentiation of human beings and their inextricable connectedness across those differences. Arendt argues for a democratic public space constituted by common interests, but at the same time she maintains that commonality is not the *ground* of politics but is revealed in public speeches and actions. I have also noted that in *The Human Condition* Arendt breaks off this train of thought without completing it because she fails to specify the institutions and practices in which individuals can be bound together and separated "in an articulate way." I turn now to examine Arendt's critique of the Western political tradition in greater detail.

Promise-Making—An Alternative Conception of Power

When Arendt looks at Western political philosophy through the lens of her new lexicon, the results are startling. She finds that "Our political tradition is almost unanimous in holding that freedom begins where men have left the realm of public life inhabited by the many, and that it is not experienced in association with others but in intercourse with one's self (BPF, 157). If the tradition is any example, then "political philosophy" is an oxymoron. It "tends to derive the political side of human life from the necessity which compels the human animal to live together with others, rather than from the human capacity to act," regards plurality as an "unfortunate" weakness, and aims to "enable the philosopher at least to live undisturbed by

it."[43] Philosophy is irreconcilably at odds with politics because solitude, not plurality, is for the philosopher a "way of life and a condition of work" (OT, 476). The effort to escape plurality is evidenced in
philosophers' attempts to "replace acting with making [which] is manifest in the whole body of argument against 'democracy' [and] which,
the more consistently and better reasoned it is, will turn into an argument against the essentials of politics (HC, 220).

This orientation toward solitude and contemplation gives philosophers a distorted understanding of power and freedom. She claims that
they mistake strength—"the fallacy of the strong man who is powerful
because he is alone"—for power(190), and sovereignty—"the ideal of
uncompromising self-sufficiency and mastership"—for freedom(234).
Where valuing strength identifies power with leverage, valuing sovereignty identifies freedom with free will. The philosophical view is ultimately self-defeating because, as Arendt remarks, "If it were true that
sovereignty and freedom are the same, then indeed no man could be
free, because sovereignty, the ideal of uncompromising self-sufficiency
and mastership, is contradictory to the very condition of plurality"(234).
This preoccupation with sovereignty in the Western political tradition
might be deemed a kind of "philosophical onanism"—the wish that
politics were something one could do with oneself and power and freedom could be enjoyed without interference by others.

It is tempting to read Arendt's critique of this traditional confusion
of power with mastery in terms of contemporary feminist theory. There
is an intimation of that work in her references to the "fallacy of the
strong man who is powerful because he is alone" and to historical "examples of the impotence of the strong and superior man who does not
know how to enlist the help, the co-acting of his fellow men"(188–189).
These references bear some similarity to feminists' claim that the purportedly abstract ideal of the rational individual is not neutral but male
and that its autonomy is an illusion sustained by some form of dominance.[44] But Arendt's is not a "feminist" critique of power, at least not

---

43. Hannah Arendt, "Concern with Politics in Recent European Philosophical Thought,"
undated, Library of Congress, MSS Box 63 02348.
44. Jane Flax, for example, has argued that the gender socialization of privileged males

in the sense of an argument in which gender is a central category and for which discerning sexism is a principal hermeneutic objective.

Arendt explains the traditional misconceptions about freedom and power in terms of the fact that the men responsible for them were *philosophers*, not that they were privileged as *men*. The problem with the philosophical perspective is that it identifies freedom exclusively with contemplation and reduces all worldly activity with necessity, thereby blurring "the distinctions and articulations within the *vita activa* itself"(17). It is because they disregard the differences among the tasks of politics and those of labor and work that they mistake power, which Arendt calls a "potentiality in being together," for a physical property that can be "possessed like strength or applied like force"(201). Arendt reconfigures this traditional conception of power to be conditional on plurality.

Although Adrienne Rich judged it to be irredeemably misogynist in 1976, it is precisely Arendt's silence about gender, ironic as it may seem, that makes a partial connection to contemporary feminist work. Specifically, her reconfiguration of power intersects with efforts to reposition gender in feminist theory and politics. This is a response to the charge that the unquestioned primacy of gender directed feminist theory toward analyses of women's difference from and oppression by men at the expense of recognizing differences of race, class, and ethnicity among women. In turn, it focused the movement on the needs of white middle-class professional women, which is probably the only social group that could perceive gender to be a sole or exclusive obstacle to its life chances.[45] In this context, the task of feminism is not to define "feminine" models of power but to define and practice democracy in what

---

inclines them to mistake strength for power, and that it is a projection of their separation anxiety to mistake freedom for sovereignty. See "Political Philosophy and the Patriarchal Unconscious: A Psychoanalytic Perspective on Epistemology and Metaphysics," in *Discovering Reality*, ed. Sandra Harding and Merrill B. Hintikka (Boston: D. Reidel, 1983), 245–281.

45. The relevant literature here is too numerous to list, but it includes bell hooks, *From Margin to Center* (Boston: South End Press, 1984), Nancy Fraser and Linda Nicholson, "Feminism without Foundations," in *Feminism/Postmodernism*, ed. Linda Nicholson (New York: Routledge, 1990), and Donna Haraway, "A Manifesto for Cyborgs: Science, Technology, and Socialist Feminism in the 1980s," *Socialist Review* 80 (1985): 82.

Iris Young calls a "heterogeneous public."[46] It would be rash to attempt to recover Arendt as a feminist in spite of herself, given that she quite explicitly distanced herself from the movement; nonetheless, I agree with Maria Markus that given Arendt's treatment of themes such as plurality, her work has received less attention from feminist theorists than it merits.[47]

Public power is Arendt's counter to the Archimedean ideal of power as leverage. But in contrast to the civic public, which Young has criticized for its aspiration to "transcend particularities of interest and affiliation to seek a common good," Arendt begins from the assumption that if power is public, then it can be held only on the condition of plurality, *the* condition of public space.[48] If power, like the public space, is contingent on plurality, then it depends on being connected to and distinct from others in an articulate way. Power cannot be exercised as leverage over others; it exists only *in relationships with* them. It is "generated when people gather together and 'act in concert,' [and] disappears the moment they depart" (HC, 244). Consequently, it "is always, as we would say, a power potential and not an unchangeable, measurable, and reliable entity like force or strength"(200). Where leverage is calculable, power *in relationship* is uncertain; it rests "upon the unreliable and only temporary agreement of many wills and intentions" and so shifts with the ebb and flow of those alliances(201). Like articulated solidarity, this power is not founded on a pre-political ground like truth, faith, shared identity, or even force. Rather, it is constituted by a "mutual promise" to act on a specific response to an interpreted situation (HC, 245).[49]

46. Young, *Justice*, esp. chap. 6.
47. Maria Markus attributes the reluctance to engage with Arendt's work to a "disturbing tendency in contemporary feminist theory . . . [to be] prepared to re-think, re-evaluate, re-interpret, or even simply learn from different theoretical propositions produced by males," but to dismiss as male-identified those women thinkers who neither identified with feminism nor employed gender as an analytic category. "The 'Anti-Feminism' of Hannah Arendt," *Thesis Eleven* 17 (1987): 76.
48. Young, *Justice*, 97.
49. Steven Lukes is simply off the mark when, basing his argument solely on the abbreviated account in Arendt's *On Violence*, he claims that she conceives of power as an

Promise-making is the alternative Arendt proposes to the Archimedean fiction of power as sovereignty or leverage. Unlike the fiction of mastery, which is an attempt to escape the web of plurality and to deny "the impossibility of foretelling the consequences of an act within a community of equals where everybody has the same capacity to act," promise-making acknowledges those limits and attempts to work within them. She calls promising "the only alternative to a mastery which relies on domination of one's self and rule over others," because promising brings into being a sovereignty that is necessarily shared (because you cannot make a promise to yourself) and limited by "an agreed purpose." Promising creates "isolated islands of certainty in an ocean of uncertainty" by defining an action to which the promisers agree to be bound. Mutual promise serves to mitigate the uncertainty of acting under the conditions of natality and plurality while protecting those conditions. It is because a promise is only a partial abrogation of both natality and plurality that it focuses individuals on a *limited* common purpose. That this purpose be a precisely specified short-term goal is crucial to the legitimacy of a promise, because the "basic unreliability" of human beings conditioned by natality puts it beyond their capacity to commit to anything absolutely. Human beings "never can guarantee today who they will be tomorrow" and so cannot bind themselves exclusively to a purpose that supercedes all others in perpetuity (HC, 244–245).

This stipulation that promising temporarily unite actors around a specific "agreed purpose" may seem at odds with Arendt's insistence that action not be reduced to its motives or goals. This critique of political instrumentalism is central to her critique of modernity as an era that has eroded the distinction between action, which is meaningful, and work, which is merely useful. That utility had increasingly become a political imperative she took to be a consequence of the rise of the social, with its constriction of public space and denigration of human ideals.

" 'ability', not a relationship." Missing altogether what I have called Arendt's critique of power as leverage, the centrality of plurality to an Arendtian "public," and her attempt to define a uniquely activist conception of power, Lukes deems her work to be a conceptualization of " 'influence' but not of 'power.' " In *Power: A Radical View* (London: Macmillan, 1974), 31.

Although it seems inconsistent, her insistence that action be meaningful (rather than determined by utility) and that it be limited by a specific purpose is not a contradiction but an insight that follows from her analysis of totalitarianism.

One difference between politics and totalitarianism is that where the former is organized by the articulation of common interests, the latter is unified by propaganda that plays on mass sentiment. The goal of a mass movement is not power, but strength. Power, which comes to be in the "interspaces" when human beings are joined together *and* distinguished from one another by their participation in speech and action, respects the condition of plurality. By contrast, strength is accomplished by fusion: "Masses are not held together by a consciousness of common interest and they lack that specific class *articulateness* which is expressed in *determined, limited, and obtainable goals*" (OT, 311; emphasis added). What Arendt rejects here is the way in which mass movements conflate meaningful action with the pretense to world-historical significance. Where a mass movement demands that its followers be unconditionally loyal to unspecified goals such as world conquest, the "concrete content" of a political program is the condition on which its participants lend their support and the standard against which they evaluate its success (OT, 324). There is something more to this action's "concrete content" than its goals: its principles. As I have argued, the principles of action are concrete in the sense that they cannot just be held intellectually but must be enacted. But the concreteness of enactment is distinct from instrumentality in that principles, in contrast to goals, can be neither implemented nor exhausted.

How well does Arendt's promise-making counter the traditional model of sovereignty? As Hanna Pitkin has argued, there is nothing revolutionary about promises; on the contrary, promising is fundamental to the concept of liberty as understood by the tradition of social contract theory against which Arendt claims to be in "manifest contradiction."[50] Where Pitkin might say there is nothing unique about promises, Michel Foucault would argue that there is nothing liberating about them. Foucault claims that promises "efface the domination intrinsic to power"

---

50. Pitkin, "Justice," 337.

by establishing what seems to be reciprocity of obligation between sovereign and subjects. Contrary to the claim to set the parameters of legitimate power by the device of mutual entailment, Foucault argues that the discourse of right "puts in motion relations that are not relations of sovereignty but of domination." Such domination is not enforced overtly as leverage, "that solid and global kind of domination that one person exercises over others, or one group over another"; rather, it is insinuated into putatively cooperative relations through the norm of integrity that is taken to be a condition of intersubjective agreement.[51] In the very ideal of concerted action in accord with a "mutual promise," it would seem that Arendt has not offered a democratic alternative to coercion; instead, she has reiterated what Peter Digeser calls the "fourth face of power" that produces "the responsible subject and the practice of promising, [and] is conveyed only by acting upon specific intentions and goals."[52]

There are some important differences, however, between promising as Arendt describes it and promising in the modern social contract tradition to which both Pitkin and Foucault refer. In that tradition, a promise is understood as a contract that is binding because it occurs in a context where obligatory acts are already stabilized either by an explicit prior agreement (as in the Hobbesian contract with the sovereign) or by common recognition of the practice of giving one's word (as in Rawls's original position). Typically, then, a promise is a private contract whose reliability is secured either by the guarantee that the sovereign will enforce it or (in the more nearly just society) by the confidence that people can be trusted to keep their word. Arendt's innovation is to attempt to define promising as a public act, not in the ordinary sense of something that can be concluded "in" public, but in the sense of a capacity that is conditional on natality. The uniqueness of promising, as animated by

51. Foucault, *Power/Knowledge*, 95–96. Dana Villa argues that both Foucault and Arendt are critics of sovereignty, claiming that they "present complementary narratives about the closure of the space for action in the modern age." Both see this closure as a consequence of the normalization of this space by mechanisms of social power that discipline bodies, thereby precluding the enactment of natality. See "Beyond Good and Evil: Arendt, Nietzsche, and the Aestheticization of Political Action," *Political Theory* 20 (1992): 274–308.
52. Peter Digeser, "The Fourth Face of Power," *The Journal of Politics* 54 (1992): 984.

natality, is that it need not rely on a previously secured context of relations but brings new publics into being. Drawing attention to its innovative aspect, Bonnie Honig calls Arendt's promises "performative
utterances" whose purpose "is to bring something into being that did
not exist before."[53] The performative quality of promising gives it the
capacity to authorize political power without reference to anything outside the practice of promising itself.[54] Thus, promising does not serve to
fix the boundaries of individuals but opens up new possibilities by means
of new connections. It is oriented to action, not exchange.

Against Honig's claim, it could be argued that far from bringing something new into being, promises originate in and express individuals' authentic, prepolitical identities. This would mean that Arendt does not
reconfigure the autonomous individual subject of Enlightenment political thought but reinstates it. Once again, however, it is deceptively easy
to assimilate Arendt's work to the conventions she resists; although she
seems to work with it, her account of promising goes against the grain.
Arendt argues that it is not the *self* that makes the promise, but the
promise that makes the self: "Without being bound to the fulfillment of
promises, we would never be able to keep our identities; we would be
condemned to wander helplessly and without direction in the darkness
of each man's lonely heart, caught in its contradictions and equivocali-
ties—a darkness which only the light shed over the public realm through
the presence of others, who confirm the identity between the one who
promises and the one who fulfills, can dispel" (HC, 237).

Arendt locates the moral force of promises not in the integrity of a
putatively inner self but in the presence of those who witness the promise. She argues, in effect, that the self exists as a reliable entity only in

53. Bonnie Honig, "Declarations of Independence: Arendt and Derrida on the Problem of
   Founding a Republic," *American Political Science Review* 85 (1991): 101.
54. Honig notes that Arendt's account of promises is incomplete in that she addresses
   neither "the question of the legitimacy of the practice" nor that "of its own techniques
   of self-legitimation," ibid., 103. This is consistent with my claim that Arendt's account
   of publicity is partial because she gives no account of the processes by which to distinguish common interests from forced consensus. I suggest here, however, that Arendt
   rules out some of the techniques of self-legitimation that usually accompany promise-
   making by her unconventional account of the self.

public.[55] The inner self known through introspection is no more than "an ever-moving stream" of fragmentary perceptions.[56] The return to companionship is a relief to solitary thinkers because "it makes them 'whole' again, saves them from the dialogue of thought in which one remains always equivocal, restores the identity which makes them speak with the single voice of one unexchangeable person" (OT, 476). Despite the fact that we commonly speak of making promises "to ourselves," Arendt's denial of the "inner self" renders this claim nonsensical. She insists that the "moral code . . . inferred from the faculties of forgiving and making promises, rests on experiences which nobody could ever have with himself, which, on the contrary, are entirely based on the presence of others."[57] Contrary to subject-centered understandings of promises, Arendt suggests that the belief that promises are proof of character and integrity has always been fundamentally misconceived. The moral force of a promise derives not from a continuity internal to the self who utters it but from that which is conferred by the presence of others before whom it is performed; it is not subjectivity but intersubjectivity that makes promises morally binding.

Arendt's discussion of promises is unusual, then, in that far from

55. Bonnie Honig makes a similar argument in a poststructuralist idiom, claiming that "Arendt's actors do not act because of what they already are, their actions do not express a prior, stable identity; they presuppose an unstable, multiple self that seeks its, at best, episodic self-realization in action and in the identity that is its reward." Bonnie Honig, "Toward an Agonistic Feminism: Hannah Arendt and the Politics of Identity," in *Feminists Theorize the Political*, ed. Judith Butler and Joan W. Scott (New York: Routledge, 1992), 220.

56. Ibid., 282.

57. HC, 238. I found this to be especially true for me when I was in graduate school, and it is demonstrated to me over again in my work now with graduate students. The commitment to write a dissertation is an unusually difficult one to make precisely because in the beginning it is a promise that you have no choice but to make largely to yourself. It is unusual because at that stage neither you, nor your advisors, nor even your best friends know what you are doing, no matter how engaged they are in your project. It is only as you progress in an academic career that you establish a public space for your work by virtue of the way it is received and the expectations it generates, not just among those who sympathize with it but also among those who question it. Beginning the dissertation is so difficult because of what Arendt calls the "unbearable isolation" of being without "the most elementary form of human creativity," which is the trust that your work will have a place in the world (OT, 475).

confirming the fiction of an "inner self," she shifts the locus of the moral force of commitment from that self to the world. As in the redefinition of sovereignty, this shift depends on conceiving of promises in performative terms. That is, it depends on the understanding that promises do not originate in subjectivity but rather bring new agency into being by constituting new relationships. Even understood in its capacity to enact new relationships, promising is still double-sided in that relationships engender new expectations, the aspect of power that Foucault identifies with discipline.

Second, promising does not establish a sovereign power with leverage "over" subjects. If power is collaborative, if it "springs up between men when they act together and vanishes the moment they disperse," then there can be no fulcrum external to the web of plurality from which to exercise control "over" it (HC, 200). Obviously, no one can be in public in a web of relations with others and at the same time be at a vantage point outside the public realm. This means that leverage—power exercised *over* others—could not pass itself off as legitimate in Arendt's public space.

Most important, promising does not confirm the fiction of sovereignty in Hobbes's sense of a total, all-encompassing, and perpetual power—or even in the sense of Rousseau's general will. In the first place, the power that promising authorizes can be neither all-encompassing nor perpetual because the selves who constitute it are multiple and shifting. Arendtian solidarity is a partial consensus, limited to the particular locality defined by a specific problem. In addition, this local consensus is partial with respect to each individual who enters into agreement with the others; that is, there is no expectation that they identify themselves exclusively in terms of any one particular locality and, hence, no expectation that they will be permanently allied and perfectly in harmony with each other.

Shortcomings of the New Lexicon

Up to now, I have been engaged in demonstrating the connections between Arendt's uniquely public understanding of solidarity and the problem, identified by contemporary democratic theorists, of the unitary public. Having shown how I think Arendt's work connects to that problem, I now want to take the more critical tack of asking just how democratic she is. This question brings me to a direct confrontation with the problem of Arendt's pronouncements about the rise of the social and requires that I re-evaluate her lexicon. Before reconsidering plurality and natality, the "conditions" of the public space, I want to examine the term *condition* itself.

The concept of "human condition" expresses her sense of the fragility of human existence. She introduces it in opposition to "human nature," which is the purportedly natural foundation to which many Western political thinkers appeal to validate their claims about the limits of and possibilities for human freedom in politics. Consistently with her critique of rulership, Arendt refutes the appeal to "human nature" as an entity that is both impossible to study and would be self-defeating if it could be known. Studying human nature, she claims, is as impossible for human beings as "jumping over our own shadows" (HC, 10). Further, knowing human nature presupposes that human beings can look upon themselves from a God's vantage point, from which they must be reduced from agents to objects of study. If political knowledge is, as Arendt claims, knowledge of human agency, then such a vantage point is inevitably self-defeating.

Arendt introduces the concept of "condition" to establish a frame for political theory that is not deterministic. The "human condition," she claims, amounts to "the conditions under which life has been given to man," and the "self-made conditions" that men create by the activities of labor, work, and action (HC, 9). The term *condition* has two distinct meanings for Arendt: the present state of things, as in a "given" condition, and a requisite that must be met in order for something else to occur, as in an "enabling" condition. Because Arendt frequently uses this term in both senses at once, she undercuts the distinction she attempts to draw between the "natural" and the conditioned.

For example, Arendt claims that plurality is both a "human condition," and *the* "condition" of politics (HC, 7). As a human condition, she means that plurality is given in the facts of human multiplicity, interconnectedness, and sameness in difference, as well as in the faculties

of speech and action that mean that humans are not "endlessly repro-
ducible repetitions of the same model"(8). As an enabling condition of
politics, plurality means the formal institution of equality before the law
in spite of differences, which must be artificially constructed by the constitution of public space. By her ambiguous use of the term *condition*,
Arendt suggests that the mere fact of plurality is sufficient to guarantee
the institution of equality. This ambiguity is explicit in the claim that
the "reality of the public realm relies on the simultaneous "*presence* of
innumerable perspectives and aspects in which the common world *presents itself*"(57; emphasis added). The language of "presence" gives an
account of the public space that is at odds with her discussion of the
Socratic dialogue. Where the former suggests that publicity is simply
there wherever people come together, in the latter she argues that differences must be voiced, acknowledged, and contested in order to be
public. In turn, this dispute cannot take place without some kind of
constitutional guarantees equivalent to public friendship. The language
of presence, then, permits her to avoid specifying the constitutional
guarantees that are necessary to make the "given" of human plurality a
meaningful part of public institutions. Absent an account of the requisites and practices of political dialogue, Arendt's "public space" is more
a metaphysical concept than a political one.

There is a similar ambiguity with respect to the term *natality*. Arendt
claims that natality is a possibility for new beginnings that is given to
everyone "by virtue of being born," and that the challenge of natality is
to make this beginning in a distinctive way (HC, 204). She also claims
that it is an enabling condition of power, which exists only where people
speak and act together in public. Again, by calling natality a condition
in both senses of the term, she suggests that the capacity for action is
sufficient to guarantee the constitution of a public realm that is open to
the entrance of every individual on his or her own terms. But as she
acknowledges in her own writings on the phenomenon of assimilationism among European Jews in the eighteenth and nineteenth centuries,
entrance is a dilemma for marginal groups (OT, chap. 5). Just as the
mere presence of plurality seems sufficient to secure equality, so too the
mere presence of natality appears sufficient to guarantee everyone equal
access to public power.

The features that Arendt attributes to "plurality" and "natality" are classic ideals of democracy. Together, they promote a conception of heterogeneous community in which there is equality in light of differences, civility in disagreement, and transformation in response to criticism. According to Arendt's own historical writings, they are not given "conditions" but, rather, achievements of political action. Taking the various aspects of plurality for example, it may be fair to say that multiplicity and differentiation are "givens" of the human condition; equality in difference, however, must be politically constructed. Similarly, interconnectedness may be endemic to the human condition, but it is not a spontaneous condition of politics. Organizations must be built before actions are possible, and the connections that constitute an organization are not "given" but must be secured by political organizing.[58] Further, where Arendt constructs natality as a problem of distinguishing oneself in order to generate power, for members of groups that have been excluded from a public realm, the problem is to have one's distinctiveness recognized as an excellence, not a deviation from existing norms. In that case, the problem is not to distinguish oneself in order to be accorded power but to seize power in order to redefine the standards by which distinctiveness is recognized. Finally, power does not "spring up between men when they act together" (HC, 200). On the contrary, action must be public to generate power, publicity requires organizing, and organizing takes resources. Thus, every individual who acts or group that attempts to organize is not assured of public visibility.

The argument so far suggests that Arendt's ambiguous use of the term *condition* is inherently conservative because it constructs political guarantees that are the *achievements* of democratic politics as "givens" of the human condition. Far more serious, Arendt protects the assumption of their "given-ness" from questioning by the opposition she sets up between the "public" and the "social." She characterizes the two in terms of a simple dichotomy. Where the public is the realm of speech, action, and freedom, the social is the realm of necessity. It pertains to activities devoted solely to the preservation of life, in which "the fact of mutual dependence for the sake of life and nothing else assumes public signif-

58. Isaac makes a similar observation in *Arendt, Camus, and Modern Rebellion*, 244.

icance and where the activities connected with sheer survival are permitted to appear in public" (HC, 46). It is a realm in which humans
are equal not by virtue of their uniqueness but by the need for survival
that they share with each other and with other species. Where public
equality is premised on the display of one's unique excellence in front
of one's peers, social equality is premised on sameness. It is a realm of
behavior that tends toward conformity, "imposing innumerable and various rules, all of which tend to 'normalize' its members, to make them
behave, to exclude spontaneous action or outstanding achievement"(40).
Finally, Arendt asserts that the social can be a realm without language.
As needs are open to neither interpretation nor principled disagreement,
to make them known, "to *express* fear, joy, etc., we would not need
speech. Gestures would be enough, and sounds would be a good enough
substitute for gestures if one needed to bridge long distances" (LKPP,
70). Freedom depends on the segregation of the public and social, because when social problems enter into the public realm, there is nothing
to say and no way to act.

The possibility of public life rests on an artificial agreement to begin
with individuals who are not just different and incomparable with respect to their excellences but also the same in their basic needs, and
accord them equal respect in political speech and action. This agreement
effects a structural separation of the private, the social, and the public
that guarantees privacy on one hand and publicity on the other. These
guarantees protect individuality in two distinct but complementary ways.
Privacy is necessary to secure a "tangible, worldly place of one's own"
as a respite from the monotonous struggle for physical survival, as well
as from the intensity of public appearance (HC, 70). When the public
and the social overwhelm the private, it is impossible to perform any
activity that requires deep concentration—thinking, writing, conversing
with an intimate, and more.

The guarantee of publicity is necessary to protect the distinction between equality, which presupposes plurality, and sameness. The more the
social encroaches on the public, the more assimilation, which is requisite
to membership in society, becomes a criterion for public participation.
This is, according to Arendt, the problem of modernity: that "society
has conquered the public realm and that distinction and difference have

become private matters of the individual" (HC, 41). The task of a political constitution, or its equivalent, is to construct a public artifice that can reconcile the fact of differences with the possibility for equality without reducing the former to normalcy and the latter to sameness.

One problem with this dichotomous opposition of the social and public is that the same conservatism that is inherent in Arendt's use of the term *condition* manifests itself here. To assert that public equality must be protected from encroachment by differing social conditions is to assume already that the state does not discriminate against groups by virtue of "social" characteristics such as race, class, gender, sexuality, and so on. Here again, Arendt posits what can only be an *achievement* of political struggle as a structural *prerequisite* of public life.

Even more troubling, Arendt understands the Greek *polis* to exemplify the proper ordering of public and social. She claims that the Greeks managed to guarantee political freedom by securing public equality against social conformism. She writes: "the [ancient] public realm was reserved for individuality; it was the only place where men could show who they really and inexchangeably were" (HC, 41). This is, as many have argued, a view of the *polis* that is idealized to the point of sheer fantasy. Greek citizens secured the integrity of their public space by making its separation from the social a matter of class. It was the task of laborers, women, and slaves to tend to necessity, and these classes were denied citizenship for that reason. The *polis* was a realm of freedom only for a social elite that was segregated by race, class, and gender; by the standards of any modern democratic polity, then, it was far from plural. In a comment for which she has been greatly criticized, Arendt seems to bemoan the loss of so neat a separation between the public and social, writing: "The fact that the modern age emancipated the working classes and the women at nearly the same historical moment must certainly be counted among the characteristics of an age which no longer believes that bodily functions and material concerns should be hidden"(73).

Sheldon Wolin argues that it is precisely this separation that makes Arendt's conception of politics "incompatible with democratic ideals." He characterizes it as "a politics of lofty ambition, glory, and honor, unsullied by private interest or the material concerns in the larger society 'outside'."[59] According to this interpretation, the "plurality" that constitutes Arendt's public space refers only to differences in opinion and perspective that Arendt holds to be categorically distinct from differences determined by race, class, or gender. Wendy Brown is more generous to Arendt, arguing that her work inspires the project to develop "feminist postmodern political spaces," but she cautions that feminist politics must ultimately be unlike Arendtian politics in that "these spaces cannot be pristine, rarified, and policed at their boundaries, but are necessarily cluttered, attuned to earthly concerns and visions, incessantly disrupted, invaded, and reconfigured."[60] As Brown suggests, the public/social separation is especially antagonistic to feminist theory and politics, in that it appears to deny the legitimacy of the principal achievement of feminist theory and politics which was to politicize the "household" and women's putatively "natural" functions within it. To Wolin and Brown, the claim that Arendt writes in opposition to the Archimedean norm would seem implausible, to say the least; they suggest that she recommends Archimedean disembodiment by her categorical separation of social needs from public principles.

Critics such as Wolin and Brown bring to the fore a question about Arendt's plurality that is important for any democratic appropriation of her work. To what kind of differences does this term refer? It would seem that by the public/social distinction, Arendt constrains plurality to refer only to individual differences in talent, opinion, and perspective, which she holds categorically distinct from group differences determined by social location such as class, gender, color, ethnicity, age, and sexuality, to name a few. Strictly speaking, Arendt's work evidences the disregard for social groups that Iris Young has argued is typical of Western political philosophy.[61] In addition to the elitism of Arendt's nostalgia for the ancient *polis*, it also seems that her work is at odds with democratic theory by virtue of the classically liberal separation between the economy and politics that she instantiates by means of the public/social dichot-

---

59. Wolin, "Hannah Arendt: Democracy and the Political," 3, 7.
60. Wendy Brown, "Feminist Hesitations, Postmodern Exposures," *differences: A Journal of Feminist Cultural Studies* 3 (1991): 79–80.
61. Young, *Justice*, esp. introduction and chap. 2.

omy.[62] Although Arendt's use of the term *plurality* to insist that politics is intersubjective is an invitation to democratic appropriation, her stipulation that private and social matters be excluded from public discourse is a deterrent to such a reading.

Following several other interpreters of Arendt's work, I will suggest a less dichotomous reading of the public/social split. However starkly she asserts them at some points, the distinctions among the public, private, and social are not categorical ones. As Paul Ricoeur has argued, "These categories are not categories in the Kantian sense, i.e. a-historical structures of the mind. They are themselves historical structures." But first, I propose a more provocative defense against Arendt's democratic critics: that these distinctions do not simply invoke elite privilege but make it visible in what Ricoeur calls its "temporal traits."[63] One justification Arendt gives for her insistence on the structural separation of the public, private, and social is that it protects mortality, which she calls the "hallmark of human existence" (HC, 18). Although humans share with other animals the fact that they will eventually die, she observes that human mortality is unique in that it is not just biological but historical. That is, the distinctiveness of human mortality "lies in the fact that individual life, with a recognizable life-story from birth to death, rises out of biological life. This individual life is distinguished from all other things by the rectilinear course of its movement, which, so to speak, cuts through the circular movement of biological life. This is mortality: to move along a rectilinear line in a universe where everything, if it moves at all, moves in a cyclical order" (HC, 19). When the public and private realms are taken over by the demands of the biological necessity, what is lost is this "rectilinear line" that interrupts these repetitious processes. This means that there is no choice but to labor without interruption. An existence in the absence of this "rectilinear line" is defined, as Paul Ricoeur puts it, by the "absence of durability."[64] Durability is the intangible privilege

---

62. Arendt is by no means a liberal. For one thing, she blames liberalism for contributing to the eclipse of the public realm by making the public "a function of the private" and making individuality a private concern (HC, 69).

63. Ricoeur, "Action, Story, and History," 61, 64.

64. Ibid., 63.

of those who enjoy an audience for their work and who can afford the privilege of time "off" for thinking, reading, or contemplation of some other kind. Of the person from whom no public appearance is demanded and who has no private space to which to repair, no story can be told.

Lars Eighner, a writer who was homeless for three years in the late 1980s, has written what might be termed a critical travel narrative about living in the absence of durability. Eighner characterizes homelessness as a condition in which the activities connected with sheer survival are not just permitted but *required* to appear in public. It is, in Arendt's terms, the epitome of a social existence whose principal characteristic is the "unrelenting ennui" of exposure to natural processes, uninterrupted by either public expectations or private relief. He writes: "In spite of the challenges that homelessness presented, the chief characteristic of my experience of homelessness was tedium. . . . Our immediate needs I met with more or less trouble, but once that was done I could do no more. Day after day I could aspire, within reason, to nothing more than survival. Although the planets wandered among the stars and the moon waxed and waned, the identical naked barrenness of existence was exposed to me, day in and day out."[65] Suggesting that a homeless existence is not, in Arendt's sense, a "mortal" existence, Eighner writes: "A homeless life has no storyline. It is a pointless circular rambling about the stage that can be brought to happy conclusion only by a deus ex machina."[66] Juxtaposing Eighner's account of homelessness against Arendt's account of the necessary distinctions among the public, private, and social suggests that the fact of separating these is not, in itself, enough to justify labeling her an elitist. Not only is there some merit in the insistence that they be separate, but the very capacity *to* maintain a distinct articulation of these various temporal dimensions may be an intangible social privilege that Arendt's work makes visible. To insist on their separation as a *prerequisite* of publicity, however, is to confuse as a structural precondition of politics something that, in a society that is unequal to begin with, must be politically achieved.

---

65. Lars Eighner, *Travels with Lizbeth: Three Years on the Road and on the Streets* (New York: St. Martin's Press, 1993), x–xi.
66. Ibid., 97.

Even if it is not as elitist as Wolin and others have argued, to assert a categorical distinction between the public and the social is to sidestep a primary question of democratic politics: How to sustain a tension between plurality—the condition of differences not just in perspective but also of social and "temporal" privilege—and publicity. Without differentiation, as Arendt has argued, there would be no need for politics. Yet, in the face of vast disparities in wealth, there can be no mutuality. To assert a categorical distinction between the two in this second instance is an offense against justice in its most rudimentary sense because it insulates such disparities from criticism.

Against those who argue that this kind of insulation is just what Arendt wants to accomplish with the distinction she makes between the social and public realms, I suggest that there is some ambiguity in Arendt's work with respect to the status of that distinction. Certainly, there are many places in her writing where she argues for a classic separation between the social realm of material interests and needs, and the public realm of principle. For example, she attributes to social questions "an irresistible tendency to grow, to devour the older realms of the political and private as well as the more recently established sphere of intimacy" (HC, 45). This image of an insatiable organism suggests that the "social" cannot enter the public realm without overwhelming it and that there is nothing to do but to stamp it out. I propose to call this classic construction of the relationship between the "public" and the "social" Arendt's "disciplinary" public realm. It is, as Brown argues, an image of a space that must be "policed" at its boundaries in order that it be "uncluttered."

Alongside the disciplinary public space, Arendt gives a much different account of the public/social distinction that constructs what I propose to call the "overgrown" public space. In the following passage, she describes the public realm as a space in which the "givens" of physical existence intertwine with contested actions. She writes that the public is a space created by "words and deeds" that "are *about* some worldly objective reality in addition to being a disclosure of the acting and speaking agent. Since this disclosure of the subject is an integral part of all, even the most 'objective' intercourse, the physical, worldly in-between *along with its interests* [emphasis added] is overlaid and, as it were, overgrown with an altogether different in-between which consists of deeds and words and owes its origin exclusively to men's acting and speaking directly *to* one another" (HC, 182–183). This passage both connects to and reconfigures her earlier account of the social. Here, the public space is an unmanageable garden in which the interested "worldly" in-between is overgrown with deeds and words that are conditioned but not determined by worldly interests. In contrast to some passages where Arendt romanticizes the public as a clearing or open space, here it seems that worldly interests inevitably clutter up that space so that there can be no categorical separation of the public from the social.

Lewis and Sandra Hinchman suggest an alternative interpretation of the public/social distinction that accords with Arendt's description of the "overgrown" public space. They claim that "almost all of Arendt's crucial terms are in fact 'existentials' and not 'categories'."[67] That is, they are not meant to be valid from the "outside" to empirical researchers looking for absolute distinctions between "public" and "social" issues. Instead, they are meant to express subtle differences that are apparent from the 'inside' to participants in various social activities. For example, the differences between labor and work, the former which Arendt argues is for the sake of immediate consumption and the latter for producing lasting objects, may not be evident to the social scientist studying the activities of a group of wage laborers. But various jobs may be experienced quite differently by the wage-earner depending on the social conditions of production.

On a panel discussion late in her life, Arendt remarked on the relationship between public and social problems in a manner that is consistent with her description of the "overgrown" public space and supported the interpretation of these terms as "existentials." Suggesting that this distinction is not categorical but rather a matter of framing, Arendt stated that political problems have a "double face," one public and the other social. The former involves things that "we cannot figure out with certainty," and the latter involves things "where the right meas-

---

67. Lewis P. Hinchman and Sandra K. Hinchman, "In Heidegger's Shadow: Hannah Arendt's Phenomenological Humanism," *Review of Politics* 46 (1984): 197.

ures can be figured out." This distinction turns on plurality, which, in this context, is the condition of the possibility of disagreement. Arendt claimed that it is "phony and a plague" to debate the social face of a problem because it has an obvious answer dictated by the requisites of human survival. Using housing as an example, she asserted that its social "face" is that "everybody should have decent housing," and its public "face" is the question whether "adequate housing means integration."[68] It may be more a matter of naivete than—as Wolin might read it— elitism that makes Arendt so sure that there is a fundamental consensus regarding basic human needs.[69]

If it is the case that "public" and "social" are not inherent properties but "faces," then it follows that *both* are open to dispute. This means that maintaining a separation between these two realms cannot be a structural prerequisite of democratic politics. Further, although political communities may recognize a distinction between public and social problems, this distinction could not be settled in advance but would have to be politically fought over. As Seyla Benhabib has argued, for Arendt to maintain the public/social divide as a categorical distinction and structural requisite of politics is inconsistent on her own terms. Benhabib claims that Arendt offers two ways of differentiating between the two realms, either by the activities that go on in them—the public is concerned with "action as opposed to work or labor"—or by the "*substantive content*" of the dialogue about public problems. Either way, the boundary turns out to be permeable because problems that arise out of the social activities of work and labor can be framed for "public" discussion. Benhabib points out that, "the struggle to make something public is a struggle for justice," suggesting that to rule in advance on what is and is not public is inconsistent on Arendt's own terms. For one thing, a categorical determination of the two would have a more stultifying effect on speech and action than the "phony" debates about social

---

68. Hannah Arendt, "On Hannah Arendt," in *Hannah Arendt: The Recovery of the Public World*, ed. Melvyn Hill (New York: St. Martin's Press, 1979), 317–318.
69. Lewis P. and Sandra K. Hinchman note that "it is not that Arendt is indifferent to social justice, but that she thinks, perhaps naively, that the demands of justice are (or should be) self-evident and, to that extent, unpolitical." "Existentialism Politicized: Arendt's Debt to Jaspers," *Review of Politics* 53 (1991): 466n.

problems that Arendt so despised, by shutting down political debate before it could begin. Further, given Arendt's assertion that it is acting in concert that opens public spaces and her belief in the spontaneity and unpredictability of political action, the boundaries of the public space are necessarily uncertain. As Benhabib puts it, "Even on Arendtian terms, the effect of collective action in concert will be to put ever new and unexpected items on the agenda of public debate."[70]

Based on the assumption that the public/social distinction can not be a categorical one, Nancy Fraser makes a radical appropriation of Arendt's terminology. She suggests that the social be viewed as the "site where . . . rival need interpretations are transformed into rival programmatic conceptions, rival alliances are forged around rival policy proposals, and unequally endowed groups compete to shape the formal policy agenda."[71] If needs are not "given," as Arendt seems to believe, then the social would not be the realm of the uncontestable, but rather that in which contests over the boundaries of the public realm take place. In sum, Benhabib argues that even if Arendt sometimes suggests an Archimedean separation of the public and the social, that separation is inconsistent on her own terms, and Fraser's work demonstrates that Arendt's theory gives rise to more radical interpretive possibilities than she herself may have allowed.

Besides the inconsistencies it introduces into her thought and the hermeneutic obstacles it presents to those who would like to appropriate Arendt's work into contemporary democratic and other critical debates, the public/social distinction presents a special problem for the interpretation I have begun to spin out. The classic version of this distinction typifies a narrative strategy that is not at odds with the Western political tradition at all. She asserts the separation absolutely and categorically and illustrates its importance with her stories of ephemeral moments of freedom—the Greek *polis* and the American Founding—that will be lost forever unless the social can be newly contained.[72] These classic aspects

70. Benhabib, *Situating the Self,* 94, 95.
71. Nancy Fraser, *Unruly Practices* (Minneapolis: University of Minnesota Press, 1989), 170.
72. Seyla Benhabib identifies this as one strain in Arendt's thought that derives "from an *Ursprungsphilosophie* which posits an original state or temporal point as the privileged source to which one must trace back the phenomena such as to capture their 'true'

of Arendt's work contravene the two principal claims I make: that
Arendt writes explicitly in opposition to political philosophers who have
written about politics from an Archimedean vantage point; and that she
practices a kind of storytelling that does not merely transmit traditions
or re-invent them but also stimulates autonomous critical thinking. Although these contravening aspects of Arendt's work are important, as
Jeffrey Isaac has recently observed, they "have been vastly exaggerated
out of an inattention to her own historical concerns."[73] The arguments
I make about Arendt's work are premised on an interpretive decision
that, like Isaac's, accords greater weight to the pariah theme than to her
classicism. But because the former cannot simply be made to erase the
latter, I return throughout this work to the problems that the classic
version of the public/social split poses for a democratic appropriation
of her thought.

---

meaning." She argues that this strain is countered by an equally pervasive "fragmentary
history" that is opposed to such nostalgia. In *Situating the Self,* 92.

73. Isaac, *Arendt, Camus, and Modern Rebellion,* 15.

3 The Critique of Abstract Impartiality

∎

Arendt objects to Archimedean philosophizing because it purports to be outside the web of plurality and, as such, confuses power with leverage and makes abstraction a condition of reliable knowledge. In the preceding chapter, I explicated one aspect of Arendt's critique of Archimedean thinking—the construction of power as leverage—and explained her answer to the problem of the unified public. She offers a model of democratic action in which the cohesiveness of the public is sustained, in the absence of a deeply felt, shared identity or an established tradition of abstract principles, by the articulation of a common problem and specific response. In this chapter I turn to Arendt's critique of the Archimedean presupposition that abstraction is requisite to impartiality and to the problem of public judgment, the second aspect of contemporary democratic theory that her work anticipates.

The Archimedean ideal of abstract impartiality poses a difficulty for democratic theory in that it makes the problem of public judgment impossible to resolve. If impartiality is necessarily abstract, then there can be no critical understanding absent an independent ground of justification. This means, in turn, that there is no way to conclude a public debate in a principled decision without appealing to an independent ground that compromises publicity. Thus, the Archimedean norm rules out the possibility of distinguishing force from power in judging and acting alike. Arendt counters this norm with a conception of knowledge that is neither subjective and particularist nor objective and abstract but situated *and* critical.

Interestingly, Arendt's critique of abstract impartiality has been ap-
propriated into contemporary critical debates by theorists who position
themselves on opposing sides of the question of humanism. She is
claimed as an intellectual ancestor by proponents of aesthetic resistance
to the normalizing forces of humanist conventions and by those who
argue that it is within the very tradition of humanism that the possibility
of a transformative critique of Western civilization is contained. This
debate can be characterized roughly as a contest between radical critics
of humanism and neohumanist critics of modernity. Radical critics of
humanism are involved in a wholesale rejection of reason that, it is
argued, promised liberation through mastery of nature—that is, of the
natural world purportedly external to the civilized world and of the
natural forces purportedly within the self. This emancipatory promise
could play itself out only in the proliferation of deadly technologies and
interest-driven objectifying relations.[1] Thus, it is not that Enlightenment
humanism failed to live up to its emancipatory promise, but that by
means of that very promise it committed Western civilization to its own
subjugation and to the subjugation of the civilizations it would inevitably
colonize.

Although neohumanist critics of modernity do not contest the
claim that the legacy of Enlightenment humanism has been one of
violence and subjugation, they take issue with the assertion that this
is *all* it has been and that, given the form of Enlightenment reason,
it could not have been *otherwise.*[2] The promise of liberation through

---

1. This position has a rich and varied history. The following could be considered among
   its proponents: Jean-Jacques Rousseau, Friedrich Nietzsche, Max Horkheimer and Theodor Adorno, Michel Foucault, and Jean-François Lyotard.
2. There are, of course, conservative defenders of Western civilization who do contest the
   claim that its history has been violent and antihumanist. I mean to distinguish this
   group, which is outside the debate that interests me, from those I take to be neohumanist critics of modernity. These two groups are lumped together when contemporary
   debates are characterized as a struggle between critics of Western civilization and its
   defenders. I am interested in an aspect of this larger struggle that is taking place not
   between critics and defenders of the political history and intellectual tradition of the
   West but *among* critics of this history and intellectual tradition. I choose to frame this
   aspect of the larger struggle as a debate among critics of modernity who position themselves differently with respect to the tradition of humanism, and I attempt to do justice
   to what I see as the complexity of the conflict: a consequence of the fact that critics of

mastery is grounded in only one aspect of reason, that which is oriented toward strategic action and conceives of the world in terms of instrumental or subject-object relations. To assume that strategic action is all that reason has to offer is to identify reason with purposive rationality and knowledge with technology. Neohumanists assert that reason has a second aspect, communicative rationality, that conceives of the world in terms of intersubjective (subject-subject) relations and is oriented toward mutual understanding.[3] This aspect of reason holds out the possibility for achieving noncoercive consensus on theoretical propositions, moral propositions, and aesthetic propositions. It opens up the possibility of generating power by "the unforced force of a better insight."[4]

Hannah Arendt's political philosophy enters into these debates by means of two competing strains that Seyla Benhabib has identified in her work. In Arendt's "panegyric" to Ancient Greece, Benhabib discerns an urge to recover the true meaning of public life by a return to its lost origin in the *polis*. Against this tradition-affirming project, Benhabib claims that there is also a fragmentary and discontinuous historiography whose aim is not to reestablish coherency but to collect mementos of past moments of resistance in the hope of inspiring continued struggle in the present. She finds this in Arendt's "odd methodology which conceives of political thought as 'storytelling'." Benhabib goes on to argue that Arendt's conception of public space gives rise to two distinct understandings of politics, depending on which of these two supplies the context in which it is read. In the

---

modernity share a common ground as critics of imperialism, colonialism, and ethnocentrism but *disagree* on the question of whether these are a necessary and inevitable outcome of Enlightenment humanism.

3. I do not mean to suggest that Jürgen Habermas and his students are the only neohumanist critics of modernity or that instrumental reason and communicative rationality exhaust the possible meanings of reason. A thinker who makes similar arguments, framed as critiques of "rationalism" and "enterprise association," is Michael Oakeshott. His unique understandings of skepticism, conversation, and conservatism offer a conception of critical reason that rivals that of Habermas. See *On Human Conduct* (London: Oxford University Press, 1975) and *Rationalism in Politics* (New York: Methuen, 1962, rpt. 1981).

4. Jürgen Habermas, *The Philosophical Discourse of Modernity*, trans. Frederick Lawrence (Cambridge: MIT Press, 1990), 305.

Greek context, Arendt's is an "agonistic" or competitive politics that takes place in a public space where "moral and political greatness, heroism and preeminence are revealed, displayed, shared with others." But in the context of storytelling, politics is cooperative and takes place in any space in which people gather to engage in "common action coordinated through speech and persuasion," and especially action oriented toward resistance. Benhabib calls this the "associational" public space.[5] I suggest that this nuanced and provocative reading maps the contours of the contest over Arendt's work that is currently taking place between radical critics of humanism and neohumanist critics of modernity.

The argument that Arendt's work is an agonistic celebration of "greatness," conceived as an aesthetic disregard for the practical consequences of political action, is an identifiable "camp" among interpreters of Arendt's political philosophy. This claim was initially deployed to discredit Arendt as a theorist of democracy.[6] Noel O'Sullivan writes that Arendt's "conception of politics as the sphere in which each man seeks to establish his identity by great deeds that impress his peers means that fellow actors are consistently assigned the role of an appreciative but essentially passive audience; they are treated, that is, as spectators watching a drama unfold."[7] Similarly, Sheldon Wolin calls her conception of politics "essentially dramaturgic," writing that it consists "of public performances staged in a clearly defined public realm and witnessed by an audience of equals engrossed in what was taking place and indifferent to calculations of material benefit or consequence."[8] Thus, on Wolin's account, citizens "attend" the spectacle of Arendtian politics as they would a good adventure film: it distracts them from the material concerns that might otherwise prompt them to demand radical political change. More recently, George Kateb has argued that Arendt's vision of

5. Seyla Benhabib, *Situating the Self* (New York: Routledge, 1992), 91, 92, 93, 93.
6. See, for example, Martin Jay's contribution to "Hannah Arendt: Opposing Views," *Partisan Review* 45 (1978): 348–368.
7. Noel K. O'Sullivan, "Politics, Totalitarianism, and Freedom: The Political Thought of Hannah Arendt," *Political Studies* 21 (1973): 197.
8. Sheldon Wolin, "Hannah Arendt and the Ordinance of Time," *Social Research* 44 (Spring 1977): 96.

political action is, in its antiutilitarianism and disregard for traditional moral values, structurally similar to totalitarianism.[9]

Interestingly, the "agonistic" reading of Arendt's public space has taken on a completely different relationship to democracy in the more recent work of poststructuralist theorists. It is now deployed to capture Arendt's work for the project of a radical transformation of democratic theory and practice. Bonnie Honig, for example, appropriates Arendt's rejection of identity-based claims to solidarity as a possible starting place for heterogeneous democratic and feminist movements. Attempting to break the identification of agonal politics with the elitism and masculine bravado of classic *virtu*, she argues that it is precisely the "agonistic and performative impulse of [Arendt's] politics," that could inform radical democratic and feminist conceptions of politics.[10] She argues that a politics that puts contest and resistance ahead of stability is especially pertinent to feminists who are concerned to get beyond the essentialism of a movement based in sisterhood and to democrats who want to move beyond the unitarian vision of community premised on loyalty and authenticity. Whether it is constructed as a reason to celebrate Arendt's democratic impulses or to deride her elitism, the "agonistic" interpretation of Arendt's politics tends to emphasize competition over association and plurality at the expense of publicity.[11]

By contrast, the "associational Arendt" is a proponent of a deliberative public space in which citizens come together to debate a common situation or problem from a plurality of positions. This line of argument comes out of Jürgen Habermas's interpretation of Arendt's work. Ap-

9. George Kateb, *Hannah Arendt: Politics, Conscience, Evil* (Totowa, N.J.: Rowman and Allanheld, 1983), chaps. 1 and 2.

10. Bonnie Honig, "Toward an Agonistic Feminism: Hannah Arendt and the Politics of Identity," in *Feminists Theorize the Political*, ed. Judith Butler and Joan W. Scott (New York: Routledge, 1992), 215.

11. One exception to this is Fred Dallmayr, who describes "agonal" politics as a "serious-playful contest revolving around the quality of excellence . . . [that] can also be described as the cultivation of a particular interhuman 'practice': namely the practice of 'friendship'—a term denoting not so much personal intimacy as a public relationship steeped in mutual respect and a willingness to let one another 'be'." *Polis and Praxis* (Cambridge: MIT Press, 1984), 9. Dallmayr suggests, as I have done, that the uniqueness of Arendt's terms "plurality," "natality," and "publicity" is precisely that they sustain a tension between individuality and intersubjectivity.

propriating her thought into his own project to define a communicative ethic, Habermas argues that Arendt counters the Weberian realist model of instrumental power with a definition of power as "the formation of a *common* will in a communication directed to reaching agreement."[12] Where the "agonistic" reading of Arendt emphasizes contestation at the expense of publicity, the "associational" reading emphasizes commonality at the expense of plurality.

I argue that Arendt is neither a champion of skepticism nor a defender of Enlightenment universalism; instead, she offers an alternative to both of these in her remarks on storytelling and storytellers. Through the storyteller, Arendt stakes a claim to the possibility of criticism from a pariah position without defining that position as one of abstract impartiality. Storytellers initiate political reconciliation. Their work is to tell stories that accord permanence to fleeting actions, crafting them into events whose meaning can be opened to public disputation. This reconciliation is neither retrospective nor passive, but the quintessential realization of natality, the condition that makes way for new beginnings. I explore this suggestion, and both the agonistic and associational readings in greater detail in the following sections of this chapter.

The Agonistic versus Associational Arendt

One of the most striking statements of the theme of Arendt as theorist of agonistic politics is Hanna Pitkin's: "Arendt's citizens begin to resemble posturing little boys clamoring for attention ('Look at me! I'm the greatest!' 'No, look at *me!*') and wanting to be reassured that they are brave, valuable, even real. . . . Though Arendt was female, there is a lot of *machismo* in her vision."[13]

12. Jürgen Habermas, "Hannah Arendt's Communications Concept of Power," *Social Research* 44 (1977): 4.
13. Hanna Pitkin, "Justice: On Relating Private and Public," *Political Theory* 9 (1981): 338. Pitkin's choice of the term *machismo* is probably disconcerting to an audience broader today than fifteen years ago. She uses the term to bring to mind the exaggeratedly narcissistic style of masculinity that is stereotypically associated with Latin men. Gloria Anzaldúa contests this one-dimensional stereotype, writing that "for men like my fa-

Pitkin's claim that the Arendtian actor is a narcissistic celebrity whose arrogance and competitive striving typifies masculine bravado, together with similar arguments by Noel O'Sullivan, Sheldon Wolin, and others, have practically established the Homeric hero as the prototypical Arendtian political actor. This interpretation is based on a particular reading of two aspects of *The Human Condition*—Arendt's references to Achilles and her use of metaphors from theater to describe public life—that disregards their context in Arendt's new political lexicon. Reading Arendt's work in light of the very traditions and ideologies against which she claims to write "in manifest contradiction," these scholars close off radical and innovative aspects of Arendt's writing.

Pitkin attributes a competitive, narcissistic conception of action to Arendt by interpreting her remarks on Achilles as an uncritical assimilation of Homeric heroism. Pitkin attributes to Arendt a competitive understanding of heroism by asserting that "Arendt *acknowledges* that *her* concept of public action 'stresses the urge toward self-disclosure at the expense of all other factors,' and therefore 'is highly individualistic'."[14] But Pitkin wrings this apparent concession by excerpting these phrases from a larger passage in which it is quite clear that Arendt is not talking about her own conception of action but about that of ancient Greece. Arendt's passage is as follows:

> No doubt *this* [Homeric] concept of action is highly individualistic, as we would say today. *It* stresses the urge toward self-

---

ther, being 'macho' meant being strong enough to protect and support my mother and us, yet being able to show love." Anzaldúa argues that "machismo" is not the essence of Latin manhood but a reflection of "hierarchal male dominance" that puts the ideal of a protector who can be both strong and loving out of reach for many Latinos. Gloria Anzaldúa, "La conciencia de la mestiza: Toward a New Consciousness," in *Making Face, Making Soul*, ed. Gloria Anzaldúa (San Francisco: Aunt Lute Foundation, 1990), 382.

14. Ibid., 336; emphasis added; citing HC, 194. Dana Villa replicates this interpretation in "Beyond Good and Evil: Arendt, Nietzsche, and the Aestheticization of Political Action," *Political Theory* 20 (1992): 285. See also Wendy Brown, *Manhood and Politics* (Totowa, N.J.: Rowman and Allanheld, 1988), chap. 2. Bonnie Honig is the only other interpreter I know of who also notes that this reading attributes to Hannah Arendt a conception of action that Arendt both identifies as a feature of Greek politics and criticizes. See "Toward an Agonistic Feminism," 234, n. 30.

disclosure at the expense of all other factors and therefore remains relatively untouched by the predicament of unpredictability. As such it became the *prototype of action for Greek antiquity* and influenced, in the form of the so-called agonal spirit, the passionate drive to show one's self in measuring up against others that underlies the concept of politics prevalent in the city-states. (HC, 194; emphasis added)

Where Pitkin attributes to Arendt a competitive conception of action, Arendt herself cites this model as the "prototype of action for Greek antiquity." Furthermore, Arendt calls up the Homeric prototype not to recommend but to criticize it. She argues that the "agonal spirit . . . eventually was to bring the Greek city states to ruin because it made alliances between them well nigh impossible and poisoned the domestic life of the citizens with envy and mutual hatred."[15] By excerpting the comments on Achilles in a way that makes it sound as if Arendt recommends his life as a model for citizenship, Pitkin quotes Arendt out of context.

That Arendt calls up Achilles not to praise but to criticize his model of citizenship becomes apparent only if her discussion of that hero is read in light of the arguments against sovereignty and mastery that Arendt makes in presenting her oppositional vocabulary. Achilles is a classic example of the "identification of sovereignty with freedom" and of the deep-seated resistance against plurality that, as I have argued, Arendt criticizes in philosophers (HC, 234). Arendt describes Achilles as "the indisputable *master* of his identity and possible greatness, because he *withdraws* into death from the possible consequences and continuation of what he began" (193–194, emphasis added). This withdrawal into death is a repudiation of natality, and the attempt to master his identity is a refusal to accept the condition of plurality. Arendt explains that the only way to "master" identity is "by foregoing the continuity of living in which we disclose ourselves piecemeal, by summing up all of one's life in a single deed, so that the story of the act comes to its end together with life itself." Although she calls Achilles the "hero par excellence, who

15. Hannah Arendt, "Philosophy and Politics," *Social Research* 57 (1990): 82.

delivers into the narrator's hands the full significance of his deed," there is no reason to assume that heroes "par excellence" make the best citizens (194). In fact, there is a suggestion that this model of heroism is a cheat. Achilles attempts to be both the actor and maker of his own story. As such, he may be actually *less* bold and courageous than the leader who risks the unpredictability of initiating an action and letting it play out "piecemeal," without attempting to control either its outcome or the stories that others make of it. Achilles represents simply another strategy for the escape from plurality for which Arendt criticizes philosophers.

The second aspect of Arendt's work on which scholars rely for their construction of Arendt's action as self-glorification is a much-quoted passage in which Arendt contends that political action has an extraordinary moral status:

> Unlike human behavior—which the Greeks, like all civilized people, judged according to "moral standards," taking into account motives and intentions on the one hand and aims and consequences on the other—action can be judged only by the criterion of greatness because it is in its nature to break through the commonly accepted and reach into the extraordinary, where whatever is true in common and everyday life no longer applies because everything that exists is unique and *sui generis*. . . . Greatness, therefore, or the *specific meaning of each deed*, can lie only in the performance itself and neither in its motivation nor its achievement. (205–206; emphasis added)

The key phrase in this passage is Arendt's claim that "action can be judged only by the criterion of greatness." Scholars who take this passage to justify reading Arendt's action as narcissism interpret "greatness" as the expression of a Homeric preference for the short and glorious life together with a Nietzschean disdain for "herd" morality. They read greatness, that is, as a synonym for glory.

This argument both interprets the passage on "greatness" out of the context of the new political lexicon of plurality, natality, and publicity and depends, so to speak, on cutting Arendt off before she has finished. The passage is usually excerpted just up to the point where Arendt claims that political action is "unique and *sui generis*," ending it at a point where Arendt seems to be arguing that great actions are unique for breaking through the constraints of everyday morality. This definition of greatness is at odds with Arendt's conception of public power, suggesting that it involves acting not in but *out* of concert with others. The final sentence of the passage on greatness suggests a different interpretation. That greatness "can lie only in the performance itself" does reaffirm the distinction she draws between acting and making. But it does *not*, as proponents of the agonistic interpretation have argued, identify action with the narcissistic *performance* of the aesthetic rebel. Rather, the gloss on "greatness" that Arendt herself provides is not the performance itself but its "specific meaning." By claiming that greatness is not the performance itself but the meanings that it "discloses," Arendt displaces the actor from the center of an act and, so, *redefines* glory.

Just what is "disclosure" and how does it make possible Arendt's contrary definitions of glory and heroism? To answer these questions, it is necessary to recall Arendt's argument against philosophers' attempts to cast action in the mode of making. In the preceding chapter, I explicated Arendt's claim that action cannot be understood in instrumental terms because an act can be real only insofar as it appears in public. In turn, to appear in public, it must always be mediated through plurality— the "already existing web of human relationships, with its innumerable, conflicting wills and intentions." It is because of the interference of this web that action "almost never achieves its purpose" (184). Disclosure suggests that the distinctive quality of an action is that it is *meaningful* rather than *purposive*. Action is the expression of natality, the possibility of second birth, and it achieves "a disclosure of the acting and speaking agent" (182). Disclosure is making an entrance; it is, in other words, a public appearance.

For the same reason that action can never achieve its purpose, this meaning cannot be voluntary or intentional. She writes that disclosure "can almost never be achieved as a willful purpose, as though one possessed and could dispose of this 'who' in the same manner he has and can dispose of his qualities. On the contrary, it is more than likely that the 'who,' which appears so clearly and unmistakably to others, remains hidden from the person himself" (179). Arendt's claim that action "discloses" the agent, then, is not to be understood to mean that action reveals the authentic inner core of the actor. On the contrary, Arendt claims that this inner core cannot appear in public at all, because it "cannot withstand the implacable, bright light of the constant presence of others on the public scene" (51).

It is useful here to recall Arendt's peculiar definition of interest as a *principled* "in-between." It is not surprising that she rejects the typical assumption that meaning resides in the "inner core" of the actor, given her insistence that action must not be reduced to motives and goals that "operate from within the self" (BPF, 152). To postulate motives and goals and then claim to deduce action from them means not only to reduce action to behavior but also to commit the fallacy of "speak[ing] about a 'who' as though it were a 'what' " (HC, 10). A human being is not the cause of an action but its performer, and what is disclosed in public performance is the principle that inspired it. The "disclosing" self, then, is uniquely political in that it is defined exclusively by the various and potentially conflicting interpretations of its inspiring principle to which its performance gives rise. The appropriate mode of knowing it is not self-discovery, to be achieved by solitary introspection, but self-revelation. And the mode of revelation is not confession (which amounts to little more than the public voicing of the discoveries of introspection) but enactment: taking a stand in public.

Just what does it mean to attribute a capacity to take a stand to the disclosing self? If disclosure disconnects the public self from an inner moral center, on what basis can Arendt claim that the actions of such a self are not simply arbitrarily and opportunistically responsive to its environment? How, in other words, does she justify her claim that action can be meaningful even though it is not purposive?

There is an answer to this question in Arendt's remarks about the relationship between action and stories. She claims that it is because plurality is the "medium" of action, "in which action alone is real, that it 'produces' stories with or without intention as naturally as fabrication produces tangible things" (HC, 184). This claim displaces the meaning of an act from the heart, mind, or conscience (whatever one takes to be the seat of motive and intent) of the actors to the stories that come to be told about it. This parallels the shift she makes in her critique of leverage by decentering meaning as she does solidarity from the self to the public space. As Lewis P. and Sandra K. Hinchman observe, for Arendt, "meaning became a jigsaw puzzle, whose pieces are distributed among actors in the public realm, spectators, poets, historians, and philosophers."[16] This decentering reframes the task of analyzing an act, which is customarily posed as a question of who did it and why, to a question of understanding the meanings the act takes on in the eyes of spectators in different times and places. By the assertion that action "produces" stories, Arendt plays out the implications of her critique of the Archimedean conception of power on the Archimedean conception of knowledge: if public power cannot be exercised as leverage, then the analysis of power and its effects cannot be causal or predictive but must be interpretive.

The effect of the argument about disclosure is to publicize knowledge as Arendt publicizes power. An action can only be an action if there is a public space in which it can appear. Further, if the public space is no more than "the organization of the people as it arises out of acting and speaking together," then it exists only as long as they are so organized (HC, 198). Without dispersing the public realm, no actor can withdraw to a vantage point outside it to observe and adjudicate political conflict, unless actors could be in two places at once: simultaneously acting "in" public and standing "outside" to observe themselves. As I have shown, however, it is precisely this separation that Arendt refuses in her critique of rulership. Given Arendt's twofold insistence that actors must be knowers, and that publics exist only where citizens speak and act, it follows that there would be nothing to observe or adjudicate if citizens attempted to exercise those capacities from a vantage point outside that realm. Consequently, political actors must understand their public worlds from within them.

This is not to say, of course, that every decision of political import is always made in public. The fact is that much of what passes for politics

---

16. Lewis P. Hinchman and Sandra K. Hinchman, "Existentialism Politicized: Arendt's Debt to Jaspers," *Review of Politics* 53 (1991): 435–468.

is conducted in the mode of rule. The implication of Arendt's claim is simply that to render a decision on something other than public criteria is to depoliticize the decision. As Ernst Vollrath explains, the political actor who withdraws to an external vantage point for purposes of judging violates the "phenomenal nature as well as the political status of political phenomena."[17] It is not impossible to adjudicate a conflict from an external vantage point, but to do so is to reframe that conflict in terms that are no longer public.

Disclosure publicizes knowledge by decentering and pluralizing the meaning of an act, taking meaning out of the mind of the actor and leaving it open to interpretation by the various participants in the public space. David Luban refers to the Archimedean ideal in laying out the consequences that publicizing knowledge has for objectivist notions of impartiality. He writes that in politics "the objective state of affairs is radically decentered: it offers us no Archimedean point from which it can be comprehended because every point is Archimedean."[18] The definitive quality of the public space is particularity: that the plurality of perspectives that constitute it is irreducible to a single common denominator. A claim to decisive authority reduces those perspectives to a single one, effectively discrediting the claims of other political actors and closing off public discussion. Meaning is not inherent in an action, but public, which is to say, constituted by the interpretive contest among the plurality of perspectives in the public realm that confer publicity on action and thereby make it real. Thus, Arendt redefines meaning as she does solidarity, by decentering its locus.

While Arendt does make a connection between action and glory, the latter takes on a most unconventional meaning in light of the dependence of the former on publicity. She claims that "Because of its inherent tendency to disclose the agent together with the act, action needs for its full appearance the shining brightness we once called glory, and which is possible only in the public realm" (HC, 180). Note that Arendt does not claim that only "glorious" deeds count as action or that it is the

17. Ernst Vollrath, "Hannah Arendt and the Method of Political Thinking," *Social Research* 44 (1977): 165.

18. David Luban, "Explaining Dark Times: Hannah Arendt's Theory of Theory," *Social Research* 50 (1983): 228.

desire for personal glory that motivates action. Instead, she claims that action "needs" glory in order to appear. Glory, in this context, is synonymous with publicity, the visibility that action has in the public space or "common world [that] gathers us together and yet prevents our falling over each other."[19]

Similarly, although the extraordinary performance of an individual may be necessary to initiate collective action, that performance is not political in itself. It is only political if it is public, and only public if it generates power. She cautions, "without power, the space of appearance brought forth through action and speech in public will fade away as rapidly as the living deed and the living word" (HC, 204). An heroic act requires power to sustain it, and power, in turn, is not an individual property but a possibility of plurality that "springs up between men when they act together and vanishes the moment they disperse" (200). An heroic performance can initiate action only when it mobilizes a network of actors.

Plurality, which accounts for the potency of action, also accounts for its "predicaments" (236). Under the condition of plurality, one acts always into situations whose contingencies cannot be mastered. This is why acting, in contrast to fabrication, carries with it certain ineluctable risks. One of these is the possibility that an act will take on meanings in the eyes of others that the actor did not intend or anticipate. Another is that it will have unforseen and unwanted consequences. These risks, of course, are consistent with Arendt's distinction between action and behavior and her differentiation of principles from motives and goals. For action to be free in the way she describes it, it necessarily entails the "predicaments" of unpredictability and irreversibility.

Given the risks of plurality, heroism need not consist in extraordinary physical bravery but simply in having the courage to take a stand for which one will almost certainly be misunderstood. Disassociating action

---

19. HC, 52. Lewis P. and Sandra K. Hinchman have argued that this conception of glory is one of Arendt's "quiet appropriations" from Martin Heidegger, who viewed glory as not simply the reward or acclaim that is attached to action after the fact but rather the condition of the possibility of action's coming into being. See "In Heidegger's Shadow: Hannah Arendt's Phenomenological Humanism," *Review of Politics* 46 (1984): 201.

from military bravado, Arendt claims that the hero "needs no heroic qualities; the word 'hero' originally, that is, in Homer, was no more than a name given each free man who participated in the Trojan enterprise and about whom a story could be told." She goes on to state that heroism consists simply in the "courage and even boldness" it takes to make a public stand; it is "present in leaving one's private hiding place and showing who one is, in disclosing and exposing one's self." Far from requiring extraordinary valor, Arendt claims that action "is not less great and may even be greater if the 'hero' happens to be a coward" (HC, 186–187). There is no need for the hero to display death-defying bravado because the risks of self-disclosure are enough.[20]

This association with publicity, in turn, distinguishes glory and heroism from self-aggrandizement. If meaning is neither up to the actor to determine nor determined by motives or intent, then actors do not own their acts. It follows that the greatness of an act cannot be self-glorifying in any simple or straightforward way. Furthermore, Arendt makes it clear that self-disclosure differs from competitive striving. She claims that "action loses its specific character and becomes one form of achievement among others . . . whenever human togetherness is lost, that is, when people are only for or against other people" (HC, 180). Arendt makes a distinction here between action and achievement, which, in turn, rests on the distinction she makes between the social and the public. Achievement pertains to the social realm, a realm of competition for status, of consumption, and of conformity. It cannot but pit people for or against one another, because it is defined in terms of a life-style that neither this society nor this planet can support for all. The public realm, in contrast, is a space in which to seek an intangible. That intangible is excellence, which comes from earning respect in accordance with the tastes of those whose company one has chosen to keep.

Proponents of the agonistic interpretation of Arendt's public space

20. Jennifer Ring makes a related claim, arguing that the Greek hero is "something of an aberration" in Arendt's conception of action and that "it is the humble notion of the individual who chooses to speak out rather than retreat to the relative security of his own household or even his own hunger, who constitutes the sustained image of the political activist in Arendt's work." See "The Pariah as Hero: Hannah Arendt's Political Actor," *Political Theory* 19 (1991): 450.

interpret this decentering and pluralizing of meaning as a celebration of sheer virtuosity that renders undecidable the moral status of a performance or its outcome(s). Political action, then, becomes a game in which excellence in competition becomes an end in itself. Bonnie Honig lauds Arendt's "disdain for our concern for physical safety and comfort; the glorification of performances which are spontaneous and surprising; and the claim that the glory of action is not a function of its goodness."[21] Where Honig celebrates virtuosity as the ultimate expression of subjectivity unconstrained by the disciplinary ideal of self-consistency that is integral to the Kantian model of autonomy, for George Kateb, this is precisely what makes Arendt's thought so dangerous. He writes that there are phenomena that can be played out in the mode of unconstrained virtuosity: "But they are games: they are restricted and self-enclosed activities and do not reach to the integrity of the person. They have no moral point: Politics may."[22] Kateb reads Arendt in light of the tradition she attempts to reconfigure by imposing a standard—integrity—that is inappropriate to the disclosing self.[23]

By contrast, Honig lauds Arendt's break with rationalism as "an activist, democratic politics of contest, resistance, and amendment." The difficulty here is that, although she calls it a *democratic* activism, Honig, in her description of the Arendtian hero as a performer of "virtuosic action," reiterates the very narcissistic qualities that Pitkin found inimical to democratic citizenship. Although acknowledging that Arendt's virtuosity (in contrast to Nietzsche's), is never a solo performance, Honig offers no account of "virtuosic" citizenship to explain how an individual who braves the risks of the public space out of an "agonal passion for distinction and outstanding achievement," would act in concert with others.[24] Whether out of fear or delight, proponents of the "agonistic" interpretation play up the disruptive implications that na-

---

21. Bonnie Honig, "Arendt, Identity, and Difference," *Political Theory* 16 (1988): 95.
22. Kateb, *Hannah Arendt*, 32.
23. Regarding Kateb's claims, James Bernauer has argued that "he is a prime example of the conceptualism in political science with which her thought wishes to break." "On Reading and Mis-reading Hannah Arendt," *Philosophy and Social Criticism* 11 (1985): 18.
24. Bonnie Honig, *Political Theory and the Displacement of Politics* (Ithaca: Cornell University Press, 1993), 77, 80.

tality and plurality have on the model of the political actor as responsible, self-contained subject at the expense of attending to the ways in which Arendt's concept of publicity counters the subjectivism and narcissism of the agonistic model.[25]

I suggest an alternate reading of the performance metaphor: that Arendt uses the language of performance to emphasize the public and participatory aspects of political action and its meanings. When Arendt talks about politics as a performing art her emphasis is precisely not on individual star performances but on the physical and social organizations that make performance possible. She introduces the theater analogy with the claim that theater is "the political art par excellence" because it "is the only art whose sole subject is man *in his relationship to others*" (HC, 188; emphasis added). The performing arts and politics are both conditional on plurality and publicity so that no one individual can assume credit or responsibility for an event. Instead, "Performing artists—dancers, play-actors, musicians, and the like—need an audience to show their virtuosity, just as acting men need the presence of others before whom they can appear; *both need a publicly organized space* for their 'work,' and *both depend upon others for the performance itself*" (BPF, 156; emphasis added). Arendt does not define either the performing arts or politics exclusively or even primarily in terms of what goes on centerstage; rather, she argues that action depends on publicity, which in turn requires being recognized, responded to, and later remembered by others.

Arendt points out that action without remembrance would be even less durable than labor, whose products are immediately consumed. As Paul Ricoeur has so poetically written, absent remembrance, action suffers "a frailty more formidable than any futility."[26] Arendt's answer to this frailty is the craft of storytelling. Deeds and words would not exist

25. Villa develops a similar line of argument against a one-sidedly Nietzschean reading of Arendt, arguing that Arendt attempted "to reconcile the imperative of greatness (the distinctive quality of 'aesthetic' action) with the preservation of genuine plurality," turning to the notion of taste as the means by which the interpretations of an action are publicly contested. The point of such contestation is, he argues, not to achieve moral consensus but to counter the subjectivism of individual performances with the publicity of contests over their meanings. See "Beyond Good and Evil," 291.

26. Paul Ricoeur, "Action, Story, and History," *Salmagundi* 60 (1983): 72.

beyond the moment of their enactment without the work of storytellers—historians, poets, essayists, novelists—who hand them down orally
and in writing.

> The "doing of great deeds and the speaking of great words"
> will leave no trace, no product that might endure after the
> moment of action and the spoken word has passed. If the
> *animal laborans* needs the help of *homo faber* to ease his labor
> and remove his pain, and if mortals need his help to erect a
> home on earth, acting and speaking men need the help of
> *homo faber* in his highest capacity, that is, the help of the artist,
> of poets and historiographers, of monument-builders or writ-
> ers, because without them the only product of their activity,
> the story they enact and tell, would not survive at all (HC,
> 173).

Words and deeds depend for their reality on being made "objective" by
artists whose work is not objective in the sense of "telling it how it is"
but in making the ephemeral performances of actors publicly visible. No
action can be "judged . . . by the criterion of greatness" without the mediation of storytellers to preserve it beyond its moment of enactment.

The mediation of the storyteller suggests an alternative to the agonistic
reading of the "greatness" passage. Recall that interpretations of this
passage, whether deriding Arendt as a nihilist or celebrating her as a
radical democrat, begin from the assumption that great performances
are, by their virtuosity, incommensurable. In contrast to both of these,
I suggest that Arendt introduces the storyteller as a worker whose craft
is necessary to the possibility of intersubjective "reality." It cannot be
on the basis of performances *in themselves* that citizens contest the meaning of actions, because these are singular and unique. Further, actions
are fleeting and, in themselves, cannot command widespread attention.
Thus, the task of storytellers is to make action public by crafting the
story of a performance that makes it visible to a broader audience and
initiates the process of disputing its meanings. As publics emerge not
around an action in itself but around the various stories that make it a
public event, there is no reason to assume that Arendt's public space is

singular and all-encompassing. Just as there will be plural accounts, so too will there be a plurality of publics and "counter-publics." [27]

Publicity suggests an alternative interpretation of Arendt's remarks about action and greatness. This is that self-disclosure depends on plurality: being in a web of relationship with other individuals whose participation in one's action is necessary to confer excellence on it. Even if narcissism and the desire for fame contribute to the inclination toward public life, that does not cancel out the inescapable fact that it is impossible to take a stand without a public space in which to do so. As Arendt puts it, "Every activity performed in public can attain an excellence never matched in privacy; for excellence, by definition, the presence of others is always required, and this presence needs the formality of the public, constituted by one's peers, it cannot be the casual, familiar presence of one's equals or inferiors" (HC, 49). Arendt's insight is that individuality is not a property of the self but a public achievement. Excellence, then, is not an innate quality but a possibility that is suggested to us by the regard of others.

These insights suggest that even if the public realm encourages narcissism, it cannot tolerate it. If one cannot recognize excellence in solitary contemplation of one's own reflection, but only in the public of a company of peers, then excellence requires the participation of at least a few others. A virtuoso performance, then, cannot be self-absorbed but must appeal to others as equals. Their participation may consist in admiring a performance and caring that it succeeds or even in criticizing it. They are peers by the fact that—allied or opposed—they understand the work and do it the honor of acknowledging its excellence by posing questions and voicing their reactions.

To their credit, proponents of the agonistic interpretation seize on the riskiness and highlight the excitement of acting in Arendt's public space.

27. In this, I think Arendt's work more closely approximates the conception of public discourse Nancy Fraser proposes with her claim that "in stratified societies, arrangements that accommodate contestation among a plurality of competing publics better promote the ideal of participatory parity than does a single, comprehensive, overarching public." See "Rethinking the Public Sphere: A Contribution to the Critique of Actually Existing Democracy," in *Habermas and the Public Sphere*, ed. Craig Calhoun (Cambridge: MIT Press, 1992), 66.

The disadvantage of this interpretation is that it feeds the perception that the Arendtian hero is more concerned with self-aggrandizement than with the public "inter-est." I have suggested that many of these interpreters take Arendt's use of the language of performance too literally, interpreting it to mean that Arendt's actors are all prima donnas who strive for celebrity. As Hanna Pitkin claims, for example, Arendt's citizens are instrumental actors who are drawn to the public realm because "each needs the other for his audience, as a means to his personal end."[28] This literalism constructs the relationships of the public realm as subject-object relationships. Insofar as the agonistic reading of the public space presents Arendt as a proponent of competitive interaction that fosters instrumental relations (among actors as well as between actors and spectators), it assimilates her ideas to aspects of the Archimedean norm that she explicitly questions.

The "associative" interpretation of Arendt's public space also blunts the force of Arendt's opposition to the Archimedean norm, but in a different way. Where the agonistic reading celebrates differentiation and plurality over publicity, the associative reading emphasizes public consensus over contestation and difference. The "associative" interpretation has the advantage of bringing to the fore Arendt's effort to displace subject-object relationships with relations of intersubjectivity. It does so, however, at the cost of domesticating the public space by reinstating the norm of mutual understanding.

Jürgen Habermas is principally responsible for the "associative" interpretation of Arendt's public space. Although he does not acknowledge it there, Arendt's influence is evident in Habermas's account of the underpinnings for his proposed shift from subject-centered reason to communicative reason, which he describes as a conceptual shift from "the paradigm of the knowledge of objects" to "the paradigm of mutual understanding between subjects capable of speech and action."[29] This shift rests on the possibility of making analogous two distinct realities that positivism takes to be incommensurable: that of subject-object relations

28. Pitkin, "Justice," 336.
29. Habermas, *Philosophical Discourse*, 295–296.

about which it is possible to make claims of fact, and that of intersubjective relations about which it is possible to make claims of right and truthfulness. Habermas writes:

> if normative rightness and subjective truthfulness are introduced as validity claims analogous to truth, "worlds" analogous to the world of facts have to be postulated for legitimately regulated interpersonal relationships and for attributable subjective experiences—a "world" not only for what is "objective," which appears to us in the attitude of the third person, but also one for what is normative, to which we feel obliged in the attitude of addresses, as well as one for what is subjective, which we either disclose or conceal to a public in the attitude of the first person.[30]

Habermas argues that the "philosophical discourse of modernity" since Descartes has been a series of failed attempts to reconcile these two worlds, involving a search for a way to justify claims of right and truthfulness *without* violating the intersubjectivity of the relations from which they issue. This means finding a way to justify nonobjective assertions without assessing their validity from a vantage point that reduces the subjects who assert them to objects of inquiry. Habermas suggests that if intersubjective reality, with its worlds of normative and expressive relationships, admitted of validity claims analogous to (but not the same as) those that can be made about the world of fact, then it would be possible to justify intersubjective norms just as it is possible to verify facts *without* appealing to an Archimedean vantage point.

Habermas's construction of the problem of justification as a problem of recognizing that the worlds of subject-object and subject-subject relations are equally real, though not real in the same way, recalls Arendt's account of the "overgrown" public space that I introduced in the preceding chapter. Just as Habermas does in the quoted passage, in her account of the "overgrown" public space, Arendt describes two distinct realities that are constituted by different kinds of relations. One is the

30. Ibid., 313.

"worldly objective reality" constituted by subject-object relations and recognized by positivism (HC, 182). The second she calls a "subjective" reality that is constituted by "men's acting and speaking directly *to* one another." She describes it: "This second, subjective in-between is not tangible, since there are no tangible objects into which it could solidify; the process of acting and speaking can leave behind no such results and end products. But for all its intangibility, this in-between is no less real than the world of things we visibly have in common. We call this reality the web of human relationships, indicating by the metaphor its some-what intangible quality" (183). It is interesting that Arendt deems this second world "subjective" in that it would seem more accurate to call it "intersubjective," given her claim that it is constituted by relations of speech and action. In any case, the connection to Habermas's work is Arendt's claim that the intersubjective world is no less real than the objective realm, though it is real in a different way.

One important difference between Arendt and Habermas, however, is in the answer each makes to the problem of justification. Habermas argues that intersubjective legitimacy is justifiable on the basis of con-sensus achieved by noncoercive public dialogue. He claims, moreover, that the possibility for "noncoercively unifying, consensus-building" dis-cussion is implicit in communication itself.[31] As I have argued, Arendt makes solidarity conditional on publicity, "which can form only in the interspaces between men in all their variety" (MDT, 31). "Interspaces" exist only where plurality, the irreducible particularity of individuals' positions, is valued more highly than the ideal of consensus.[32]

31. Ibid., 315.
32. As Thomas McCarthy has argued, Habermas's ideal of rational consensus is moralistic in its emphasis on mutual understanding at the expense of bargaining and disagree-ment, as if contestation and even sometimes arriving at a mutual agreement to disagree were not legitimate outcomes of public dialogue. "Practical Discourse: On the Rela-tionship of Morality to Politics," in *Habermas and the Public Sphere*, ed. Craig Calhoun (Cambridge: MIT Press, 1992), 59. Similarly, Margaret Canovan has argued that "Arendt did not share Habermas's crucial belief in the possibility of rational consensus on political questions." Canovan takes this difference to mean that Arendt is ultimately more of a republican than Habermas, whom she terms a participatory democrat. This conclusion seems at odds with Arendt's evident enthusiasm for many spontaneous eruptions of participatory democratic movements. See "A Case of Distorted Com-munication: A Note on Habermas and Arendt," *Political Theory* 11 (1983): 108.

If proponents of the "agonistic" interpretation of Arendt's public space emphasize the particularity of these perspectives to the point of forgetting Arendt's fine distinction between incommensurability and irreducibility, Habermas's "associative" interpretation emphasizes publicity at the cost of particularity. However different they are in their descriptions of the kinds of activities that would go on in the public space, both the agonistic and associative interpretations of Arendt's work pose a problem because each puts her in opposition to only one aspect of Archimedean thinking. As I have argued, there are two aspects of this norm. It constructs power instrumentally, as leverage, and knowledge in terms of a separation between thinking and acting, as abstract impartiality. Those who claim that Arendt's public space is agonistic recognize her appeal to greatness as a resistance to the disciplinary force of permitting acting to be ruled by abstract thinking. But insofar as they go on to claim that greatness defies principled judgment altogether, they obscure Arendt's distinction between power and force. In contrast, proponents of the "associative" reading of the public space recognize the metaphor acting in concert as an opposition to instrumental power and strategic rationality, but they assume that concerted action is impossible without an immanent consensus on moral principles. I now focus in on storytelling to make visible Arendt's opposition against *both* aspects of Archimedean thinking.

Storytelling as Resistance

I have argued so far that Arendt's opposition to the Archimedean norm involves redefining both power and knowledge in terms of publicity. Whereas acting in concert decenters power, ruling out the notion that there can be a fulcrum outside the public space from which to exercise control over political events, disclosure decenters knowledge, ruling out the appeal to a vantage point from which the meaning of public events can be unequivocally decided. The problem is that these arguments, however carefully constructed from the details of her texts, seem to reduce Arendt's work to a relativism that is utterly at odds with the spirit of her writing and intellectual project. Judging is certainly a defining purpose of Arendt's work, and she was neither tentative nor hesitant in passing judgment on the events of her time. As Dagmar Barnouw writes, the "provocative, irritating, and illuminating energy of Arendt's perspective on cultural and political history has been a curiously compounded partial impartiality." In other words, Arendt was a polemical writer whose arguments were tempered by "a view of the whole on which the particulars depend for meaning; but this whole has been openly and forcefully partial as a result of her acts of judging."[33]

Is this "curiously compounded partial impartiality" merely incoherence on Arendt's part? Was it simply inconsistent of Arendt to write so eloquently about what it means for plurality to be *the* condition of public life and, at the same time, to insist that totalitarianism was not simply one of many possible perspectives *in* the public realm but an insupportable crime *against* it? By what right could one assert such a judgment from within an Arendtian public space?

Like Habermas, I discern the intimation of an answer to this problem in Arendt's description of the "overgrown" public space. But where Habermas attaches great importance to Arendt's claim that the worlds of "words and deeds" are no less real for being less tangible than the "physical" world, I note how Arendt's description of the "overgrown" public space stands out from other statements she makes about the public realm. In it she makes the claim that the "words and deeds" by which actors appear in public, "are *about some worldly objective reality* in addition to being a disclosure of the acting and speaking agent" (HC, 182; emphasis added). This suggests that the social realm of objective necessity is intertwined with the public realm of freedom; facts grow together with principles, and worldly interests emerge together with deeds and words that are conditioned but not determined by them. It is crucial that she not only declares that principles and interests are intertwined but also affirms that judgments about both the normative realm and the realm of physical objects can be justified in accordance with standards that are to some degree independent of the subjective preferences of its hegemonic interests. Matters of principle can be *dis-*

---

33. Dagmar Barnouw, *Visible Spaces: Hannah Arendt and the German-Jewish Experience* (Baltimore: Johns Hopkins University Press, 1990), 18.

tinguished from worldly interests and the relations of power to which they give rise, but they cannot be *disentangled* from them.[34] Perhaps this begins to get at the crux of what Barnouw calls Arendt's "partial impartiality." This passage intimates a conception of judgment whereby one would take a public stand that is not justified *in the abstract*, but in terms of accountability to the interests from which it emerged.

Some may object to this reading, claiming that Hannah Arendt could not have held so contextual a notion of judgment, because anything—even genocide—can be made accountable to a set of interests, however perverse. There seems to be an irreconcilable tension between Arendt's claim that totalitarianism shattered the framework of universal truths by which it could be understood and judged and her insistence that this is precisely why it should be considered a political evil. Her denunciation of genocide is at odds with her claim that "Totalitarian domination as an established fact, which in its unprecedentedness cannot be comprehended through the usual categories of political thought, and whose 'crimes' cannot be judged by traditional moral standards or punished within the legal framework of our civilization, has broken the continuity of Occidental history" (BPF, 26). The paradox is that in taking a stand against genocide, one denounces as crime an event that is neither named nor proscribed by any commandment.

Arendt works through this paradox, somewhat surprisingly, on the occasion of her acceptance of the Lessing Prize of the Free City of Hamburg. The argument of this diffuse and digressive lecture is that Götthold Lessing should be understood as the exemplar of humanism in these "dark times." By means of the remarkable thought experiment with which she closes the talk, Arendt demonstrates to her audience that Lessing could have exposed genocide as an unjustifiable act without violating its status as an unprecedented crime. She describes Lessing as a distinctively public thinker, who chose his positions not from an Archi-

---

34. Carried to its furthest implication, Arendt's account of the public space suggests that truth claims about "worldly objective reality" would also be entangled in intersubjective relations. Publicity and plurality would not be restricted to the explicitly normative realm of politics but would be a constitutive aspect of scientific objectivity as well. See, for example, Helen Longino's argument for "contextual empiricism" in *Science as Social Knowledge* (Princeton: Princeton University Press, 1990).

medean position but based on "how the matter in question was being judged by the public and *quite independently of the degree to which it was true or false*" (MDT, 7; emphasis added). He was less concerned, in other words, with the correctness of a doctrine than with guaranteeing its visibility as just one position among others in public discourse. She called this Lessing's "partisanship for the world" (8) which was an approach to criticism that she admired for "the astonishing lack of 'objectivity' in Lessing's polemicism . . . his forever vigilant partiality, which has nothing whatsoever to do with subjectivity because it is always framed not in terms of the self but in terms of the relationship of men to their world, in terms of their positions and opinions" (29). Despite the apparent relativism of such a way of thinking—or perhaps because of it—it is through partisanship for the world that Arendt justifies the possibility of refusing unequivocally to permit Nazism a position in the world.

Typically, Arendt makes her claim for Lessing's greatness in an oppositional fashion, first setting his conception of disputational friendship against the romanticism of Rousseauist fraternity, then setting his "forever vigilant partiality" against Kantian rationalism. I will focus on the second of these because I think that Arendt's account of what she takes to be Lessing's method is an implicit justification of her own. She opposes Lessing to Kant by claiming that Lessing explored an "antinomy" that is invisible to both religious and secular humanism: "the possible antagonism between truth and humanity" (MDT, 28). Such an antinomy would be inconceivable within the framework of Kantian rationalism, where truth is quite plainly *not* the antagonist of humanity but its ground. As Arendt observes, Kant "would scarcely have agreed with Lessing than the truth, if it did exist, could be unhesitatingly sacrificed to humanity, to the possibility of friendship and of discourse among men" (27). She goes on to assert that it is by virtue of this commitment to truth that "the inhumanity of Kant's moral philosophy is undeniable . . . because the categorical imperative is postulated as absolute and in its absoluteness introduces into the interhuman realm—which by its nature consists of relationships—something that runs counter to its fundamental relativity" (27). The argument is not that Kant or Kantians are inhumane; rather, consistently with the concept of publicity and anticipating the argument of the lectures on judging, she affirms that an abstract imperative is necessarily incompatible with a public space that is conditional on plurality.[35]

Can Arendt seriously mean to accuse Kant of dogmatism and inhumanity? As she herself attests, she knows quite well that Kant was no dogmatic proponent of reason's mastery, but a critical theorist whose "great object" was to chart the "limitations of the human understanding" (MDT, 26). Nonetheless, in lecture notes for a seminar she offered at the New School for Social Research, she argues that Kant's moral philosophy is inherently contradictory due to a "self-misunderstanding in Kant" that prompted him to formulate the principle of autonomy as an "imperative, instead of defining it as a proposition." [36] Arendt observes that the *Critique of Practical Reason* makes no sense as an account of self-legislation unless there is a "rebellious aspect" to the categorical imperative that would consist in differentiating carefully between the duty to "act my part as legislator of the world," and the duty to obey "someone else's law."[37] Insofar as the categorical imperative is understood not as the responsibility to *legislate*—in one's own actions—as if one prescribed a law for all to follow, but as the duty to *obey* the dictates of reason, this "rebellious aspect" is effaced.

By means of an idiosyncratic reading of his theatrical masterpiece *Nathan the Wise*, Arendt uses Lessing to bring out the "rebellious aspect" of humanism. The work is typically read as confirmation of Enlightenment humanism: a teaching about tolerance that somewhat paradoxically affirms human progress through faith in both divine providence and the perfection of reason.[38] By contrast, Arendt claims that the play's "dramatic tension . . . lies solely in the conflict that arises between friendship

---

35. In her fine explication of the Lessing address, Margaret Canovan takes up this line of argument to formulate an Arendtian critique of Habermasian discourse ethics. "Friendship, Truth, and Politics: Hannah Arendt and Toleration," in *Justifying Toleration: Conceptual and Historical Perspectives*, ed. Susan Mendes (Cambridge: Cambridge University Press, 1988), 188–190.

36. Hannah Arendt, "Some Questions of Moral Philosophy," New School for Social Research, 1965, Library of Congress, MSS Box 45, 13.

37. Ibid.

38. Henry Allison, *Lessing and the Enlightenment* (Ann Arbor: University of Michigan Press, 1966). Leonard Wessel, *G. E. Lessing's Theology, A Reinterpretation: A Study in the Problematic Nature of the Enlightenment* (The Hague: Mouton, 1977).

and humanity with truth," and she lauds Nathan for the "wisdom" of "his readiness to sacrifice truth to friendship" (MDT, 26). What makes Arendt's reading of this play so curious is that its two pivotal events— Nathan's pledge of friendship to the Crusader who saved the life of his foster-daughter and his telling the ring parable to the Sultan—ground friendship and tolerance quite solidly in a universalist conception of humanity.[39] Alluding to both of these scenes, she flatly contradicts their teaching, asserting: "As for the statement with which Nathan the Wise (in effect, though not in actual wording) countered the command: 'Step closer, Jew'—the statement: I am a man—I would have considered as nothing but a grotesque and dangerous evasion of reality" (MDT, 18). In effect, Arendt reads this antinomy into the play to reverse the categorical imperative, arguing that the test of humanity is not the capacity to prefer the putatively universal claim of duty to the demands of particular attachments, but, on the contrary, to resist abstract imperatives for friendship's sake.

Explaining how truth can be at odds with humanity, Arendt argues that people who believe themselves to be in the possession of an abstract imperative are reluctant to deviate from it to accommodate the ambiguous demands of friendship. They believe "that to do so would be to violate a higher duty, the duty of 'objectivity'; so that even if they make such a sacrifice they do not feel they are acting out of conscience but are even ashamed of their humanity and often feel distinctly guilty about it" (28). She goes on to imply that the rhetoric of duty to an abstract imperative provided German religious leaders and intellectuals with a convenient rationalization for their failure to resist Hitler's regime in its early years. Though Arendt knows of course that the race laws of the Third Reich could not be farther from the spirit of Kantian critical theory, she nonetheless asserts that both contravene critique and resistance by confronting the political subject with an imperative.

39. This is evident in the text of Nathan's pledge of friendship to the Crusader, by which he urges the young man not to disavow the good deed he did for a Jew, but, instead, to acknowledge their common humanity:"—O come, we must, / We must be friends! Disdain my folk. Are we our folk? What is a folk? / Are Jew and Christian sooner Jew and Christian / Than man? How good, if I have found in you / One more who is content to bear the name / Of man!" Götthold Ephraim Lessing, *Nathan the Wise*, trans. Bayard Quincy Morgan (New York: Frederick Ungar, 1955), act 2, scene 6.

Arendt's insistence on the priority of friendship to truth cannot be understood outside the context of her interpretation of her experiences as a German Jew in the first half of the twentieth century. Prior to 1933, Hannah Arendt was, like other "secular middle-class Jews," a relatively assimilated German citizen. The separation between that time and the years that followed is one of what Elisabeth Young-Bruehl calls the many divisions of Arendt's life into "'Then' and 'Now'." In this instance, "Then" meant being at home in Germany; "Now" was being pronounced a stateless person and then becoming a Jewish refugee.[40] Given the proximity of their lives in many parts of the country at that time (Hamburg among them), Arendt suggests that non-Jewish Germans had to act against their experience of Jews as friends in order for the Holocaust to occur. This was not Rousseauist fraternity but friendship in the sense that German Gentiles knew German Jews on the streets and in school as people whose businesses they patronized, as their doctors or lawyers, and in the milieu of art and literature.[41] Thus, from Arendt's perspective, the Holocaust not only shattered the abstract principles of Western humanism but also disrupted public relationships.

To illustrate the "antinomy" between friendship and truth to her Hamburg audience, Arendt tells a story. She invites her listeners to imagine "the case of a friendship between a German and a Jew under the condition of the Third Reich," and asks them to consider under what circumstances such a friendship would count as a "sign of humanness" (MDT, 23). She answers that it would not be so if the friends were "to have said: Are we not both human beings?" Reprising her critique of Lessing, she asserts that rendering their situation in abstract universal terms "would have been mere evasion of reality and of the world com-

40. Elisabeth Young-Bruehl, *Hannah Arendt: For Love of the World* (New Haven: Yale University Press, 1982), 11, 3.

41. Young-Bruehl describes German society as a world in which, although not fully integrated, Jews and Germans were at home together: "The Jewish business and professional families lived in a district called the Hufen, near the spacious Tiergarten, in middle-class comfort. . . . It was unusual for a Jew to hold a local or provincial government appointment, but the Jews contributed schoolteachers and artists to the larger community, in addition to the more prevalent doctors and lawyers. Jews were not appointed to professorships at the university, though they held honorary positions and were permitted to teach Judaic studies." Ibid., 10.

mon to both at that time; they would not have been resisting the world as it was." But it would be an act of resistance, "a humanness in the midst of the reality of persecution," if they addressed each other by their particular identities, saying "to each other: A German and a Jew, and friends" (23). With this, each recognizes the other in terms of what the reality of the world has defined—for each of them—as a crime and releases the other for the sake of friendship.

It would be crude oversimplification to take Arendt to mean that the Holocaust would not have happened if German Gentiles had been better friends to German Jews. Instead, she tells this story to demonstrate both the conflict between friendship and truth, and the inadequacy of abstract humanism to challenge the phenomenon of totalitarianism. Although it has political significance by virtue of the circumstances within which it occurs, this hypothetical friendship turns not on critical judgment but on sympathy. It is an example of a political resistance prompted by private affection; as such, it is no answer to the dilemma of proscribing an unprecedented crime. Such a proscription would have to be agreed upon by people who do not like each other and may not even know each other. The question is whether Arendt can reformulate this exceptional instance of friendship as a general principle without appealing to an imperative grounded in truth.

There is a second model of friendship in the Lessing address that does not turn on personal affection and, as such, bears directly on the problem of public judgment. This second model is disputational. Arendt attributes it to Lessing whom she describes as someone who sought engagement with others not for the warmth of brotherhood but for argumentative companionship. Though "polemical to the point of contentiousness," Lessing was deeply committed to sustain friendship—not to "fall out with someone with whom he had entered into a dispute"—out of a concern to humanize "the world by incessant and continual discourse about its affairs and the things in it" (MDT, 30). This is a model of friendship that is humanizing not because it brings about consensus but because it fosters dispute.

Lessing's disputational friendship gives Arendt a way out of the paradox of political judgment: how to take a principled stand in a public dispute without contravening the "fundamental relativity" of plurality?

The answer is by refusing the model of systematic scholarly argument in favor of what Lessing termed his *"fermenta cognitionis,"* critical essays that provoke others to dispute.[42] Arendt explains that, "Because Lessing was a completely political person, he insisted that truth can exist only where it is humanized by discourse, only where each man says not what just happens to occur to him at the moment, but what he 'deems truth'" (MDT, 30). This requirement to say what one "deems truth" suggests a set of crucial distinctions between flippancy, dogmatic pronouncement, and political discourse. These first two are not conducive to public or disputational friendship because while they assert differences, they do not forge connections. Where the problem with flippancy is that it is commentary without conviction, dogmatism does not engage questioners but rather seeks to secure a position against them. These two may be contrasted against what Arendt calls Lessing's "curious kind of partiality," which is a model of critical thinking that consists in "always taking sides for the world's sake, understanding and judging everything *in terms of its position in the world at any given time*" (5, 7–8; emphasis added). Arendt's account of Lessing's principled "partiality" suggests a way to think about what Barnouw calls Arendt's "curiously compounded partial impartiality." In spite of the dissonance between the distinctive, "self-authorized" voice of many of Arendt's writings and her rejection of Archimedean pronouncement, Arendt crafted her essays to invite discussion in the way that she thought Lessing's did.[43]

But the problem of relativism remains. Given Lessing's (and Arendt's) commitment to a many-sided public space, and given his (and her) belief that a doctrine might be publicly valid even if it were not literally true, by what right would one refuse genocide a position in the world? She prompts the audience to think with her through this problem by telling a second story.

Addressed to an audience of Germans just fifteen years after the war, the story she tells must have made her listeners uncomfortable.[44] It be-

---

42. MDT, 8. This is a metaphor not unlike the idiom "food for thought." It is more colorful in a literal translation, however, which would be something like yeasts of thinking or inquiry.

43. Barnouw, *Visible Spaces*, 18, 13.

44. The letters Arendt exchanged with Karl and Gertrude Jaspers around that time suggest

gins with a proposal: "let us assume for the moment that the [Nazi's] racial theories could have been convincingly proved," which would mean
that the Jews are actually biologically inferior. With this stipulation,
Arendt puts her audience in an argument against genocide on *Nazi*
terms. That is, they are not to debate the justifiability of genocide in the
abstract but as if they had to make a response to it from within a totalitarian regime. Given that "the practical political conclusions the Nazis
drew from these theories were perfectly logical," if the theories themselves had been true, there would have been no rational opposition
against genocide *except* on moral grounds. Having ruled out its refuta-
tion in accordance with the conventions of argument—truth and self-
consistency—Arendt draws them into the dilemma of judging an
unprecedented crime. She tells them it is "too easy" to ask the hypothetical opponent whether the proven biological inferiority of a race would
"justify its extermination," because this implicitly invokes the first and
fundamental commandment: "Thou Shalt Not Kill." The challenge, she
tells them, is to pose the problem of genocide by means of "a way of
thinking governed by neither legal nor moral nor religious strictures."
She meets this challenge by invoking Lessing whom she says would have
"posed [it] thus: *Would any such doctrine, however convincingly proved, be
worth the sacrifice of so much as a single friendship between two men?*"
(MDT, 29). By this answer, Arendt resolves the dilemma of formulating
a general rule that does not violate the priority of friendship over truth.
By contrast to the earlier hypothetical that relies on private affection, or
friendship in a literal sense, this rule relies on plurality, which might be
conceived as the principle of friendship. In other words, Arendt argues
that there is justifiably no space in the public realm for a doctrine that
denies human plurality, its condition of possibility.

It is fair to argue that Arendt treats plurality as a kind of foundational
principle. It is the premise from which she launches her attack on abstract impartiality, leverage, and the subject conceived as a responsible
individual. If it is a foundation, however, it is an unusual one, in that it
embodies her claim that totalitarianism shattered the founding prin-

---

that it was probably calculated to do so, in order to break what she described to
Gertrude Jaspers as the "dreadful" atmosphere of "unarticulated" resentment in Germany at the time (C, 385).

ciples of modern Western philosophy. This is not to deny that Arendt's use of this term establishes its own certainties that insulate political questions from debate. As I argued in the final section of the previous chapter, the assertion that plurality is a "condition" constructs what is actually an achievement of political struggle as an existential given.

Arendt's description of nonfoundational and nonconsensual public judgment as "partisanship for the world" raises one further question. If Lessing's concern is to foster "incessant and continual discourse" about worldly affairs, how do people conclude a discussion in an instance where they need to take action? To put it differently, how do they decide to proceed not against perpetrators of crimes against humanity, but in more mundane circumstances of conflict? Can the many-sidedness of the public realm survive only insofar as decisions are endlessly deferred?

Arendt assigns to storytellers the task of bringing a public matter to a provisional conclusion, on the basis not of consensus but of reconciliation. Partisanship for the world is, in fact, a metaphor for reconciliation, and the Lessing address, in turn, is not just a lecture *about* reconciliation but an instance of its *performance*. Tacking once again from the realm of abstract philosophy to the "painful example" of current history, Arendt remarks on the Germans' "profound awkwardness, which strikes every outsider, in any discussion of questions of the past," and on their difficulty finding "a reasonable attitude" toward their relationship to "Hitler Germany." Noting that some suggest this awkwardness could be dispelled if the past were to be "mastered," Arendt dismisses this assessment as an Archimedean fantasy of a transcendent perspective from which to incorporate totalitarianism into a narrative of progress. She rejects this "cliche" with the assertion that the "best that can be achieved is to know precisely what it was, and to endure this knowledge, and then to wait and see what comes of knowing and enduring." Storytellers are indispensable to this process, for they initiate the "ever-recurrent narration" that makes the past available to be "experienced a second time in the form of suffering by memory operating retrospectively and perceptively. Such memory can speak only when indignation and just anger, which impel us to action, have been silenced— and that needs time. We can no more master the past than we can undo it. But we can reconcile ourselves to it. The form for this is the lament, which arises out of all recollection." The storyteller's function is to make reconciliation possible, not by *mystifying* the past, but by calling the present to account. But the way the storyteller does this, as distinct from a judicial or religious authority who *settles* accounts by doling out retribution or exacting penance for the past, is by "relating what has happened; but such narration, too, which shapes history, solves no problems and assuages no suffering; it does not master anything once and for all" (MDT, 20–21). It is in this sense that the past cannot be mastered: No one balances the record books, there is no release of anger, and there is no spiritual synthesis of opponents into allies.

Reconciliation effects a kind of forgiveness that Arendt first introduces in *The Human Condition*, as "one of the potentialities of action" that renews the condition of natality. Forgiveness, in other words, is not a divine gift but a political act of releasing other human beings from "the deeds of the past" (HC, 236–237). Although perhaps an extraordinary gesture, it is one that is necessarily mundane because "trespassing is an everyday occurrence which is in the very nature of action's constant establishment of new relationships *within a web of relations*, and it needs forgiving, dismissing, in order to make it possible for life to go on by constantly releasing men from what they have done unknowingly" (240; emphasis added). The discussion of reconciliation in the Lessing essay is at once more historically specific and less optimistic than the presentation of forgiveness in *The Human Condition*. By contrast to the earlier work, this is not an instance of releasing the accidental consequences of an act but of moving beyond past actions that are unforgivable. In reconciliation, persons or peoples who have violated each other's humanity face up to the web of crime that is their common history and acknowledge that to renew the condition of natality for the ones who will come after, they must relinquish their claims to justice *for what has passed*.[45]

---

45. It is difficult to imagine reconciliation as a means to restore the condition of natality, given Arendt's insistence that it is achieved through lamentation, which seems far more passive than active. But Maya Angelou's Inaugural Poem beautifully illustrates this connection. It can be read as an Arendtian public lament that begins with a recognition of the past, moves through reconciliation, and finishes by invoking a new beginning. The connection between lamentation and natality is evident even in the *double entendre*

One objection that might be raised to my claim that Arendt presents reconciliation, initiated by storytellers, as an answer to the paradoxes of public judgment is that the figure of the storyteller does not discredit the pretense to timeless moral authority but reproduces it. Among the few secondary scholars who have attempted to make any sense at all of the connection between action and storytelling, which Paul Ricoeur calls "one of the most striking themes of the whole treatise on *The Human Condition*," most assume that the storyteller reproduces the norm of Archimedean detachment.[46] Ronald Beiner, for example, argues that Arendt has two opposed theories of judgment, one framed from the point of view of the requirements of action, and the second from the point of view of contemplation. Beiner associates storytelling with this second view and describes the storyteller as a privileged spectator who is "at a remove from the action and therefore capable of disinterested reflection."[47]

It is undeniable that Arendt believes storytellers cannot be actors in the stories they tell *as* they tell them. She claims, for example, that "[A]ction reveals itself fully only to the storyteller, that is, to the backward glance of the historian, who indeed always knows better what it was all about than the participants" (HC, 192). Nowhere, however, does she claim that this "backward glance" has to be disinterested, as Beiner suggests, or that it is omniscient.[48] Instead, as Paul Ricoeur suggests, the connection Arendt so subtly insinuates between action and storytelling "repudiates . . . the substitution of a *contemplative* philosophy of history, with its escape into the 'whole,' for a political philosophy, *which remains within the borders of the vita activa*."[49] This place within the borders

---

of the title—"On the Pulse of Morning"/Mourning—which suggests that we effect reconciliation only by a recounting and courageous facing-up to the violations of humanity that are our common history. Only when we have *mourned* do we engender *morning* with its renewal of the possibility of action.

46. Ricoeur, "Action, Story, and History," 67.

47. Ronald Beiner, "Interpretive Essay," LKPP, 91.

48. In Chapter 4 I explore in detail Arendt's regard for Thucydides, who had been an actor in the story he came to tell and who was far from disinterested in it. This exploration will support my claim that the storyteller's vantage point is not Archimedean.

49. Ricoeur, "Action, Story, and History," 71; emphasis added.

cannot be properly appreciated without taking seriously the implications of plurality as a condition of action. Plurality, the concept Arendt uses to decenter and multiply both power and meaning, together with the web metaphor she uses to describe it, rules out three strategies for invoking absolute moral authority.

Remember that Arendt claims no one can act except into a web of relations that she describes as "a medium where every reaction becomes a chain reaction and where every process is the cause of new processes" (HC, 190). Consequently, the principle of natality or new beginnings is, as Arendt puts it (likely with unintentional irony), "never *consummated* unequivocally in one single deed or event . . . " (233; emphasis added). Although so far I have interpreted plurality in terms of the public space, this web of relations is also a web in time, a web that spins out from the consequences that an act sets into motion. The "backward glance" of the storyteller is not privileged for being *outside* the web, but for coming after the beginning. The storyteller, then, is positioned closer to its *margins* than either the leader who initiated the action or the followers who helped spin it out. One aspect of Archimedean impartiality the web metaphor rules out is the strategy of claiming to tell a story from outside.

A second Archimedean strategy that the web metaphor makes unavailable is the claim to exclusivity of understanding. If not on the pretense to an external and, hence, objective standpoint, the claim to exclusivity depends on there being a position from which to know the "inside scoop." This account is typically supplied by the actors. Arendt undercuts the privilege of the "inside scoop," arguing that the account from an actor's perspective is never definitive. She writes "All accounts told by the actors themselves, though they may in rare cases give an entirely trustworthy statement of intentions, aims, and motives, become mere useful source material in the historian's hands and can never match his story in significance and truthfulness" (HC, 192). This provision does not grant exclusive privilege to the storyteller; rather, it discredits the claim of exclusivity altogether in that once actors are ruled out as authorities on the events they set in motion, it becomes very difficult to sustain the fiction that anyone could offer a definitive account. That fiction depends on another assumption that Arendt rejects, the belief that the significance of an action lies in its cause and that its cause can be reduced to the motivations and intentions of a central perpetrator or perpetrators.

The third Archimedean strategy that the web metaphor refutes is the claim to tell the "whole truth." Appearing to claim that one can tell the "whole truth" when an event is over, Arendt writes that "whatever the character and content of the subsequent story may be, whether it is played in private or public life, whether it involves many or few actors, its full meaning can reveal itself only when it has ended" (HC, 192). The peculiar quality of a web, however, is that it can be extended indefinitely. New margins are forever being created, which means that there is a multiplicity of positions from which the story of any action can be told. She remarks that, "even if the spectacle were always the same and therefore tiresome, the audience would change from generation to generation; nor would a fresh audience be likely to arrive at the conclusions handed down by tradition as to what an unchanging play has to tell it" (LM: 1, 96). No story can ever be told "once and for all" because every retelling engenders new contests over the meaning of the event, spinning an ever larger and more intricate web. In sum, by introducing the storyteller, Arendt does not reinstate the ground from which to make an Archimedean claim to comprehensive and exclusive knowledge of an event; the storyteller is a pariah critic whose vision is not objective or omniscient and who does not claim to have the last word.

Arendt's "publicity" suggests a way out of the oppositional contest between the assertion that knowledge claims are incommensurably particularist and the assertion that claims can be rendered commensurable in terms of common abstract principles. She claims that public spaces are constituted not by speech and action—i.e. performance—*in itself*, but by the multiple meanings an action discloses to its spectators. Her account of publicity is distinctive because it is the telling and retelling of the story of an event that make that event public. Thus, it is not consensus but the activity of interpretive contestation that sustains both the integrity of the public realm and its plurality. If consensus about meaning sustains "inter-est," and if, in turn, "inter-est" generates power, then Arendt's concept of "publicity" supports the claim that interpretive contestation is contestation for power.

In the preceding two chapters I laid out the theoretical framework of

Arendt's opposition against the Archimedean norm; arguing that she proposes acting in concert as an alternative to the ideal of power as leverage and worldly "partisanship" as an alternative to Archimedean abstraction. In the following chapter, I detail Arendt's attempts to use storytelling in the practice of political theory by analyzing the dilemmas she encountered in writing about totalitarianism.

4 More Truth than Fact

■

A well-crafted story shares with the most elegant theories the ability to bring to light a version of the world that so transforms the way people see that it seems never to have been otherwise. Under certain conditions, a story can be a more powerful critical force than a theoretical analysis. As Arendt wrote, "My assumption is that thought itself arises out of incidents of living experience and must remain bound to them as the only guideposts by which to take its bearings" (BPF, 14). In a society where the abstraction of social theory and social science sometimes masks real conflicts, a skillful narrative can reveal the assumptions buried in apparently neutral arguments and challenge them. Storytelling invites critical engagement between a reader and a text and, more important, among the various readers of a work in a way that the impersonal, authoritative social science "voice from nowhere" cannot.

In this chapter I tell a story that Hannah Arendt did not tell because she considered it inappropriate to do so. It concerns the methodological innovations she made—but would not call attention to—while writing about totalitarianism. Early on, she claims that "history has known no story more difficult to tell" than that of the concentration camps ("IH," 292). The camps and the regime that produced them "cannot be comprehended through the usual categories of political thought" or "judged by traditional moral standards or punished within the legal framework of our civilization" (BPF, 26). In sum, Arendt argues that totalitarianism was not just a moral crisis, but an unprecedented "problem of understanding."[1] That problem of understanding is to find a way to make a spontaneous but principled response to the phenomenon of total domination. In the absence of the traditional categories and standards that ordinarily serve as guideposts to critical thought, she argues that such a response must take its bearings from the "personal experience" of the thinker.[2] "Storytelling" is the term she uses to describe critical understanding from experience.[3]

What Hannah Arendt called "my old fashioned storytelling" is at once the most enigmatic and provocative aspect of her political philosophy ("A," 11). Elisabeth Young-Bruehl observes that "Arendt's political theory always grew up out of . . . thought exercises, attempts to capture experience and find the experiential base of positions, decisions, and policies," but that she rarely revealed these processes to her readers.[4] The apologies she sometimes made for this way of proceeding are well-known, but few scholars have attempted to discern from these "scattered remarks" a statement of epistemology or method.[5] Although Arendt alluded to the importance of experience to critical understanding through-

1. Hannah Arendt, "Notes for Six Lectures"; "The Great Tradition and the Nature of Totalitarianism," The New School, March 18–April 22, 1953, Library of Congress.

2. "R," 79. Although positivists in Arendt's time may have modeled their research more closely after that of objective science, few political scientists today sustain the belief that theories can be perfectly detached from the commitments of the scientist who espouses them, and few deny that methodology and results are mutually conditioning. If read for her critique of positivism, these early essays would be of little interest because they address a well-worn debate, and not very persuasively at that. But the attraction of these essays lies not so much in the case she makes *against* positivism as in the case she makes *on behalf of* storytelling. Arendt is exceptional because she actually tells stories about Dreyfus and Disraeli, uses passages from Proust, and refers to *Lawrence of Arabia* in support of the theoretical claims she makes in *The Origins of Totalitarianism.*

3. Seyla Benhabib argues that "the historiography of National Socialist totalitarianism presented Arendt with extremely difficult methodological dilemmas with normative dimensions, and that while reflecting upon these dilemmas Arendt developed a conception of political theory as 'storytelling'." See "Hannah Arendt and the Redemptive Power of Narrative," *Social Research* 57 (1990): 170.

4. Elisabeth Young-Bruehl, *Hannah Arendt: For Love of the World* (New Haven: Yale University Press, 1982), 308.

5. Ernst Vollrath, "Hannah Arendt and the Method of Political Thinking," *Social Research* 44 (Spring 1977): 161. Along with Benhabib, Vollrath's essay is a noteworthy exception, as is David Luban's, "Explaining Dark Times: Hannah Arendt's Theory of Theory," *Social Research* 50 (1983): 215–247.

out her writings, often in offhand comments such as the one quoted at the beginning of this chapter, she left an important question unanswered: How can thought that is "bound" to experience as its only "guidepost" possibly be critical? I discern an answer to this question in Arendt's conception of storytelling, which implicitly redefines conventional understandings of objectivity and impartiality.

Arendt failed to explain what she herself termed a "rather unusual approach" ("R," 77) to political theory because she considered methodological discussions to be self-indulgent and irrelevant to real political problems.[6] She did herself a disservice by this reticence, because her failure to explain how storytelling creates a vantage point that is both critical and experiential left her open to charges of subjectivism.[7] As Richard Bernstein has argued, however, what makes Hannah Arendt distinctive is that she is neither a foundationalist nor a subjectivist but rather attempts to move "beyond objectivism and relativism."[8]

Storytelling is not a term Arendt defines precisely or uses consistently throughout her writings. Consequently, there is more than one "theory" of storytelling in her work. Drawing largely from Arendt's remarks in *The Human Condition*, Seyla Benhabib characterizes Arendt's storytelling as "redemptive narrative" whose purpose is "redeeming the memory of the dead, the defeated and the vanquished by making present to us once more their failed hopes, their untrodden paths, and unfulfilled dreams."[9] There is a strikingly different account of storytelling in the unpublished outlines, research memoranda, and lesser-known essays Arendt composed while she wrote *The Origins of Totalitarianism*. In these writings, storytelling is a way to chart a course of action at a time when the thread of tradition is irreparably broken so that we are confronted with the necessity "to understand without preconceived categories and to judge without the set of customary rules which is morality."[10] The consequence

---

6. Ibid., 162.
7. See, for example, Martin Jay, "Hannah Arendt: Opposing Views," *Partisan Review* 45 (1978): 348–380.
8. Richard Bernstein, *Beyond Objectivism and Relativism* (Philadelphia: University of Pennsylvania Press, 1985).
9. Benhabib, "Hannah Arendt," 196.
10. Hannah Arendt, "Understanding and Politics," *Partisan Review* 20 (July–August 1953): 391.

of this rupture in the tradition is precisely that one can no longer set a course in politics by the aspirations of the past. Although Arendt explicitly refuses the authority of tradition, she affirms that it is possible nonetheless to make responsible judgments about political events so long as judgment is situated in the experience of the theorist.

In this chapter I explicate the conception of critical thinking from personal experience that is implicit in Arendt's remarks on storytelling. I chart its development from the earliest publications, where, in spite of her distaste for polemic, her writing is quite polemical. Next, I look at her discussions of methodology in the research outlines and memoranda she composed while writing *Origins*. In these unpublished writings, she begins to justify the difference between her storytelling and simple polemic. I then treat the exchange between Voegelin and Arendt that occurred after the publication of *Origins*. It is only when she is attacked by social scientists for her use of metaphor as a substitute for empirical research,[11] and by humanists for her partiality[12] that Arendt attempts to explicate her method. She argues for a redefinition of validity to be achieved not by abstract, neutral writing but by storytelling from a committed moral perspective. In this chapter, I explore the early writings where Arendt attempts to practice storytelling. In the next chapter, I carry this methodological debate into the lectures on Kant's *Third Critique* where Arendt uses Kant's concept of taste to defend storytelling as a critical practice. Before turning to the early writings, I situate that practice in the context of Arendt's resistance to the Archimedean norm.

Why Storytelling as *Critical* Thinking?

As I have argued, Arendt's storytelling proposes an alternative to the Archimedean model of impartiality as detached reasoning. The argument for storytelling as a practice of constructing knowledge complements the argument she makes against rulership. Plato's theory of the forms, she

11. Luban, "Explaining Dark Times," 247.
12. Eric Voegelin, a review of *The Origins of Totalitarianism*, *Review of Politics* 15 (1953): 68–76.

argues, is the epistemological justification of rulership. It opened an "abyss between philosophy and politics" that parallels the hierarchical articulation of action into command and execution.[13] Arendt proposes storytelling to bridge this abyss and to question the inevitability with which rulership seems to follow from the Archimedean model of knowledge.

Both aspects of the Archimedean norm, the myth of power as leverage and the ideal of abstract impartiality, are perpetuated by the very style of philosophical writing, according to Arendt. Principles that appear timeless and universal when couched in abstract arguments really began as particular experiences, so "no matter how abstract our theories may sound or how consistent our arguments may appear, there are incidents and stories behind them which, at least for ourselves, contain as in a nutshell the full meaning of whatever we have to say" ("A," 2–3). Storytelling both situates our theories in the experiences from which they came and engages an audience in a different kind of critical thinking than an argument does. A story can represent a dilemma as contingent and unprecedented and position its audience to think from within that dilemma. It invites the kind of situated critical thinking that is necessary when we are called upon, in Arendt's words, to think "without a banister."[14]

In the context of the Western political tradition, it is strange to describe *critical* thinking as storytelling. Much of that tradition has always taken it for granted that conceptual thought is the principal weapon against the prejudices carried by "old fashioned" stories. It is even stranger to associate storytelling with discontinuity, to argue that the time to tell stories is when the past has "lost its authority," given the belief that stories preserve continuity, transmitting tradition from one generation to the next (BPF, 28). Alasdair MacIntyre, for example, identifies stories with tradition, writing that "there is no way to give us an

13. Hannah Arendt, "Philosophy and Politics: The Problem of Action and Thought after the French Revolution," 1954, Library of Congress, MSS Box 76, 32.
14. Hannah Arendt, "On Hannah Arendt," in *Hannah Arendt: The Recovery of the Public World*, ed. Melvyn Hill (New York: St. Martin's Press, 1979), 336–337. Margaret Canovan also notes that the "banister" metaphor is evidence that Arendt's work anticipates antifoundationalism. *Hannah Arendt: A Reinterpretation of Her Thought* (New York: Cambridge University Press, 1992), 278.

understanding of any society, including our own, except through the stock of stories which constitute its initial dramatic resources."[15] Strangest of all is the claim that stories invite argumentation when, in a traditional society, storytelling is a consensus-building practice that serves to hand down "a common understanding of the meaning and purpose of human life."[16] Contrary to these assumptions, Arendt argues that it was the very abstraction of moral categories that made it possible for the Nazis to supplant the familiar guideposts of moral life with "language rules." These rules kept Nazi functionaries from equating the crimes made legal under that regime "with their old, 'normal' knowledge of murder and lies."[17] Under such conditions, when "thought and reality have parted company," Arendt argues that telling stories is a way to remind ourselves of the reality to which our abstract concepts are no longer adequate, and to bring to light the discrepancies between those categories and our experiences (BPF, 6).

In *The Fragility of Goodness*, Martha Nussbaum explains how stories work as a critique of Archimedean thinking. Nussbaum contrasts the abstract, rule-governed model of critical understanding in rationalist philosophy with the particularist method of tragedy. She argues that where rationalist philosophy aims to rule out irreconcilable ethical conflict by rendering "all values commensurable in terms of a single coin," tragedy presents unique situations in which the choice is among values that cannot be calibrated against a common measure. Tragic dramas, she claims, teach a "horizontal drawing of connections," so that one reflects on an incident "by burrowing down into the depths of the particular, finding images and connections that will permit us to see it more truly, describe it more richly." If tragic dramas teach us to think horizontally, rationalist philosophy teaches us to think vertically, to construct ethical problems in terms of "pre-articulated" rules. These two modes of critical thinking, one spontaneous and horizontal, the other "pre-articulated" and vertical, require altogether different ways of telling sto-

15. Alasdair MacIntyre, *After Virtue* (Notre Dame: University of Notre Dame Press, 1981), 201.

16. Benjamin R. Barber, *The Conquest of Politics* (Princeton: Princeton University Press, 1988), 183.

17. Hannah Arendt, *Eichmann in Jerusalem* (New York: Penguin, 1963, rpt. 1983), 86.

ries. The Archimedean thinker is not really engaged in storytelling but in illustration, treating a story as "a schematic philosopical example" of an abstract principle. In contrast, the tragic story traces "the history of a complex pattern of deliberation" and so "lays open to view the complexity, the indeterminacy, the sheer difficulty of actual human deliberation."[18] Tragic storytellling serves not to settle questions but to *un*settle them, and to inspire spontaneous critical thinking in its audience.

The implicit claim of Arendt's earliest writings and final work on judgment echoes Nussbaum's argument that storytelling both exhorts and teaches spontaneous critical thinking. Like Nussbaum, Arendt argues that when the salient feature of a dilemma is that it cannot be understood in terms of "pre-articulated" rules, it is best represented by telling a story. Archimedean thinking is inadequate to the challenge of an unprecedented event, because such an event brings "to light the ruin of our categories of thought and standards of judgment."[19] The new lexicon of politics suggests that although totalitarianism may have provoked Arendt's turn to storytelling, situated criticism is not unique to the study of that phenomenon; rather, totalitarianism accentuates the features of politics that require the political theorist to be a storyteller. To discern the salient features of a political phenomenon one must begin not with the categories of moral and legal philosophy but with its stories.

Polemic or Storytelling?

In the early essays, Arendt argues that totalitarianism is an unprecedented regime that precipitates not simply a crisis of morality but a "problem of understanding" because it is incomprehensible in terms of the existing conceptual categories of the Western political tradition.[20] As Luban puts it, Arendt judged totalitarianism to be a moral and, more

18. Martha C. Nussbaum, *The Fragility of Goodness* (Cambridge: Cambridge University Press, 1986), 58, 69, 14, 14.
19. Arendt, "Understanding and Politics," 388.
20. Arendt, "Notes for Six Lectures."

important, an "epistemological" crisis.[21] She defines this "epistemological" crisis as the problem of understanding when "we are confronted
with something which has destroyed our categories of thought and standards of judgment."[22]

She begins to lay out this problem of understanding in a very early
book review of *The Black Book*, a denunciation of the Nazis that came
out soon after the war. Arendt criticizes the book for purporting to be
a "bill of indictment" against the Nazis.[23] The book fails to persuade
precisely because the authors take it as their mission to resurrect truth
and justice and attempt to do so by stating true facts to displace Nazi
falsehoods. Arendt argues that this strategy is naive. Without the total
power to fabricate "a false reality according to a lying ideology, [the]
propaganda and publicity of the style embodied in this book can only
succeed in making a true story sound unconvincing" ("IH," 292). What
its authors do not understand, according to Arendt, is that the Nazis
have called into question the belief that truth can vanquish power. They
understand "that gigantic lies and monstrous falsehoods can eventually
be established as unquestioned facts, that man may be free to change
his own past at will, and that the difference between truth and falsehood
may cease to be objective and become a mere matter of power and
cleverness, of pressure and infinite repetition" (OT, 333). The problem
is that in the wake of a political regime that exercised power by means
of the fabrication of reality, it must be acknowledged that "truth" can
be a *construct* of power. As she remarks in a letter to David Riesman at
about the same time, "truth may disappear from the human community
if we do not want it; after all, we can also lie and—to a very large
extent—we can make our lies stick. This is a question of power."[24] To
propagandize on behalf of the "truth" as if true stories simply compel
our assent is to miss the point of what the Nazis accomplished. The
Nazis did more than lie. They proved that under a totalitarian regime

21. Luban, "Explaining Dark Times," 218.
22. Arendt, "Understanding and Politics," 382.
23. *The Black Book: The Nazi Crime against the Jewish People*, comp. and ed. World Jewish
    Congress, the Jewish Anti-Fascist Committee, the Vaad Leumi, and the American Com-
    mittee of Jewish Writers, Artists, and Scientists (New York: Duell, Sloan and Pearce,
    1946). Quoted in Arendt, "IH," 291.
24. Hannah Arendt to David Riesman, June 13, 1949, Library of Congress, MSS Box 12.

"fact depends entirely on the power of man who can fabricate it" (OT, 350).

One cannot answer the Nazis by opposing truth against falsehood because both truth and falsehood "stick" equally well. This is not because truth and fact are merely relative but because the propaganda that totalitarian rulers deploy erodes citizens' critical faculties. Arendt suggests that propaganda was successful in Hitler's and Stalin's regimes because it preyed on the more widespread modern phenomenon of the credulity of public opinion in mass societies. According to Arendt, it is a characteristic of modernity to have great agnosticism about natural law coexisting with dogmatic confidence in scientific fact so that "it is rare to meet people who believe they possess the truth; instead, we are constantly confronted by those who are sure that they are right" (MDT, 28). Totalitarian leaders prey on this credulity by crafting propaganda that lends the appearance of "scientificality" to its claims. She claims that this is a phenomenon of mass society, noting that the "strong emphasis of totalitarian propaganda on the 'scientific' nature of its assertions has been compared to certain advertising techniques which also address themselves to the masses" (OT, 345). The task of the critic in such an age is not to correct false views with true ones, but to invigorate the practice of critical skepticism. The challenge Arendt sees for herself and other critics and analysts of totalitarianism is to craft its story in a way that does not compel assent but rather stirs people to think about what they are doing.[25]

Arendt alludes to "scientificality" in a sarcastic moment of the mercurial essay "We Refugees," where she remarks on the difficulty of bringing "modern people" to understand the suicidal despair of the displaced Jewish bourgeoisie and intelligentsia:

> I speak of unpopular facts; and it makes things worse that in order to prove my point I do not even dispose of the sole arguments which impress modern people—figures. . . . I am

---

25. In the preface to BPF, Arendt also argues that it is not by logical consistency or factual descriptions that one counters falsehoods but by inciting one's audience to critical thinking.

quite sure those figures [on Jewish suicide rates] are no longer correct, but I cannot prove it with new figures, *though I can certainly with new experiences*. This might be sufficient for those skeptical souls who never were quite convinced that the measure of one's skull gives the exact idea of its content, or that statistics of crime show the exact level of national ethics. (JP, 58–59; emphasis added)

This is, of course, a caricature of that dogmatic confidence in science that Arendt attributes to "modern people." But alongside the polemical commentary on science, Arendt makes the provocative suggestion that it is by means of stories that one speaks to those "skeptical souls" who are inclined to take neither facts nor truths at face value. She proposes, in effect, to respond to the problem of understanding by moving from the level of objective universals to that of particularity. What she does not justify, however, is the implicit suggestion that stories—which would seem to foster credulity, not combat it—encourage skepticism.

In letters that she wrote at about the same time to Mary Underwood, editor at Houghton Mifflin for her book on totalitarianism, Arendt considers the problem of understanding in relation to her own project on totalitarianism.[26] Arendt complains to Underwood that she is having difficulty formulating an outline of the project because she is unsure how to write the history of totalitarianism as a critique of that phenomenon. In one draft memo she writes, "the coherence of this book which is essentially a book against should not be the coherence of continuity."[27] The dilemma, as she presents it in another draft memo, is that her subject matter calls for a history written against what she calls "the inherent law of all historiography which is preservation and justification and praise." She wants "to present its result in such a way that it serves the opposite and intrinsically unhistoric purpose of destruction."[28]

26. See also Young-Bruehl's discussion of these methodological difficulties, *Hannah Arendt*, 200–206.
27. Hannah Arendt, draft of memo to Mary Underwood, probably August 1946, Library of Congress, MSS Box 76.
28. Hannah Arendt, draft research outline, " 'The Elements of Shame. Antisemitism—Imperialism—Racism.' or (The Three Pillars of Hell. Antisemitism—Imperialism—Racism.)" August 1946, Library of Congress, MSS Box 76.

Arendt claims that other historians faced with this kind of task have engaged in "polemical writing," but that this "is permitted only as long as the author can fall back upon a firm ground of traditional values which are accepted without questioning and on which judgments can be formed." Because she believes that totalitarianism takes this ground out from under her, she concludes "I, therefore, had to avoid [sic] carefully the polemical style, much as I was tempted by it, because polemical attitudes today degenrate [sic] into cynism [sic] or are superficial triteness."[29] Polemic is, then, a kind of Archimedean thinking that relies on a "pre-articulated" normative framework and functions not to initiate discussion but to settle it. Arendt's objection to *The Black Book* was that it was a polemic about the very event that rules out polemical writing, precisely by shattering the ethical certainties to which polemic needs to refer.

Although she rules out polemical writing, Arendt is not calling for detached, politically neutral social science. On the contrary, in an essay titled "Social Science Techniques and the Study of Concentration Camps," Arendt claims that totalitarianism is an epistemological crisis as much for positive science as it is for moral philosophy. The essay opens with the dramatic claim that "Every science is necessarily based upon a few inarticulate, elementary and axiomatic assumptions which are exposed and exploded only when confronted with altogether unexpected phenomena which can no longer be understood within the framework of its categories." She claims that the camps explode the presupposition of falsifiability that guarantees the possibility of objectivity in the social sciences. The camps are organized in accordance with an "inflexible logic" characteristic of paranoia, "where everything follows with absolute necessity once the first insane premise is accepted" ("SST, 49–50). What makes totalitarianism "total" is precisely its capacity to "fabricate" reality; that is, the knowledge that it is possible to take a particular hypothesis and "in the course of consistently guided action, [ensure that] the particular hypothesis will become true, will become actual, factual reality" (BPF, 87). This capacity to fabricate reality puts the totalitarian system beyond the "objective necessities conceived as the

29. Draft of memo to Mary Underwood, probably August 1946.

ingredients of reality itself" ("SST," 61). Techniques of positive social science are discredited when confronted with a power that can make facts in the image of its own hypotheses. The epistemological crisis of totalitarianism, then, is precipitated by the capacity to "make" reality that renders objectivity meaningless.

The ethical crisis of totalitarianism is engendered by the systematic dismantling of "the individual" through the concentration camp system. In contrast to the murder, which is a crime against a distinct person, the destruction of "the individual" is an unprecedented crime against humanity itself. Western ethics is premised on the assumption of an autonomous individual that is responsible for its actions and identical with itself over time. Arendt argues that deportation to a concentration camp dismantles this premise by systematically violating the three conditions on which individuality depend–legality, publicity, and natality.

First, autonomy, which is defined legally in terms of action and intent, is rendered meaningless by an arbitrary arrest that "stands in no connection whatsoever with the actions or opinions of the person." Second, she argues that identity over time is ruptured by the violation of publicity that, in this context, simply means the continuity of one's appearances in a neighborhood, work at a job, and relationships with friends. This continuity is interrupted by deportation, which effects the total disappearance of the person from his or her place in the world. By secreting the camps from public view and discouraging inquiries about them, the Nazis ensured that neighbors never knew where a deportee had gone or even whether he or she had died, "it is as if he [sic] had disappeared from the surface of the earth" ("SST," 60). Elsewhere, Arendt describes this loss of publicity from the perspective of the deportee who survived or escaped the camps by an ironic reference to a "nice little fairy tale" that features "a forlorn emigre dachshund [who], in his grief, begins to speak: 'Once, when I was a St. Bernard...'" (JP, 60). This "fairy tale" confirms that many who survived or escaped the camps did so at the cost of a displacement that they experienced not just as a change of place, but as a rupture of identity.

Third, the institutionalization of experimental torture destroys natality, the condition of spontaneous human action, by creating an environment in which individuals are reduced "to the lowest possible

denominator of 'identical reactions.' " The crime perpetrated by the totalitarian regime is unprecedented because arbitrary arrest, disappearance from public view, and routinized torture effect a fundamental
transformation of human nature. Totalitarian political philosophy begins
from the discovery that "limitations which usually are thought to be
inherent in the human condition could be transcended" ("SST," 61).
The concentration camp is more than a site for mass murder: its mechanisms function not simply to kill people but to negate their humanity.

The controversial part of this argument is that Arendt denies that
humanity is a distinctive quality or property that is somehow essentially
in all human beings; on the contrary, it is a capacity that depends on
legal, civil, and social conditions. Autonomy depends on legal constructions of intentionality and responsibility, as well as on civil guarantees
against the arbitrary exercise of police power. Identity over time, which
is typically understood to be internal to the person, is not secured by a
private faculty such as memory or a moral core such as integrity but by
one's appearances over time in a particular social milieu. Finally, the
capacity for action depends on a mutuality of respect that is not a natural
right of persons in virtue of their humanity but is, rather, secured by
legal, civil, and social convention. The concentration camps make it clear
that there is no basis in "nature" for the autonomous "individual" of
humanism. By abrogating those protections, the camps "show that human beings can be transformed into specimens of the human animal,
and that man's 'nature' is only 'human,' insofar as it opens up to man
the possibility of becoming something highly unnatural, that is, a man"
(OT, 455). What is left when the public artifice is stripped away is not
the essential core of humanity but the natural fact of the vulnerability
of the human animal, which is the "common denominator" of species.

The camps are "the image of hell" because they are the antithesis of
the democratic ideal of "public space" she defends in *The Human Condition*. Where the public space is constituted by political equality, the
concentration camp constitutes a "monstrous equality" of undifferen-
tiated beings "without fraternity or humanity" ("IH," 292). Fraternity
and humanity are lost because without a public space, human plurality—
which is the condition of fraternity and individuality—has no place to
appear.

This essay is almost never mentioned in studies of Arendt's political thought, and with good reason.[30] It is not tightly argued, and its critique of positivist social science is incomplete. Even worse, Arendt defends the claim that totalitarianism is a crime against human individuality as if everyone would understand what she means by terms like *natality* and *publicity*. Although these terms are critical to her claim that *mass* murder is not simply analogous to murder but constitutes a genuinely unprecedented crime, she did not define them for almost ten years, when she published *The Human Condition*.

Consequently, the essay is probably less important for its clarity and persuasiveness than for its remarkable prescience. In it, Arendt demonstrates the storytelling techniques that are innovative even now. In describing the concentration camps, Arendt sets aside the *literal* idiom of social science for the *resonant* "voice of poetry."[31] The style of a more conventional argument would be at cross purposes with Arendt's substantive theme, that totalitarianism is incomprehensible in conventional terms. Metaphor, oxymoron, and hyperbole permit her to express this claim in an idiom that matches it. She categorizes the camps through oxymoron, calling them "extermination factories," or "death factories" for the "fabrication of corpses" ('SST,' 50, 51, 58). The incongruity in the juxtaposition of opposites—production and annihilation—calls attention to the fact that the phenomenon being described violates common sense. This language dramatizes the insanity of the camps. "Factories" that exist to "produce" death are absurdity made real. This language further refutes the analogy to mass murder. Where mass murder is only quantitatively unprecedented, the systematic dismantling of individuality by the production of corpses—dead and alive—is incomprehensible in terms of existing categories of crime.

If oxymoron frames this analysis, moral hyperbole punctuates the statistical and historical evidence that constitutes the body of the argument.

---

30. Luban's "Explaining Dark Times" is a noteworthy exception. This essay is a most illuminating explication of Arendt's critique of positive social science. Although Luban criticizes Arendt for relying too much on passing references to theoretical physics and too little on explicit argument, he nonetheless draws from Arendt's various assertions about social science a more plausible critique of positivism than she makes herself.

31. See Michael Oakeshott, "The Voice of Poetry in the Conversation of Mankind," in *Rationalism in Politics* (New York: Methuen, 1962, rpt. 1981).

The camps are the "image of hell" where inmates exist in "monstrous equality." The Nazis' crime is not just wicked but "deformed wickedness," and the victimization of the Jews is "deformed . . . innocence" ("IH," 292). Like the incongruous language of the categories, the hyperbole in her judgments about the evidence works to illustrate Arendt's point that this event cannot be understood in terms of traditional categories such as guilt and innocence. But although she intends the literary devices she employs to dramatize her belief that totalitarianism is incomprehensible, the effect is that the early essays have a moralizing and polemical tone, in spite of Arendt's critique of polemical writing. Arendt herself was well aware of this tendency in her writing and joked about it with Karl Jaspers while she was correcting the final proofs for *Origins*: "With me there's always something dogmatic left hanging around somewhere. (That's what you get when Jews start writing history)" (C, 176).

Jokes notwithstanding, there must be some meaningful distinction between what she took herself to be doing and the style for which she criticized works such as *The Black Book*. What makes Arendt juxtapose explicitly judgmental writing and empirical evidence, as if the resonant idiom of literature and the literal idiom of social science were perfectly compatible? She defends this style of writing in a letter to Karl Jaspers, reacting to one German critic's appraisal of *Origins* as having been written in an exaggerated style. She begins by accepting this appraisal, explaining that "My 'exaggerated' kind of thinking . . . is at least making an effort to say something adequate in a tone that is, if possible, itself adequate." But she finishes the sentence by refuting the charge, suggesting that what comes off as exaggeration is actually critical historiography. She asserts that such a style "will of course sound wildly radical if you measure it not against reality but against what other historians, going on the assumption that everything is in the best of order, have said on the same subject."[32] The implicit distinction between storytelling and polemic might be analogous to that between literature and pulp

---

32. C, 150. Seyla Benhabib explains Arendt's technique this way: "the moral resonance of one's language does not primarily reside in the explicit value judgments which an author may pass on the subject matter; rather such resonance must be an aspect of the narrative itself. The language must match the moral quality of the narrated object." "Hannah Arendt," 186.

fiction; where the latter capitalizes on shock value for the sake of titil-
lation, the former attunes its style to the substance of its vision. If Arendt's analysis is radical, her style must be too. Its implicit complexity
notwithstanding, because Arendt does not make the underlying logic of
this approach public until much later (in her response to Eric Voegelin's
critique of *Origins*), these earliest writings appear more dogmatic than
innovative.

This examination of the early essays and unpublished memos shows
that Arendt's claim that totalitarianism poses a problem of understanding is not just an analytical argument but also a practical dilemma she
encountered in the course of trying to tell the story. In response to that
problem of understanding, she experiments with a kind of storytelling,
using literary devices to present her analysis in affective terms. But in
these early writings, Arendt merely identifies the problem of totalitarianism and experiments with storytelling techniques as a response. She
neither refers to her work as storytelling nor attempts to defend storytelling as a response to either the epistemic crisis of totalitarianism or
the conditions of politics more generally. I turn now to *Origins* to begin
to discern Arendt's defense of storytelling as critical theory.

Storytelling as New "Objectivity"

It is curious that the methodological dilemmas of the early essays never
make their way into print, despite their connection to Arendt's principal
thesis that totalitarianism precipitates an epistemic breakdown. It turns
out that one of the most interesting accounts of her storytelling is an
untold story about the change from the working title of the totalitarianism project to *Origins of Totalitarianism*, the title under which it was
published in the United States. This story can be inferred from the discrepancies between the unpublished outlines and memos to Mary Underwood and the published title and preface.[33]

33. In England the book appeared as *The Burden of Our Times*, a title less in the style of
    social science than that under which it appeared in the United States, but still missing
    the allusion of the working version.

In the memos to Underwood, Arendt complains of the difficulty of writing a history that does not celebrate its subject matter or present it as a necessary outcome of an evolutionary process. The title she proposes is consistent with the methodological dilemmas she spells out. The working title, "The Elements of Shame: Antisemitism—Imperialism—Racism," names the method of the book, which is to be an analysis of the "elements" of totalitarianism for which antisemitism is the "amalgamator."[34] "Elements" makes the break with historical narratives that chart the continuous evolution of an event from its causes. "Amalgamation" suggests that totalitarianism occurred from a coincidence of elements that are not necessarily or causally connected but whose intersection is not simply random. Thus, together these terms give Arendt a vocabulary for contingency. Finally, the use of the explicitly judgmental "shame" suggests that contingent events, unlike those that are either random or necessary, demand an exercise of critical judgment.

The title that actually makes it to press is inconsistent with the methodological imperatives she lays out in the memos to Underwood. Both "elements" and "shame" disappear in the switch from the working title to its published version, to be replaced by the more conventional "origins." "Origins" is a temporal concept that implies an evolutionary narrative about causally related events. This change redefines the work itself. Where "Elements of Shame" announces a study that violates the conventions of social science to explain a contingent event that is incomprehensible within that framework, "Origins" suggests a causal analysis that appears to follow those conventions.[35]

Similarly, in the brief references to methodology she makes in the preface, Arendt suppresses the uncertainty she revealed in the Underwood memos. In the published version, Arendt frames the problem of contingency as the problem of comprehending an event such as totalitarianism. She asserts that comprehension can mean neither explanation

34. Hannah Arendt, "Outline," for Mary Underwood, probably August 1946, Library of Congress, MSS Box 76.
35. Similarly, Benhabib calls the term *origins* a "misnomer" for the work, because Arendt makes it "clear that she is not concerned to establish some inevitable continuity between the past and the present of such a nature that one has to view what happened as what had to happen." "Hannah Arendt," 171.

in terms of general laws nor fatalist acceptance. Instead, it entails a critical posture, achieved by means of "the unpremeditated, attentive facing up to, and resisting of, reality—whatever it may be or might have been" (OT, xiv). Presumably, the term *unpremeditated* is an allusion to her earlier argument that totalitarianism is an unprecedented phenomenon that shatters all prior conceptual frameworks. But because Arendt only alludes to the vivid account she made in the social science essay, and because her for-publication voice is so authoritative, the preface actually serves to undermine her thesis that totalitarianism poses a problem of understanding. Where the uncertainty of Arendt's tone in the Underwood memos makes her claim that totalitarianism is an epistemic crisis all the more plausible, her for-publication voice sounds polemical and idiosyncratic.[36]

The preface is even more confusing because Arendt retains some of the physics language from the earlier version but mixes it with the evolutionary metaphor. If anything, the physics language is more emphatic in this version. Anti-Semitism is no longer the "amalgamator" but now the "catalytic agent" of National Socialism, the war, and genocide. And totalitarianism is the "final crystallizing catastrophe" that brings its "elements and origins" into the open (OT, xiv, xv). But this sentence is the problem. Arendt writes as if "elements" and "origins" meant the same thing. This is confusing because "elements" suggests a contingent formation and so is consistent with "crystallization," whereas "origins" implies that totalitarianism evolved from a primary cause. Arendt actually clarifies the distinction between these terms in a draft for the essay "Understanding and Politics," where she writes that "The elements of totalitarianism form its origins if by origins we do not understand 'causes.' . . . Elements by themselves never cause anything. They become origins of events if and when they suddenly crystallize into fixed and definite forms."[37] This passage, however, does not make it into the version of the essay that was published in *Partisan Review*. Thus, in the

---

36. This is exactly the point on which she is taken to task by critics who see her as a cold war ideologist. See Benjamin R. Barber et al., *Totalitarianism in Perspective: Three Views* (New York: Praeger, 1969).

37. Hannah Arendt, "On the Nature of Totalitarianism: An Essay in Understanding," undated typescript, Library of Congress, MSS Box 76, 7.

preface to *Origins*, her only public statement of method, Arendt mixes metaphors of physics and evolution, thereby obscuring the distinction between contingency and causality that presumably moved her to choose such peculiar words as "elements," "amalgamation," and "crystalliza-tion" in the first place.

Of course, it is possible that Arendt simply changed her mind over the course of writing *Origins*. Maybe she believed that she had solved these dilemmas and consequently had no need to carry her uncertainty into print. I suggest that she did not, in fact, resolve them, but rather suppressed them to conform to conventions of explanation. This is ev-idenced by the fact that she resurrects the arguments that did not make it into the preface in her reply to Eric Voegelin's review of the book. Because Arendt fails to make public her more detailed statement of the problem of understanding as she lays it out in the early memos—and fails to justify her method as a response to that problem—she leaves her work open to misinterpretation in terms of the very epistemic framework she claims to write against. It is just such a misinterpretation, by Voe-gelin, that prompts Arendt to be more forthcoming about her method.

Voegelin objects to Arendt's work on both methodological and sub-stantive grounds. He characterizes her approach as an "emotionally de-termined method of proceeding from a concrete center of shock toward generalizations." His objection is not to Arendt's emotional presence in the work, in fact he calls that "the strength" of the book and says it is reminiscent of Thucydides. Rather, he objects to the fact that Arendt is so caught up in the "phenomenal difference" of totalitarianism that she does not see its "essential sameness" to the crises that follow from the agnosticism of the modern age. Voegelin claims that totalitarianism is not unprecedented but, rather, the "climax of a secular evolution" that began in the High Middle Ages with the heretical notion that the per-fection of humanity could be achieved not through the grace of God but by acts of men. Although he agrees with her that it is a mass social phenomenon, he criticizes what he describes as her attempt to "make contemporary phenomena intelligible by *tracing their origin* back to the 18th century." He argues that eighteenth-century events are only surface manifestations of the deeper "spiritual disease" of the modern age, and so to penetrate the essence of totalitarianism, Arendt would have to locate its origin at "the genesis of the spiritual disease."[38] Voegelin depicts Arendt's work as an evolutionary tale that falls short of the origin and therefore misunderstands the essence of totalitarianism.

The methodological dilemmas she excised from the preface return in her response to Voegelin. In fact, the reply begins with Arendt acknowledging the shortcomings of the preface as a statement of method and admitting that she ought to have made such a statement. She writes, "I failed to explain the particular method which I came to use, and to account for a rather unusual approach . . . to the whole field of political and historical sciences as such." Arendt repeats the problem she explained to Mary Underwood, that totalitarianism made her "write historically about something . . . which I did not want to conserve but on the contrary felt engaged to destroy." Her answer to this problem was to break totalitarianism into its "chief elements" and analyze their "decisive role" in contributing to that particular phenomenon. Arendt makes it clear that she chose quite consciously not to construct an evolutionary narrative of totalitarianism because that would be the kind of laudatory, preserving historiography she wants to avoid. Thus, Voegelin's reading of her work as a story of the "genesis" of totalitarianism presupposes the continuing existence of a framework that she claims has been shattered. Arendt concludes her response to this section of Voegelin's review with a remarkable repudiation of the for-publication title: "The book, therefore, does not really deal with the 'origins' of totalitarianism—*as its title unfortunately claims*—but gives a historical account of the elements which crystallized into totalitarianism" ("R," 77–78; emphasis added). Hers is an analysis, then, of the formation of totalitarianism, not its genesis.

Nowhere is the fact that Voegelin has completely missed her point more evident than in his accusation that she is herself prey to the disease of the modern age. Voegelin makes this claim in response to Arendt's argument that an epistemic breakdown cannot but effect a transformation of human nature. Voegelin mistakes Arendt's complex argument for a mistaken use of the concept "human nature." He asserts, "A 'nature' cannot be changed or transformed; a 'change of nature' is a con-

---

38. Voegelin, review of *Origins of Totalitarianism*, 70, 69, 69, 74; emphasis added.

tradiction of terms; tampering with the 'nature' of a thing means destroying the thing."[39] Arendt responds that totalitarianism is not a "spiritual disease" but a *political* crisis and that humanity is not an essential essence but a public phenomenon. Although she agrees that the masses are spiritually empty, their problem is not that they have lost their faith but that they have lost a public space in which to act. She chides Voegelin for a cowardly escape into a comforting anachronism: "Historically we know of man's nature only insofar as it has existence, and no realm of eternal essences will ever console us if man loses his essential capabilities" ("R," 84). Voegelin and Arendt assess totalitarianism from utterly incompatible perspectives. He attributes the rise of totalitarianism to agnosticism, the loss of *faith* in fundamental truths concerning God, human nature, and the universal principles that follow from them. She attributes it to the loss of the public realm that can be restored not by the recovery of abstract truths but by reuniting thinking with acting.

To reestablish the connection between thinking and acting, Arendt must redefine objectivity. She does this in her defense against Voegelin's criticism that the structure of *Origins* is "emotionally determined." Arendt argues that she uses morally charged language because she believes, paradoxically, that explicit judgments are not less but rather more objective than ostensibly neutral categories. She writes that she "parted quite consciously" with objective historiography as it is conventionally defined, in an attempt to "describe the totalitarian phenomenon as occurring, not on the moon, but in the midst of human society" ("R," 78). Objectivity is not abstract neutral description but explicitly judgmental storytelling, situated in the "living experience" of the theorist (BPF, 87). She illustrates with a hypothetical example, positing an historian of the British working class who describes its poverty in the early industrial revolution:

> The natural human reaction to such conditions is one of anger and indignation because these conditions are against the dignity of man. If I describe these conditions without permitting

39. Ibid., 74.

my indignation to interfere, I have lifted this particular phenomenon out of its context in human society and have thereby
robbed it of part of its nature. . . . For to arouse indignation is
one of the qualities of excessive poverty insofar as poverty occurs among human beings. ("R," 78)

Arendt argues that it is a "methodological necessity" to situate the phenomenon she describes in the context of her own outrage against it,
because to describe a social phenomenon out of context of the response
it provokes is to deprive it of part of "its important inherent qualities."
She calls attention to the fact that this narrative strategy amounts to a
redefinition of objectivity, writing "In this sense I think that a description of the camps as hell on earth is more 'objective,' that is, more
adequate to their essence than statements of a purely sociological or
psychological nature" ("R," 78–79).

The reply to Voegelin raises at least as many questions as it answers,
however. The claim that indignation is a "natural" response to an affront
to the "dignity of man" assumes a shared conception of dignity and a
shared belief that poverty is "against" it. This example implies that situated thinking is not random or idiosyncratic; rather, it takes its bearings
from a general common sense. Is this a moral sense or a political sense?
If the former, how can she invoke a common moral sense in the absence
of the traditional "guideposts" whose loss she has so definitively pro-
claimed? If the latter, what would justify it as judgment (as opposed to
mere prejudice or opinion) absent an overarching ethical framework? It
is to answer this question that she turns, more than a decade later, to
Kant's *Third Critique*. Before moving on to the lectures on judgment,
however, I want to conclude the discussion of Arendt's redefinition of
objectivity by analyzing an essay on history and a lecture on epistemology in which she revisits the themes she initiates in her reply to Voegelin.
Then I use an example from *Origins* to illustrate her practice of this
redefined objectivity.

Given that Voegelin misinterprets so much of what is unusual about
Arendt's project, it is ironic that he should claim that the strength of
Origins is its similiarity to the writings of Thucydides. In her writings
on history and epistemology, Arendt offers *The Peloponnesian War* as a

model of the kind of historical writing she is trying to achieve. She sees
Thucydides' work as an exemplar of a kind of critical historical writing
that is not grounded in abstract universals but in experience. She uses
a contrast between Archimedes and Thucydides as the vehicle for a critique of objectivist impartiality that extends the themes she introduces
in her reply to Voegelin.

In her comparison of Archimedes and Thucydides, Arendt makes a
distinction between political understanding and objective knowledge.
She argues that the Archimedean model of knowledge is apolitical because of "its objectivity, its disinterestedness, its impartiality in the consequences which its pursuit of truth might have."[40] Thucydides, on the
other hand, strives for political understanding in that he attempts to
inspire his readers to engage in critical thinking. Peter Euben describes
Thucydides' project in a way that spells out the difference between objective knowledge and political understanding, writing that "By constructing a text that replicates the difficulties for the reader that he faced
as a historian describing and making sense of his real world, Thucydides
presents for us the problem of trying to reconstitute and comprehend
collective experience."[41] As Euben describes it, Thucydides' project is
precisely analogous to the problem of *Origins*, which is to write in a way
that gives one's readers the experience of interpreting a complex historical situation.

Note that the contrast Arendt draws between abstract objectivity and
political understanding does not set up a simple dichotomy between
objective and experiential thinking. That she values a kind of objectivity
is evidenced by her assessment of Thucydides whom she praises for
having "kept himself aloof, and quite consciously so, from involvement
with the events themselves. . . . Obviously, no judgment such as Thucydides'—'This was the greatest movement yet known in history'–would
have been possible without such withdrawal." As I mentioned, her objection to the Archimedean model is not that it is impartial but that it
makes abstract objectivity a requisite of impartiality and is consequently

40. Hannah Arendt, "The Archimedean Point," reprint of a lecture for the University of
    Michigan College of Engineers, 1968, Library of Congress, MSS Box 61, 7.
41. J. Peter Euben, *The Tragedy of Political Theory* (Princeton: Princeton University Press,
    1990), 197.

so far removed from political conflict that it can not "pay any attention to human interests." What she takes from Thucydides is a kind of impartiality achieved by a "much more limited" withdrawal.[42]

It is typical of Hannah Arendt to toss off a controversial statement as if it needed no explanation and also typical for such statements to touch on points of controversy and obscurity in her own thoughts. This presentation of Thucydides as a model of the kind of impartiality she thinks is appropriate to historical writing is a classic instance. If Thucydides can be considered impartial, it is not in any conventional sense of the word. In the first place, he is no disinterested observer of the Peloponnesian War. He is a committed participant, a general, who opens his account by identifying himself in explicitly partisan terms as "Thucydides the Athenian." Second, there is ambiguity over the question of whether Thucydides, who wrote in exile after the war, was in a position to *report* history or whether he *reconstructed* the events of the past. Some classicists question whether what he wrote can be considered "history" at all or whether he used the past as a means to present his own mature reflections on important events of his lifetime.[43]

Arendt seems to have viewed Thucydides as she did herself, as a political theorist for whom the question of historical objectivity is an irrelevant methodological debate. The task of the political theorist is not to report objectively but to tell a story that engages the critical faculties of the audience. Euben makes a similar claim, crediting Thucydides with "offering a new standard of accuracy" to his readers. He writes, "However personal or Athenian his work, however much he may have had ties to the aristocratic class at Athens, there is a sense in which he is absent from his discourse. Or to put it more accurately, he is trying to sustain conditions

---

42. Arendt, "Archimedean Point," 6, 25. For related discussions of the epistemological status of political understanding, see William Connolly, *The Terms of Political Discourse* (Princeton: Princeton University Press, 1983), and Tracy Strong, *The Idea of Political Theory* (Notre Dame: University of Notre Dame Press, 1990), chaps. 1 and 3.

43. For a discussion of this controversy, see John Finley, *Three Essays on Thucydides* (Cambridge: Harvard University Press, 1967). Finley's reading of Thucydides supports Arendt's position. He argues that the work is neither a simple fabrication nor a literally accurate report but rather a "possible picture of men's attitude" toward the events of the war (3). Thucydides offers a representation of things that could have been said in a work that "in style as well as in thought carries the imprint of the past itself" (89).

within the text that makes *discourse outside it* possible. . . ."[44] This is no conventional model of objective reporting, as it consists in neither a bloodlessly neutral writing style nor an attempt to avoid selectivity but, rather, in the fact that Thucydides leaves the reader with the task of interpreting the various conflicts he represents. To Euben and Arendt, then, who are political theorists, Thucydides' work achieves something more important than objectivity: political impartiality.

Political impartiality is not secured by means of detachment from politics but by fostering public deliberation, which depends on the ability "to look upon the same world from one another's standpoint." Arendt credits the practice of political impartiality to the *polis*, which she idealizes as a realm of "incessant talk" and plurality, in which "the Greeks discovered that the world we have in common is usually regarded from an infinite number of different standpoints, to which correspond the most diverse points of view" (BPF, 51). Thucydides' work fosters political impartiality by an artistic (though not fictional) creation of plurality by his representation of speeches from the multiple, divergent perspectives that constitute the public realm. Euben writes that Thucydides gives us "a form of political knowledge that respects, even recapitulates, the paradoxes and 'perspectivism' of political life."[45] This account of political impartiality, characterized not by abstraction but by the interplay among a plurality of perspectives, anticipates the conception of impartiality Arendt will discern in Kant's description of the "enlarged mentality" in the *Third Critique*. She admires Thucydides because his imaginative history makes it possible for the reader to think as if engaged in the debates of his time.

Arendt arrives at the need to invent a kind of political impartiality out of the epistemological crisis of totalitarianism. In the absence of the framework of universal moral concepts that totalitarianism shattered, its critic must proceed historically, employing categories of understanding that are given by the particular phenomenon itself. The problem is, of course, that no phenomenon simply gives rise to its categories of analysis. The theorist who would proceed in the absence of the interpretative

44. Euben, *Tragedy*, 197; emphasis added.
45. Ibid., 199.

frameworks given by philosophy or religion cannot simply invoke experience as the ground of analysis. Rather, she must choose a rival framework that is both particularistic and interpretive. Where Thucydides uses
the device of speeches to foster political impartiality, in *Origins* Arendt
employs a somewhat different technique, attempting to shift from the
general and universal to the particular by asking "what kind of basic
experience in the living together of men permeates a form of government
whose essence is terror and whose principle of action is the logicality of
ideological thinking" (OT, 474).

This method, taking a phenomenon such as genocide that was so
abhorrent from the standpoint of humanism and attempting to understand it in its particularity, was frequently misunderstood. Critics
charged Arendt with displaying heartlessness toward her friends and
sympathy toward her enemies, because she took such care to ask how
genocide could have made sense to those who cooperated with it.[46] But
to accuse Arendt of extending *empathy* or *sympathy* toward that which
calls for censure is simply to misread her analysis of totalitarianism.[47]
When it came to judging totalitarian genocide, Arendt was quite ready
to recognize it as a crime against humanity; what she would not do,
however, was to denounce it as a radical evil. She refrained, in other
words, from marking it as an "other" with respect to the principles of
humanism. One reason for her reluctance was that she assumed from
the start that the Nazis could not have succeeded without the cooperation of the German citizenry. Consequently, to denounce genocide as a
radical evil would be tantamount to calling Germany a nation of demons; this was a judgment that Hannah Arendt, who lived almost thirty
years as a German citizen, knew to be absurd. Furthermore, even if she

---

46. The question of Arendt's partisanship, or lack thereof, was a focus of contention in
the controversy that emerged over *Eichmann in Jerusalem*. See, for example, Daniel
Bell's relatively sympathetic critique, where he describes her as writing "from the standpoint of a universal principle which denies any parochial identity." In "The Alphabet
of Justice," *Partisan Review* 30 (Fall 1963): 428. For a critical response to Bell, see
Dwight MacDonald, "Arguments: More on Eichmann," *Partisan Review* 31 (Spring
1964): 262–269.

47. No doubt some of the controversy this practice engendered resulted from the fact that,
aside from some brief remarks in BPF, she did not begin to work out its theoretical
justification until the end of her life.

had thought it plausible to demonize Germany in this way, her claim that totalitarianism represented not just a political but an epistemological crisis precluded such an assertion. She believed that the moral ground from which to assert so polemical a judgment no longer existed.

Thus, there is a kind of sympathy in her method, but one that has nothing whatsoever to do with misplaced compassion. Instead, it dramatizes what Arendt describes in the lectures on judging as thinking "with an enlarged mentality" (LKPP, 43). Rather than denounce those who appear to be so radically other for their inhumanity, she undertakes to understand the experiential basis of their ideologies.[48] There is an excellent example of this method in *Imperialism*, in her analysis of the relationship between the racism of the Boers' imperialist conquests in South Africa and the racism of the Nazis. The question of *Origins* in general and the short section on the Boers is this: under what conditions can extermination appear to be a respectable political policy? Arendt draws the categories for this analysis from two novels by Joseph Conrad (OT, 197).

In the first footnote to the section in which she analyses the Boers, Arendt declares that "Joseph Conrad, 'Heart of Darkness' in *Youth and Other Tales*, 1902, is the most illuminating work on actual race experience in Africa" (OT, 185). Her analysis is interwoven with allusions to, long citations from, and interpretive paraphrasing of Joseph Conrad's *Victory* and "Heart of Darkness," which she uses to help her analyze how it could have seemed to the Boers that their relations with South African Blacks were exempt from Western moral conventions.[49] Arendt

48. Lionel Abel, whose polemic against *Eichmann in Jerusalem* sparked an extensive discussion in the pages of the *Partisan Review*, attacks Arendt for her use of this same approach in the later work. Incensed by the "banality of evil" thesis, Abel asserts that "once Eichmann is judged morally and politically, it should be perfectly clear that the contention of Prosecutor Hausner that Eichmann was a moral monster will be seen to be a valid and intelligent one, while Miss Arendt's judgment of Eichmann as an insignificant and commonplace official will be seen to be perverse and arbitrary." In "The Aesthetics of Evil," *Partisan Review* 30 (Summer 1963): 224. Abel puts this claim forth with a certainty born of his refusal to engage Arendt's argument that totalitarianism shattered the moral standpoint from which to make such a claim.

49. It could be objected that Arendt accords a far too complex political philosophy to both of these groups, whose actions can be reduced simply to an expression of power politics or to the evil of their leaders and members. One of the premises of Arendt's

suggests that "the basis in experience" of the Boers' racism was the ambivalence they felt at identifying with that which one expects to be radically different:

> Race was the emergency explanation of human beings whom no European or civilized man could understand *and whose humanity so frightened and humiliated the immigrants* that they no longer cared to belong to the same human species. Race was the Boers' answer to the overwhelming monstrosity of Africa—a whole continent populated and overpopulated by savages—an explanation of the madness which grasped and illuminated them like "a flash of lightning in a serene sky: 'Exterminate all the brutes'." (OT, 185; emphasis added).

Contrary to the notion that it is sheer hatred of difference, the insight Arendt takes from Conrad is that racism is borne out of a dissonance between identity and difference. She uses Conrad's text to argue that racism is a defense against the frightening ambivalence of an encounter with another whom one fears to acknowledge in one's self.[50]

---

analysis of Nazism (most explicitly stated in the subtitle to *Eichmann*) is that the Holocaust could not have happened without the participation of ordinary law-abiding citizens. The question of how such people, who think of themselves as moral, could be drawn into complicity with a totalitarian government is what animates this concern to understand their political philosophy.

50. Because of Arendt's failure to appreciate American racism as racism, she would no doubt dismiss much contemporary African-American social criticism as "a pose" (MDT, 18). Even so, her analysis of the ambivalence in racism brings to mind the work of Audre Lorde. Like Arendt, Lorde understands racism not as a denial of difference but a denial of common humanity. As an exercise for well-intentioned liberals, as well as for explicit bigots, Lorde recommends: *"I urge each one of us here to reach down into that deep place of knowledge inside herself and touch that terror and loathing of any difference that lives there."* In *Sister Outsider* (Freedom, Calif.: The Crossing Press, 1984), 113; emphasis in original. Both Lorde and Arendt suggest that it is not by an attempt at empathy with "the other" (imagining how they must feel as other) that one resists racism but by acknowledging that which one habitually denies in oneself as "other." If empathy is a gesture that confirms privilege by its pretense of extending pity "downward" from those who think they are immune to racism to those whom they take to be victimized by it, Lorde's exercise disturbs the complacency of the empathic subject. To "touch" otherness in one's self is to confront the fact that no one in a racist society is guiltless of practicing racism or immune to its effects.

She develops this argument further with a lengthy excerpt from "Heart of Darkness" that she inserts into her own text with very little commentary. She quotes from Conrad:

> "We could not understand because we were too far and could not remember, because we were traveling in the night of first ages, of those ages that are gone leaving hardly a sign—and no memories. The earth seemed unearthly . . . and the men. . . . *No, they were not inhuman. Well, you know, that was the worst of it—this suspicion of their not being inhuman.* It would come slowly to one. They howled and leaped, and spun, and made horrid faces; but what thrilled you was just the thought of their humanity—like yours—the thought of your remote kinship with this wild and passionate uproar" ("Heart of Darkness"). (OT, 190; emphasis added)

The "horror" of the African colonists was to have to interact with other human beings outside the boundaries of European civilization, and without the protection of its *moeurs*.[51] Under a condition of such radical displacement, they discovered that much of what passes for the distinctively and innately human is a social construct and, conversely, that much of what looks (from that constructed perspective) like uncivilized brutishness is "not inhuman." Confronted with human beings whom they recognized as kin but could not acknowledge as such without compromising what they took to constitute their own humanity, their response was to "exterminate all the brutes." Arendt suggests that genocide is a logical outcome of a perverse twist of the humanist premises of equal worth and mutual respect: it is a deliberate and calculated imposition of otherness by behaving with inhumane cruelty toward those to whom one will not accord reciprocity.

Conrad's story seems to contain "as in a nutshell" an insight about

---

51. The French *moeurs* refers to the complex of tastes, sensibilities, and habits by which one society can be distinguished, almost intangibly, from the next. It is often translated by "manners," which seems to me to be class specific and to connote a politeness that is narrower than the French term.

racism that Arendt recasts in her dense and difficult argument about the distinctively modern "perversion of equality from a political into a social concept" (OT, 54–60). She introduces this distinction as a theoretical frame for her historical observation that it was "political ignorance" for middle-class Jews in nineteenth-century Berlin and Paris not to have appreciated the differences between social and political anti-Semitism. She argues that they were "oversensitive" to the former, which consists in social discrimination, but naive about the latter, which consists in making racial intolerance into a rule of law.

She begins the argument with a pronouncement against social equality, writing: "Equality of condition, though it is certainly a basic requirement for justice, is nevertheless among the greatest and most uncertain ventures of modern mankind." She argues that it is a "great challenge" of modernity to hold political equality as a principle that is distinct from the social fact of equal condition, especially in the face of the rapid disintegration and leveling of class differences. In turn, it is a "peculiar danger" that these discrete aspects of equality will collapse into each other. When that happens, she remarks that there is only "one chance in a hundred that it [equality] will be recognized simply as a working principle of a political organization in which otherwise unequal people have equal rights; there are ninety-nine chances that it will be mistaken for an innate quality of every individual, who is 'normal' if he is like everybody else and 'abnormal' if he happens to be different" (OT, 54). In other words, the peculiar danger in the conflation of political equality with social equality is that it provides an imperative for normalization.

Arendt bases these claims on the uncertain relationship of nineteenth-century Jews to the nation-state and civil society. In the case of the Jews, equality of condition and political equality were inextricably joined. "All advocates of emancipation called for assimilation, that is, adjustment to and reception by, society, which they considered either a preliminary condition to Jewish emancipation or its automatic consequence" (OT, 56). And the Jewish case illustrates the peculiar danger of this combination. Either Jews as a group could be emancipated, at the cost (for middle-class Jews) of being social outcasts, or middle-class Jews could enjoy social acceptance at the cost of disenfranchisement for Jews as a group. Arendt writes, "Assimilation, in the sense of acceptance by non-

Jewish society, was granted them [middle-class Jews] only as long as they were clearly distinguished exceptions from the Jewish masses even though they still shared the same restricted and humiliating political conditions, or later only when, after an accomplished emancipation and resulting social isolation, their political status was already challenged by antisemitic movements."[52] Simply stated, Arendt's point is that Europeans viewed Jews as innately and ineradicably different. Jews of privilege—wealth, intelligence, or talent—could achieve social acceptance by trading on this difference as exotic appeal, but they could only be accepted socially as "exception Jews" as long as they were political outcasts. Once it seemed that Jews *as a group* could command exceptional treatment by the state, middle-class Jews were made to pay "with social insult for political success" (OT, 56). Their political emancipation triggered social and, ultimately, political backlash.

This argument is difficult to sort through, in part because it presupposes the as-yet unspecified conceptual framework of *The Human Condition*. This critique of the transfiguration of equality from a political principle to a social fact anticipates what Arendt will later criticize as the rise of the social. But there is a subtle and interesting difference in the way she articulates the distinction between public and social in the context of this historical analysis and the way she frames the distinction in theory. In the later work the importance of this separation is to preserve the sanctity of the public realm against matters that should be contained in the social. By contrast, the concern here is not with the proper boundaries of realms but with the meanings that can accrue to a concept depending on its context in one realm or the other. Arendt identifies two competing discourses: the universalist discourse of equality as a political principle, and the demographic discourse of equality as a social fact. These are distinguished in that political emancipation is the measure of the former and sameness that of the latter. When the two converge, equality is no longer recognized as a guarantee of equal rights to "otherwise unequal people" but understood either to affirm a more basic human sameness or to require assimilation as a requisite to polit-

52. OT, 56. Arendt argues that Kafka's *The Castle* is a literary analysis of this very trade-off and of the inadequacy of the discourse of universal political rights to address it. I discuss this at length in Chapter Five.

ical rights. As Joan Scott has argued, such a convergence implicitly "poses equality as the antithesis of difference" and thereby creates a discursive context of false dichotomies that give license to anti-Semitism and other expressions of racial intolerance.[53] Describing the violent outcome of such dichotomies, Arendt writes, "It is because equality demands that I recognize each and every individual as my equal, that the conflicts between different groups, which for reasons of their own *are reluctant to grant each other this basic equality*, take on such terribly cruel forms" (OT, 54). This is precisely the insight that she illustrates with the passages from "Heart of Darkness." If this "basic equality" is taken to presuppose a fundamental sameness that is contradicted by the evident differences among human religions, languages, and social organizations, then the ideal of equal rights turns out to be disproved or discredited by the fact of difference—which, as Joan Scott has argued, is precisely what occasions the demand for equality in the first place.[54]

Arendt argues that novelists are especially skilled analysts of political phenomena that result from the confusion of social and political discourses. In a passage that is reminiscent of the earlier essay on "Social Science Techniques," Arendt claims that the problem in studying a phenomenon such as genocide is that its elements are imperceptible to conventional methods of analysis. Reiterating the argument that genocide cannot be deduced from its origins by any causal logic, she asserts that

> social factors, unaccounted for in political or economic history, hidden under the surface of events, never perceived by the historian and recorded only by the more penetrating and passionate force of poets or novelists (men whom society had driven into the desperate solitude and loneliness of the *apologia pro vita sua*) changed the course that mere political antisemitism would have taken if left to itself, and which might have resulted in anti-Jewish legislation and even mass expulsion but hardly in wholesale extermination. (OT, 87)

53. Joan Scott, *Gender and the Politics of History* (New York: Columbia University Press, 1988), 172.
54. Ibid., 173.

She suggests here that novelists have access to a historical dimension that is invisible to analysts of large-scale trends and regime changes. They are uniquely suited to perceive the "decomposition of political issues into their dazzling, fascinating reflections in society" (OT, 80), and the novel—"the only entirely social art form,"—is uniquely suited to recording that decomposition (HC, 39). But the question is, If novels are particularistic, what makes them critical?

Although Arendt never explicitly answers this question in her work, I argue in the next chapter that this question—How to defend a mode of analysis that is both particularistic and critical—informs her reading of Kant's *Third Critique*. Arendt anticipates this last work in her remarks about Proust, whose *Remembrance of Things Past* is a primary source for her analysis of Jewish exceptionalism in the salons of late-nineteenth-century France. Although she calls Proust a "true exponent of this society" because he was admitted into it as an exotic representative of "'vice' of Jewishness and the 'vice' of homosexuality," she does not recommend his work on the strength of the authenticity of his experience (OT, 80). Instead, she suggests that a writer such as Proust (Conrad, Dinesen, and Faulkner are among the others whom she admires) is an exceptionally analytical observer of his world because he practices a kind of judgment that answers the epistemological crisis of totalitarianism. She writes, "Proust, born on the fringe of society, but still rightfully belonging to it though an outsider, *enlarged this inner experience* until it included the whole range of aspects as they appeared to and were reflected by all members of society" (OT, 80; emphasis added). The language she uses to characterize Proust's thinking anticipates her discussion of Kant's *Third Critique*, where she fastens on Kant's description of judgment as "enlarged thought" (CJ, 136). This capacity to represent a political situation from a multiplicity of perspectives is the common thread of her praise for Proust and Thucydides and of her fascination with Kant.

In this chapter I have reconstructed an "untold story" about storytelling from the discrepancies among the various statements of method (published and unpublished) that Arendt formulated over the course of writing *Origins*. I have documented her "unusual approach" to political theory and historiography in the shift she makes from abstract, neutral reporting to explicitly moral writing from the personal experience of the author. This shift entails a change in the method of analysis from an abstract, neutral account to explicitly moral narrative that is situated in the experience of the thinker. Furthermore, it entails a change in the way the analysis is received. It is not intended as a definitive, factual account but as a story from one perspective that elicits a plurality of divergent accounts. Her aim, though not her style, is like Thucydides': to re-present totalitarianism in a way that exhorts her readers to judgment.

Arendt adopts this approach to demonstrate and teach a kind of critical understanding that, in Nussbaum's words, "consists in the keen responsiveness of intellect, imagination, and feeling to the particulars of a situation."[55] This early work begins to describe how to make a judgment from experience, arguing that one proceeds not by applying principles from a transcendent framework but by considered attention to one's immediate response to an event. It does not yet explain what makes this contingent judgment critical. The answer to this question lies in her attempt to discern a political philosophy in Kant's *Critique of Judgement*.

In the next chapter I will argue that Arendt sustains the belief that political theory can be understood as a kind of storytelling from these early writings to her unfinished lectures on judging. This conception of political theory is, in the words of Virginia Woolf, "more truth than fact." Woolf uses this phrase in the opening pages of *A Room of One's Own*, which is ostensibly an essay on the subject of "women and fiction." Like Arendt, she apologizes to her audience that she cannot produce a "nugget of pure truth to wrap up between the pages of your notebooks" and proposes to tell a story instead. And like Arendt, her apology is disingenuous. Woolf tells a story not because it is the best she can *do* but because it is the *best* she can do. Furthermore, she does so not because she wants to illustrate her theories about women writers or to express her feelings about being a woman writer but to give the "audience the chance of drawing their own conclusions as they observe the limitations, the prejudices, the idiosyncrasies of the speaker."[56] Woolf,

---

55. Nussbaum, *Fragility*, 191.
56. Virginia Woolf, *A Room of One's Own* (New York: Harcourt, Brace, Jovanovich, 1929, rpt. 1957), 4, 3, 4.

like Arendt, suggests that the most "objective" way to write about a social question or problem is to situate it in the context of the beliefs that gave rise to it. This means telling the story of a situation in a way that makes explicit the disposition of the author and relates as many of its constituent perspectives as possible. Storytelling is "more truth" than fact, because it communicates one's own critical understanding in a way that invites discussion from rival perspectives.

The purpose of political theory, as Arendt understands it, is not to make a descriptively accurate report of the world but "to transcend the limitations of facts and information" to tell a provocative and principled story.[57] In almost so many words, it is Woolf's distinction between truth and fact that Arendt is attempting to achieve. She struggles to invent a way of writing about totalitarianism that will not define that phenomenon so much as answer its ethical and epistemological challenge: she writes to move her audience to engage with her in thinking "what we are doing" (HC, 5).

57. Arendt,"On the Nature of Totalitarianism," 6.

5   Training the Imagination to Go Visiting

▮

In the early writings on totalitarianism, Arendt seems to practice principled contextual thinking without explaining how that practice is possible. She describes critical understanding in the absence of abstract principles as a process of considered attention to one's immediate response to a particular event but does not justify how an immediate personal experience of a particular phenomenon attains the status of a judgment. Her response to Voegelin points in the direction such a question might take her, where she notes that "personal experience . . . is necessarily involved in an historical investigation that employs imagination consciously as an important tool of cognition" ("R," 79) She explains further that the kind of critical thinking she has in mind "is closely related to that faculty of imagination that Kant called *Einbild-ungskraft* and that has nothing in common with fictional ability" (79). In her lectures on Kant's *Critique of Judgement* Arendt comes back to the methodological problems she encountered over the course of those writings. She takes up the unanswered question of moving from experience to criticism by means of a creative appropriation of Kant's conception of taste. What Arendt seeks in the *Third Critique* is a possible justification for principled contextual thinking—a means by which to take a stand without attempting to resolve or disguise the ambiguity and contingency of any response that one makes to a situation that unfolds within the web of human plurality.

My claim that the lectures on judging follow from these early dilemmas is at odds with the typical view that Arendt's final work makes a break with her political writings. Several scholars have argued that where Arendt's early definition of political thinking is engaging in the interpretive contests that accompany acting in concert, in later essays she relocates this contest from the public space to the imagination of a spectator. In his valuable reconstruction of Arendt's lectures on Kant, Ronald Beiner interprets this shift as a move from a political to a Kantian conception of judgment: "The more she reflected on the faculty of judgment, the more inclined she was to regard it as the prerogative of the solitary (though public-spirited) contemplator as opposed to the actor (whose activity is necessarily nonsolitary)."[1] Beiner is careful to avoid framing the contrast as one between the engaged actor and the disengaged observer, rendering it instead as a contrast between the necessarily solitary but "public-spirited" spectator and the necessarily "nonsolitary" actor. Even so, he looks at the *Lectures on Kant's Political Philosophy* through a Kantian lens, imposing on it the opposition between acting and thinking that is peculiar to the framework of the Archimedean dilemma. He argues that together with the Eichmann book, these last writings on judgment illustrate the "tragic conflict . . . between political membership and political judgment," in which the judging subject must terminate her membership in the community.[2] Following Beiner's lead, Benjamin Barber writes that Arendt "cannot escape the embrace of Kant, into whose arms she seemed about to recommit herself at the end of her life. . . . *Vita activa* or no, judgment remained for Arendt a product of detachment, more the function of spectators than of actors."[3]

Although I agree that there is a change from the early to the late writings, to see the lectures on judgment as a decisive retreat from the political writings is to break the thread of Arendt's radical critique of the tradition and finish it off with a tidy knot. Beiner's construction of the judgment writings in terms of a "tragic conflict" between spectatorship and membership implicitly reinstates the norm of Archimedean thinking. To cast the problem of judgment in these terms is to assume, as Michael Walzer puts it, that "the conditions of collective life—im-

1. Ronald Beiner, "Interpretive Essay," LKPP, 92.
2. Ronald Beiner, *Political Judgment* (London: Methuen, 1983), 115.
3. Benjamin R. Barber, *The Conquest of Politics* (Princeton: Princeton University Press, 1988), 198.

mediacy, closeness, emotional attachment, parochial vision—militate against a critical self-understanding."[4] Contrary to Beiner, these are not the terms in which Arendt frames the problem of judgment. By imposing the dilemma of spectatorship versus membership on the judgment writings, both Beiner and Barber read the contradictions in Arendt's work in a way that renders her ideas consistent with the very traditions she is attempting to break out of. By contrast, I claim that Arendt, like Walzer, conceives of the judging subject not as a disinterested spectator of politics but as a marginal critic. As she remarks in praise of Götthold Lessing, he "never felt at home in the world as it then existed and probably never wanted to, and still after his own fashion he always remained committed to it" (MDT, 5). She would concur that the difficulty of judging is, as Walzer puts it, not that "of detachment but of *ambiguous connection.*"[5] That Arendt conceived of judging as a problem of "ambiguous connection" is evident in her lectures on Kant's *Third Critique*, where she treats this problem in the abstract, and in her writings on pariahs, where she explores the concrete historical problem of Jewish identity in Western Europe prior to World War II. It is poignantly dramatized in her correspondence with Karl Jaspers, whose friendship called upon her to plumb the complexities of her ambiguous connection to her German homeland. In this chapter I explore Arendt's lectures on Kant and in the next her ruminations about the irreconcilability of being a German Jew.

Thinking without a Banister

The questions Arendt brings to the *Third Critique* emerge out of the methodological dilemmas she encountered in writing *Origins*. Specifically, she looks to it to find the conceptual resources she needs to address the problem she calls "thinking without a banister," by which she means

---

4. Michael Walzer, *Interpretation and Social Criticism* (Cambridge: Harvard University Press, 1987), 36.
5. Ibid., 37; emphasis added. Jeffrey Isaac makes this same connection, in *Arendt, Camus, and Modern Rebellion* (New Haven: Yale University Press, 1992), 11.

thinking without traditional concepts that are no longer adequate to the phenomena they purport to explain.[6] She calls banisters "categories and formulas that are deeply ingrained in our mind but whose basis of experience has long been forgotten and whose plausibility resides in their intellectual consistency rather than in their adequacy to actual events."[7] They are, in other words, abstractions that are *imposed* on events by force of habit.

The banister metaphor is yet another way Arendt attempts to frame the opposition between particularist skepticism and abstract universalism so that it can be surmounted. Climbing or descending a staircase without a banister can be more taxing and may be more risky than it is with one, but it is not impossible. If abstract formulas are to principled critical thinking as a banister is to climbing a staircase, then it should be possible to do without formulas without abandoning a commitment to principle altogether. To call for thinking without a banister, then, is to call for a way of proceeding in which critical categories are not imposed on but inspired by one's engagement with a phenomenon.

She poses the dilemma of thinking without a banister in conjunction with her claim that totalitarianism is a problem of understanding. It must be understood without reference to conventional moral truths because it shattered those truths and so calls for "a new kind of thinking that needs no pillars and props, no standards and traditions to move freely without crutches over unfamiliar terrain" (MDT, 10). But even if it had not been a moral crisis beyond all measure, it would still be a political phenomenon that, because it is conditioned by natality, must be understood without reference to conventional measures. Anticipating the objections that would be raised to this way of framing the problem, she imagines herself in dialogue with an interlocutor who holds fast to the norm of Archimedean impartiality. The interlocutor begins:

> *How can we measure length if we do not have a yardstick, how could we count things without a notion of numbers?* Maybe it is

6. Hannah Arendt, "On Hannah Arendt," in *Hannah Arendt: The Recovery of the Public World*, ed. Melvyn Hill (New York: St. Martin's Press, 1979), 336.
7. Hannah Arendt, "Personal Responsibility under Dictatorship," 1964, Library of Congress, MSS Box 76, 27.

preposterous even to think that anything can ever happen which our categories are not equipped to understand. Maybe we should resign ourselves to the preliminary understanding, which at once ranges the new among the old, and with the scientific approach, which follows it and deduces methodically the unprecedented from precedents, even though such a description of the new phenomenon may be demonstrably at variance with the reality.[8]

What Arendt wants is a model of the kind of understanding she attempted to practice in *Origins*, a shift from a historiography that remembers, preserves, and—implicitly—justifies an event, to a fragmentary historiography that presents a phenomenon as an incomprehensible and unjustifiable outrage against common sense. Those who claim that her turn toward *Third Critique* is a turning away from politics interpret it out of context of the banister metaphor. Arendt finds in Kant's concept of taste a model of critical thinking that confronts "phenomena, so to speak, head-on, without any preconceived system."[9] It offers her a way to answer the Archimedean interlocutor, because it is a model for thinking without a banister.

It is noteworthy that Arendt, unlike Jürgen Habermas or John Rawls, turns not to the *Critique of Practical Reason* but to the *Critique of Judgement* as Kant's "nonwritten political philosophy" (LKPP, 19). To interpret her turn to Kant as a turn to moral universalism is imprecise with respect to both thinkers because Arendt looks to that text precisely to make a distinctive break with his moral philosophy.[10] Practical reason, she claims, is inappropriate to politics because it concerns the solitary individual, who, "consulting nothing but his own reason, finds the

8. Hannah Arendt, "Understanding and Politics," *Partisan Review* 20 (July–August 1953): 382–383.
9. Hannah Arendt, Remarks at the American Society of Christian Ethics, Richmond, Virginia, January 1973, Library of Congress, MSS Box 77, 9.
10. Judith Shklar makes this choice seem insignificant by interpreting Arendt's turn to the writings on judgment to advocate an "enlightened common sense [that] must be assumed to yield universally acceptable standards." In "Rethinking the Past," *Social Research* 44 (1977): 89.

maxim that is not self-contradictory, from which he can then derive an Imperative" (LKPP, 49). In the Lessing essay, as I have argued, she rejects the categorical imperative as a model of political rationality for its "undeniable" inhumanity (MDT, 27). By contrast to Kant's moral philosophy, in which Arendt finds the antipathy toward plurality that is typical of the tradition, she argues that the discussion of taste pertains to "men in the plural, as they really are and live in societies" (LKPP, 13).

Further, the reading of the lectures as a retreat to philosophy reads past the places where Arendt goes out of her way to read *Third Critique* against the grain. Specifically, it overlooks Arendt's declared goal to take Kant's work on taste in a direction he did not foresee and misses the explicit interpretive choices Arendt makes to deviate from Kant in explaining key terms such as "common sense" and "enlarged thought." Arendt declares early on that her relationship to Kant's *Third Critique* is one of creative appropriation, claiming to go "beyond Kant's self-interpretation in [her] presentation" but to remain "within Kant's spirit" (33). Against the Kantian interpretation of Arendt's lectures on judgment, I propose to take this claim seriously and to interpret these writings as an Arendtian creative appropriation of Kant.[11]

The Visiting Imagination

Kant's problem in *Third Critique* is to account for the possibility of aesthetic judgment by distinguishing judgments about beauty from idiosyncratic preferences on one hand and from moral imperatives on the other. Taste must differ not only from my interest in the pleasant, to which I am drawn by the desire for gratification but also from my regard for the good, which I am compelled to esteem by its objective worth according to the categorical imperative. Where moral judgment is "determinant" (CJ, 15), which means in Arendt's terms that it subsumes

---

11. Patrick Riley's "Hannah Arendt on Kant, Truth, and Politics," is an example of a very different approach. Reading Arendt's lectures on judging as an exercise on Kant, Riley argues that Arendt is "almost certainly" wrong to "relocate Kant's political philosophy in a region of shared, intersubjective 'judgment' that stands between pure subjectivism and objective truth." In *Political Studies* 35 (1987): 382; emphasis in original.

new phenomena under existing precedents, taste is reflective. Kant calls it "a disinterested and *free* satisfaction; for no interest, either of sense or of reason, here forces our assent" (44). Taste operates in a contingent situation, meaning one for which there can be no precedent and in which judgment takes its bearings not from general concepts or rules but from particular phenomena.

Arendt's turn to *Third Critique* is not a departure from politics and return to philosophy; rather, it follows from the methodological dilemmas of her own political writings. Arendt is drawn to this work because if she can argue that political judgment is not a version of practical reason (or moral judgment) but, instead, a kind of taste, then she can justify the possibility of thinking without banisters. The burden of that argument is also the problem of Kant's *Third Critique*: to establish that taste is rightfully a species of judgment by explaining how a spontaneous expression can be more than "groundless and vain fancy" *without* arguing that it is objectively necessary (191). I will now explain how those dilemmas correspond to the project of Kant's work on taste.

"Crystallization," the term Arendt uses in the preface to *Origins* in opposition to reconstructive historiography, is an allusion to *Third Critique*.[12] Arendt uses the term both to resist making a causal explanation of totalitarianism, describing it as an amalgam of fragments that are only contingently related, and to explain the unconventional structure and organization of her analysis of that phenomenon. Similarly, Kant introduces "crystallization" as a metaphor for contingency. Crystallization describes the formation of objects that come into being not by a gradual, evolutionary process but suddenly and unpredictably, "by a *shooting to-*

12. Seyla Benhabib concurs that Arendt uses the metaphor of "crystallization" to express what she described to Mary Underwood as writing "against" history. She argues that the term alludes to Walter Benjamin's "Theses on the Philosophy of History," where Benjamin argues that the critical historian who refuses to write from the perspective of the victor must "brush history against the grain." See *Illuminations*, ed. Hannah Arendt (New York: Schocken, 1969), 257. According to Benhabib, Arendt uses the peculiar language of "elements" and "crystallization" because she, like Benjamin, wants "to break the chain of narrative continuity, to shatter chronology as the natural structure of narrative, to stress fragmentariness, historical dead ends, failures and ruptures." See "Hannah Arendt and the Redemptive Power of Narrative," *Social Research* 57 (1990): 182–183. No doubt the crystallization metaphor is evidence that Arendt writes with Benjamin in mind, but it also points to Kant's account of taste.

gether, i.e. by a sudden solidification, not by a gradual transition . . . but all at once by a *saltus*, which transition is also called *crystallization*." (CJ, 194; emphasis in the original). Crystalline forms have a structure, but that structure is not determined by any one essential element or oriented toward a particular goal. He describes this structured spontaneity as "the form of the *purposiveness* of an object, so far as this is perceived in it *without any representation of a purpose*" (73; emphasis in the original). By denoting a kind of being that is contingent but structured and thus susceptible to critical evaluation, crystallization justifies the possibility of a kind of judgment that is both spontaneous and principled.[13]

Arendt makes an analogy between contingent beauty and unprecedented evil by calling totalitarianism "the final crystallizing catastrophe" that constitutes its various "elements" into a historical crisis. This analogy turns on the claim that totalitarianism, a phenomenon for which no existing conceptual framework is adequate, poses a problem of understanding that is similar to that posed by beauty. The events of politics, which take shape within the web of plurality, are like aesthetic objects in that they can neither be explained in evolutionary terms nor judged with reference to an external purpose or principle. Even so, actors are bound to make some sense of them or else to relinquish their freedom by playing without thinking into a situation whose various possible story lines they have not considered. The paradox Kant sustains in defining taste as a judgment that takes its bearings not from transcendental concepts but from feeling is analogous to Arendt's attempt to define political judgment as critical understanding that does not withdraw to an abstract vantage point but takes its bearings from experience.

As I read it, then, Arendt's turn to Kant's *Third Critique* for a model of political judgment is utterly consistent with the early essays. This move is motivated by her judgment that totalitarianism could not be subsumed under traditional categories of understanding and the subse-

---

13. Paul Guyer also connects the discussion of "crystallization" to contingency. He argues that Kant uses crystallization to argue that the "mechanical processes of nature" are sufficient to account for the existence of natural forms and so that "the actual existence of beautiful forms in nature does not require us to attribute any actual intentions to nature or its creator." *Kant and the Claims of Taste* (Cambridge: Harvard University Press, 1977), 349.

quent need to justify the possibility of thinking without such categories. Arendt's decision to take up *Critique of Judgement* rather than *Critique of Practical Reason* underscores this continuity. Where the latter is concerned with universal moral principles, the former is primarily concerned with questions of interpretation; it confronts the world from the start as a problem of understanding.

But Arendt does not simply assimilate Kant's work wholesale into her own. Instead, she makes deliberate interpretive choices that fit taste into her project. Kant's answer to the problem of distinguishing taste from both subjective preference and objective truth is to argue that taste is intersubjective. He claims that where the assertion that something is *pleasant* is merely subjective, meaning that something pleases *me*, the claim that something is beautiful expresses a preference that I assume others would agree with. Even though I attribute it to everyone else, my judgment that something is beautiful is not objective, because if asked to justify it, I could not do so in terms of an abstract universal concept of beauty. Instead, my judgment is intersubjective; that is to say, it rests on a purportedly common sense of pleasure in the beautiful. This common sense is, according to Kant, what makes taste "strange and irregular" because "it is not an empirical concept, but a feeling of pleasure (consequently not a concept at all) which, by the judgment of taste, is attributed to everyone." (CJ, 27). He explains further that taste speaks "with a universal voice . . . [but] does not *postulate* the agreement of everyone . . . it only *imputes* this agreement to everyone, as a case of the rule in respect of which it expects, not confirmation by concepts, but assent from others" (50–51). For taste to be intersubjective means that it cannot be *proved* but could be defended on the ground of an assumed common sense.

And here is the ambiguity in Kant's account of taste. Paul Guyer has noted that Kant gives two defenses of taste without sufficiently differentiating between them. He defends taste on cognitive grounds, that a judgment about beauty is *imputed* to everyone else, and on the grounds of communicability, that it actually secures the *assent* of others in public exchange. Guyer notes that although Kant "is at pains to show that pleasure in the beautiful may be imputed to others, he is not at equal pains to show how such pleasure may be conveyed from one who feels it to one who, in particular circumstances, does not."[14] Kant justifies the possibility of imputing an aesthetic judgment to others by means of "enlarged thought," which involves the practice of representative thinking: "comparing your judgment with the possible rather than the actual judgments of others, and by putting ourselves in the place of any other man, by abstracting from the limitations which contingently attach to our own judgment" (CJ, 136). Obviously, imputing assent to others by imagining their "possible" responses is a far cry from actually securing that assent by means of actual communication. The ambiguity in Kantian intersubjectivity consists in the fact that justifying the cognitive defense does not justify the communicability defense; imputing assent to others is clearly not equivalent to communicating with them.

If Arendt sees this ambiguity, she does not remark on it. In fact, she seems to rule it out altogether, declaring in the second lecture that nowhere in the *Third Critique* "does Kant speak of man as an intelligible or a cognitive being" (LKPP, 13). In an earlier essay, she chooses to present Kant's understanding of taste exclusively in terms of communicability, the non-cognitive defense, by selecting phrases from his text that suggest that discussion is necessary to making a judgment of taste. Shifting the weight of the defense from intersubjectivity to *publicity*, she writes: "Kant, who certainly was not oversensitive to beautiful things, was highly conscious of the public quality of beauty; and it was because of their public relevance that he insisted, in opposition to the commonplace adage, that taste judgments are *open to discussion* because 'we hope that the same pleasure is shared by others,' that taste can be *subject to dispute*, because it 'expects agreement from everyone else' " (BPF, 222; emphasis added by Arendt, citing sections 6–8 of Kant's *Third Critique*). She begins to make two significant alterations of Kant's text in this passage. Not only does she edit out the cognitive dimension of taste but also she subtly shifts the terms in which Kant defines both taste and common sense. Where Kant claims that taste "expects agreement," Arendt claims that matters of taste are—contrary to the truism "to each his own"—public. In turn, she defines public as *"subject to dispute."* In

14. Paul Guyer, "Pleasure and Society in Kant's Theory of Judgment," in *Essays in Kant's Aesthetics*, ed. Ted Cohen and Paul Guyer (Chicago: University of Chicago Press, 1982), 23. Also Guyer, *Kant and the Claims of Taste*, 279–282.

the lectures on judgment, Arendt continues with this line of argument by contending that the validity of taste turns on "publicity," which she describes as "the testing that arises from contact with other people's thinking" (LKPP, 42). Although for both Arendt and Kant, taste is intersubjective, there is a distinct difference in emphasis regarding how it is to be secured; where he speaks of imputing or expecting agreement, she speaks of dispute.[15]

Arendt departs significantly from both of Kant's defenses of taste by rendering "intersubjectivity" in terms of "publicity." In contrast to the cognitive defense, Arendt affirms that a judgment must come into "contact" with others' perspectives: it cannot simply be *imputed* to them. In contrast to the communicability defense, "contact" and "testing" in no way imply that one expects one's tastes to meet with the agreement of others or that one actually endeavors to secure their general assent. On the contrary, to the extent that the existence of the public realm depends, as Arendt claims, "on the simultaneous presence of innumerable perspectives and aspects . . . for which no common measurement or denominator can ever be devised," general assent would be both an unlikely and an undesirable outcome of a contest over taste (HC, 57). Arendt does not, then, import Kant's ideas wholesale into her own work but appropriates them creatively. She politicizes Kant's taste by calling it "public" in her distinctive sense of the term: an interpretation that is tested against a plurality of divergent perspectives.

Dagmar Barnouw notes a further instance of what I would call creative appropriation in Arendt's decision to translate *allgemein* as "general." Barnouw notes that it is customary in Kant scholarship to translate the term as *universal*, although it can also mean general, common, or public. It is used idiomatically to indicate widespread belief or common consent rather than universal truth. Barnouw claims that Arendt's decision to draw on its idiomatic use is a deliberate departure from "the desirable universal standpoint in Kant's meaning [which] is located above rather

15. Compare this argument to Richard Bernstein's discussion of Arendt's use of Kantian aesthetic judgment. He argues that her interest in *Third Critique* is motivated by its model of judging particularities, and by the notion of intersubjectivity, but he does not mention the creative departures Arendt makes from the latter. *Philosophical Profiles* (Philadelphia: University of Pennsylvania Press, 1986), 236.

than in community."[16] Arendt makes this decision to limit the validity of political judgment explicit, writing that it "is endowed with a certain *specific* validity but is *never universally* valid. Its claims to validity can never extend further than the others in whose place the judging person has put himself for his consideration" (BPF, 221; emphasis added).

The interpretive choice that Arendt makes with respect to the term *allgemein* casts some doubt on Beiner's unequivocal assertion that for Arendt one cannot exercise political judgment without subordinating membership in a particular community to a dispassionate attachment to general principles. Even though Arendt claims that judging must leave behind self-interest, it would seem that this does not extend to denying particularity and membership. On the contrary, judging is only possible within the limits of *some* community, because it is only *in* community that communicability makes sense. This point is explicit in Arendt's rejection of references to "*the* spectator," as if spectatorship were solitary. She counters that "Spectators exist only in the plural. The spectator is not involved in the act, but he is always involved with fellow spectators" (LKPP, 63). And membership need not diminish the validity of a judgment, because its purpose is not to arrive at a universal concept but, rather, to achieve a multi-perspective understanding of the particular situations in which I want to act. Further, the very processes of political thinking and political action are at odds with the universalism of the categorical imperative. The model of integrity or self-consistency that regulates practical reason is inappropriate to a judgment one reaches by considering multiple standpoints in turn because to render them consistent would be to diminish their plurality. Thus, a principle that is to be put into action in concert with others would need to be as "plural" as possible in order to be persuasive to people who inhabit different locations. The first concern of political judgment is not to safeguard the integrity of a single actor but to articulate a principle that others would be inspired to take up.

All that said, it is perfectly understandable that Beiner and others interpret Arendt's last work as a turn to Kantian philosophy because she

16. Dagmar Barnouw, *Visible Spaces: Hannah Arendt and the German-Jewish Experience* (Baltimore: Johns Hopkins University Press, 1990), 21–22.

herself presents it that way. Despite the fact that Arendt's "publicity" makes a significant departure from Kant's "intersubjectivity," Arendt attributes her innovations to him, claiming to have learned them from his concept of "common sense." Common sense means different things to each of them, however, because they have different versions of what it means to practice the representative thinking that is necessary to enlarged thought. Kant describes representative thinking as "*abstracting* from one's own contingent situation to think in the place of "*any* other man" (CJ, 136; emphasis added). In contrast, Arendt describes representing multiple standpoints in turn and holding them in her mind as a kind of intellectual public space: "The more people's standpoints I have present in my mind while I am pondering a given issue, and the better I can imagine *how I would feel and think* if I were in their place, the stronger will be my capacity for representative thinking and the more valid my final conclusions, my opinion" (BPF, 241; emphasis added). Representative thinking as Kant describes it involves abstracting from the "limitations" of a contingent situation to think as "any" man. By contrast, Arendt describes feeling and thinking simultaneously from a plurality of standpoints. In her account, it is not abstraction but considered attention to particularity that accounts for "enlarged thought." As she puts it in the *Lectures*, representative thinking is "closely connected with particulars, with the particular conditions of the standpoints one has to go through in order to arrive at one's own 'general standpoint' " (LKPP, 44). If for Kant common sense is inclusive because it is general, for Arendt this inclusiveness depends on specificity and multiplicity of detail.

In Arendt's theoretical writings about judgment, this difference between generality and specificity is almost too subtle to appreciate. It is magnified, however, in a course she designed to teach the practice of enlarged thinking called "Political Experiences."[17] Her notes for the first session explain that the purpose of the course is to develop the "reproductive imagination," the faculty for Kant's enlarged mentality, which she tells the students is the faculty that makes it possible to "relive [a]

17. Arendt taught variations of this course at least twice, at Berkeley in 1955 and again in 1968 at the New School, where she called it "Political Experiences in the Twentieth Century," Library of Congress, MSS nos. 023609–023613.

period vicariously." She explains that, "To exercise this mentality permits you to take into account the perspectives of others *as well as their circumstances.*"[18] What is interesting about this course is that although its syllabus includes some works of history, biography, and sociology, it is primarily composed of memoirs and novels.[19] The syllabus demonstrates Arendt's implicit assumption that literature makes it possible to enter into both aspects of another's standpoint: the intellectual perspective *as well as* the circumstances that give rise to it.

The difference between Kant's and Arendt's conceptions of representative thinking might be summed up as a contrast between the philosophical imagination and that of artists and storytellers. Where Kant describes representative thinking in terms that are general and philosophical, thinking from the position of "any" man, Arendt describes it in literary terms as populating one's imagination with a multiple cast of characters. The difference between these two can be further elucidated by examining the account of the antagonism between thinking and judging that Arendt makes in *The Life of the Mind.*

Arendt argues that the solitude and quiet that are the conditions of thinking are at odds with the conditions of action. She writes "we can act only 'in concert,' in company and agreement with our peers, hence in an existential situation that effectively prevents thinking" (LM:I, 91) Because it is antithetical to plurality, thinking is not only opposed to acting but also to judging. She characterizes this opposition as "an *intramural warfare* between man's common sense, this sixth sense that fits our five senses into a common world, and man's faculty of thought and need of reason, which determine him to remove himself for considerable periods from it" (81; emphasis in the original). Where acting and judging pertain to men in the plural, while engaged in "sheer thinking . . . [one] lives completely in the singular, that is, in complete solitude, as though not men but Man inhabited the earth" (47). This account of "sheer" thinking puts "representative" thinking into relief. Where the former is

---

18. Hannah Arendt, Notes for "Political Experiences in the Twentieth Century," Library of Congress, MSS 023609; emphasis added.
19. The Berkeley syllabus includes André Malraux, *Antimémoires*, William Faulkner, *A Fable* and "Victory," Jean-Paul Sartre, *Nausea*, George Orwell, *Homage to Catalonia*, Glenn Gray, *The Warriors*, and Joseph Heller, *Catch-22.*

pure egoism, the latter is public spirited. It does involve a withdrawal from action, although not into utter solitude; rather, in judging, one exercises the imagination to simulate the condition of plurality in the mind.

The trick of judging, then, is to be able to step back from acting without becoming thoroughly self-absorbed, as is the case in thinking. Her concern to spell out this difference and her belief that few Western philosophers appreciated it, prompt her critique of the Archimedean posturing of that tradition. With the exception of Kant and Jaspers, she argues that Western philosophers were unable to position themselves imaginatively in the manner of writers as varied as Thucydides, Lessing, Kafka, Benjamin, Dinesen, Faulkner, and others. By contrast, she ascribes to artists and storytellers a special facility for judging, because their craft demands that they practice a kind of detachment that stops short of an absolute, Archimedean withdrawal. About Isak Dinesen she writes that becoming an artist requires "a certain detachment from the heady, intoxicating business of sheer living that, perhaps, only the born artist can manage *in the midst of living*" (MDT, 97; emphasis added). Unlike philosophers who need solitude in order to think, storytellers need not withdraw altogether from the condition of plurality in order to practice their art and indeed *can*not if they are to have material for it.

It is precisely this capacity to exist on the margins of thinking and acting that Arendt thinks Kant lacked when writing his moral philosophy, but discovered for the aesthetic writings. In a letter to Karl Jaspers, Arendt explains the political inadequacy of Kant's *Critique of Practical Reason* as a consequence of the fact that "The power of imagination, which is as great in Kant *as it otherwise is only in poets*, left him in the lurch as far as life is concerned" (C, 318; emphasis added). Note here that the highest praise Arendt can give to the philosopher whom she most admired is that he had a poet's imagination. Philosophy is second to poetry in Arendt's view of critical understanding, not the reverse. This letter, written long before she began to lecture or write publicly on *Third Critique*, tells the story of her attraction to that work in a more personal way than she would in a formal essay. She relates that she has been rereading it with "increasing fascination" with Kant's concepts of common sense, taste, and "communicativeness," which she claims "incor-

porate the experiences young Kant had in society, and then the old man
made them come to life again" (318). This story frames Arendt's determination to argue that "Kant's real political philosophy is hidden" in
his *Third Critique* in terms of the distinction between artists and philosophers (318). In that late work she believes that Kant came closest to
writing philosophy as a poet, using abstract thinking to bring his experiences to life.[20]

The appropriation of taste does take Arendt into a public realm that
is different from what she described in *The Human Condition*. Where
the latter is a space of speech and action, the former is a metaphorical
space in the mind that is opened by critical thinking that, "while still a
solitary business, does not cut itself off from 'all others.' To be sure, *it
still goes on in isolation*, but by the force of imagination it makes the
others present and thus moves in a space that is potentially public, open
to all sides." (LKPP, 43; emphasis added). Although clearly judging takes
priority over acting, it is too quick to categorize this as a shift from the
standpoint of the actor to that of the spectator. For one, the investigation
of Arendt's own storytelling in the preceding chapter, together with her
discussion of Thucydides, demonstrate that she did not conceive of the
historian as a spectator whose job is to preserve the past and hand it on
as a tradition. Although they do not participate in the events they nar-
rate, historians are not absolutely disengaged from them either; to tell a
traditional story to a "fresh audience" that will draw its conclusions
based on present concerns is not just to transmit the past but to initiate
its re-enactment (LM:I, 96).

Furthermore, there are, as I have noted, subtle but important differences between representative thinking in Arendt and in Kant. Where
Kant describes it as thinking from the general standpoint of "any" man,
Arendt describes it as taking divergent opinions into account in the
process of making up my mind and, ultimately, locating my judgment

20. Interestingly, Riley also sees that the imagination as Arendt describes it in the *Lectures*
is more like that of a poet than a philosopher. In fact, he claims that the account of
judging she describes is more appropriately attributed to Shelley's *A Defense of Poetry*
than to Kant. Where I judge this to be a "creative appropriation" of *Third Critique*,
Riley faults her for it as a misreading that imputes to Kant an ultimately faulty conception of judgment that displaces moral truth with opinion. See Riley, "Hannah
Arendt," 383–384.

in relation to those particular views. She describes it as a process that is "always and primarily, even if I am quite alone in making up my mind, in an *anticipated communication* with others with whom I know I must finally come to some agreement" (BPF, 220; emphasis added). This anticipated communication is achieved not by imagining what "any" man might say, but by training "one's imagination to go visiting" (LKPP, 43).

"Visiting" marks the difference between representative thinking as the philosopher practices it and as the storyteller practices it. It describes the work that the imagination does in an act of judgment. In Kant's account, the imagination establishes the critical distance that makes it possible to assume a general standpoint. But for Arendt, this reflective or representative function is only one aspect of the work of the imagination. There is also a bridging function that makes present other perspectives for the purpose of visiting. Although there is no extended discussion of "visiting" in the judging lectures, in a much earlier essay she describes the work of bridging this way:

> Only imagination is capable of what we know as "putting things in their proper distance" and which actually means that we should be strong enough to remove those which are too close until we can see and understand them *without bias and prejudice*, strong enough to bridge the abysses of remoteness until we can *see and understand* those that are too far away *as though they were our own affairs*. This removing some things and bridging the abysses to others is part of the interminable dialogue for whose purposes direct experience establishes too immediate and too close a contact and mere knowledge erects an artificial barrier.[21]

In Arendt's account, the operation of the imagination is twofold: it involves "removing some things and bridging the abysses to others." In

21. Hannah Arendt, "On the Nature of Totalitarianism: An Essay in Understanding," Library of Congress, MSS Box 76, 12; emphasis added. A similar paragraph appears at the end of a much-altered published version of this essay, "Understanding and Politics," *Partisan Review* 20 (July–August 1953): 377–392.

effect, the representative imagination works together with what might be called the "visiting" imagination.

Representation is principally oriented toward creating distance. It detaches me from the immediacy of the present where there is no space in which to stop and think. It also takes a step back from the pull of self-interest, which makes it difficult for me to conceive of a situation except in terms of its effect on me. Finally, it disrupts the familiarity of the present, inclining me to stop and think about things that would otherwise pass unnoticed. Representation is a limited withdrawal that makes the present less urgent and the familiar strange but stops short of disengaging me to the point that I no longer care to wonder what a situation means.

In contrast, visiting bridges distance to that which is strange and unfamiliar, so that I can look upon it "as though it were [my] own affair." Visiting is the activity of the imagination in judging, as distinct from thinking and from deciding. Visiting involves constructing stories of an event from each of the plurality of perspectives that might have an interest in telling it and imagining how I would respond as a character in a story very different from my own. It is a kind of representation that arrives at the general through the particular. As Arendt says of poetry, its "generalizing power . . . arises out of an ultimate and absolute precision in the use of words, if it takes every word seriously" (RV, 115).

Visiting should be distinguished on the one hand from the abstract generality of Kant's account of taste, which is a kind of tourism that preserves a spectatorial distance, and from the immediacy of empathy on the other, which is a kind of assimilationism. In order to tell yourself the story of an event from an unfamiliar standpoint, you have to position yourself there *as yourself.* That is, you can neither stand apart from nor identify with that position. She writes, "This process of representation does not blindly adopt the actual views of those who stand somewhere else, and hence look upon the world from a different perspective; this is [not] a question . . . of empathy, as though I tried to be or to feel like somebody else . . . but of being and thinking in my own identity where actually I am not" (BPF, 241). Visiting is contrary to parochialism, which means simply to stay at home, contrary to "accidental" tourism, which means to ensure that you will have all the comforts of home even as you travel, and contrary to assimilationism, which means forcibly to make yourself at home in a place that is not your home by appropriating its customs.[22] To visit, in other words, you must travel to a new location, leave behind what is familiar, and resist the temptation to make yourself at home where you are not. Both the tourist and the assimilationist erase plurality. The former does so by an objectivist stance that holds to "how *we* do things" as a lens through which different cultures can only appear as other. The latter trades this spectatorial lens to assume native glasses, identifying with the new culture so as to avoid the discomfort of being in an unfamiliar place. In contrast, as a visitor you "think your own thoughts but in the place of somebody else," permitting yourself to experience the disorientation that is necessary to understanding just how the world looks different to someone else.[23]

Where Kant's philosopher transcends his own position to inhabit the standpoint of "any" man, Arendt's visitor imagines how he or she might feel and think as a character in each of the several stories to which any series of events can give rise.[24] The connections among visiting, story-telling, and critical thinking are implicit in the comments Arendt makes about writers such as Lessing and Isak Dinesen. In her essay on Dinesen,

22. "Accidental" tourism is the wry metaphor that titles Anne Tyler's 1985 novel, an exquisitely detailed study of spectatorial distance, assimilationism, and visiting that tells a story about Macon Leary, a self-contained man who writes guides for business people who want to travel without really leaving home. In keeping with the paradox of the title, Leary is a travel writer without a sense of direction. This deficiency makes him put more energy into charting and following routes than into experiencing travel; his anxiety about losing his way means that he is never at home anywhere. The narrative is propelled by Leary's trying on a series of homes, beginning by returning to his orderly ancestral household (where he finds comfort but at the cost of sexuality), then attempting to "go native" by moving into the untidy, haphazard, and deteriorating apartment of Muriel Pritchett, and finally trying to recover his marriage by moving back in with his wife. Leary is true to his name. He is cautious throughout the novel, a constant spectator who sidles through his travels as through his relationships. The resolution of the novel is almost too symmetrical, as Leary relinquishes his spectator stance to settle in with Muriel, who is his antithesis in many respects. She is poor, outspoken, spontaneous, and (as someone with a knack for training dogs) looks people straight in the eye. *The Accidental Tourist* (New York: Random House, 1985).

23. Arendt, "Political Experiences in the Twentieth Century."

24. As many feminists have argued, Kant made it quite clear that women could not be philosophers. To use anything other than the pronoun "he" would impute a false gender neutrality to his work.

she remarks that artists are uniquely suited to do the work of distancing and bridging that is necessary to critical thinking because their craft demands that they practice standing simultaneously in a particular location in the world and, in a sense, next to themselves. For Arendt, then, it is not generality but the multiplication of particularity that accounts for the possibility of critical understanding.

The difference between the model of critical thinking Arendt takes from storytelling and that which she ascribes to philosophy is not that the former is imaginative and the latter is not. On the contrary, as her praise of Kant indicates, the imagination is involved in abstract thought just as it is in visiting. The difference is that in abstraction the work of the imagination is primarily distancing. Critical rigor is thought to be satisfied so long as I am removed enough from my particular interests to make it possible for me to think in terms of what is good for others as well as for myself. The more general the terms, the more likely it is that the judgments I make will be just.

The work of the imagination in visiting is twofold. It distances me from the familiar *and* takes me to standpoints that are unfamiliar. The aim of its abstract moment is to achieve a kind of formal equality between self and others by making me an "other" to myself; the visiting moment fosters a practical equality of concern by multiplying the stories in which I imagine myself to be an actor. One assumption behind visiting is that one cannot think in terms of what is good for others who are different without knowing what they believe to be good, and that one cannot come by that knowledge by an abstract thought experiment.[25]

Recognition of the need for visiting implies that formal equality, however attractive for its promise of a neutrality that can in principle be all-encompassing, is more difficult to achieve than practical equality of

---

25. This is one of the assumptions that informs Seyla Benhabib's critique of John Rawls's "veil of ignorance." Benhabib argues that the condition of abstract impartiality that is imposed by the veil, though it is supposed to ensure moral reciprocity, actually precludes it because it does away with human plurality. She writes, "Moral reciprocity involves the capacity to take the standpoint of the other, to put oneself imaginatively in the place of the other, but under conditions of the 'veil of ignorance,' the other as *different from the self*, disappears." See "The Generalized and the Concrete Other," in *Feminism as Critique*, ed. Seyla Benhabib and Drucilla Cornell (Minneapolis: University of Minnesota Press, 1987), 89.

concern. In the absence of knowing the ways in which various "concrete others" would tell their stories of a particular situation, it is impossible to understand the problem(s) it poses, let alone to determine a response that would inspire acting in concert. Abstract impartiality slips too easily into what María Lugones calls "boomerang perception," an inclusiveness that erases plurality by accepting "others" on the assimilationist assumption that they are, deep down, like "us."[26] Boomerang perception is what happens when the philosopher's version of representative thinking falls short of the mark—when in the attempt to make me an "other" to myself I stop at making "others" into selves just like me. The preference for visiting rests on the belief that it may in practice be easier to interest myself in the affairs of others *as if they were my own* than to imagine myself as "any" man, because it is easier to imagine myself as the central character in someone else's story than to think of myself in no story at all.

Like the departures she makes from Kant's versions of intersubjectivity and representative thinking, visiting is another unacknowledged aspect of her creative appropriation of enlarged thought. Arendt erases this departure by crediting Kant with breaking from the customary assumption that abstraction is requisite to impartiality. She writes that Kantian impartiality "is not the result of some higher standpoint that would then actually settle [a] dispute by being altogether above the melée"; instead, it "is obtained by taking the viewpoints of others into account" (LKPP, 42). Her generosity notwithstanding, Kant's account of the enlarged mentality describes the solitary philosopher either securing general assent to his taste or merely imputing it to others. It is Arendt who radicalizes what it means to take particular viewpoints into account by modeling it after the artist, who uses his or her imaginative powers to inhabit a plurality of embedded standpoints, and by introducing the "visiting" metaphor to describe it. Visiting is the alternative that Arendt poses to Archimedean impartiality.

I suggest the paradox "situated impartiality" to name the elusive critical position that is achieved by visiting. Arendt herself does not use this

26. María C. Lugones, "On the Logic of Pluralist Feminism," in *Feminist Ethics*, ed. Claudia Card (Lawrence: University Press of Kansas, 1991), 41, citing Elizabeth V. Spelman, *Inessential Woman: Problems of Exclusion in Feminist Thought* (Boston: Beacon, 1988).

term. Rather, I discern it from the various places where she describes the enlarged mentality as "being and thinking" as yourself from a position in which you are not at home. Where Arendt presents the visiting metaphor as an insight that she learned from Kant, "situated impartiality" presents it as a conceptual innovation and a departure from his text. It should be clear from the preceding chapters, however, that this is not a term I am forcing onto Arendt but one that emerged out of my close reading of her work.[27] By introducing it, I attempt to address her thought as she addressed Kant's, perhaps moving beyond her "self-interpretation" but remaining within her "spirit" to appropriate it into the horizon of contemporary debates.[28]

By "situated impartiality" I mean a critical decision that is not justified with reference to an abstract standard of right but by visiting a plurality of diverging public standpoints. Though arriving at a situated impartial judgment is a public and collective process, it does not involve the absolute or definitive resolution of conflict either by transcending it or by subsuming it within an all-encompassing solution. Admittedly, with the exception of the "visiting" metaphor, Arendt's account of this process in the *Lectures* is so abstract as to be utterly vague. Her most specific statement defines it by what it is not, as she insists that the "trick of critical thinking does not consist in an enormously enlarged empathy through which one can know what actually goes on in the mind of all others." Where empathy amounts to no more than an "exchange [of] their prejudices for the prejudices proper to my own station," critical thinking consists in moving, as myself, "from standpoint to standpoint" in as large a "realm" as possible (LKPP, 43). I suggest that the process

27. Naomi Scheman characterized this way of reading to me by means of a metaphor that resonates with Arendt's visiting. In contrast to following the road signs the author leaves for you, she described it as finding a path through the work that is not so clearly marked. Some schools of interpretation would regard this as trespassing and others as sheer fantasy; Naomi recommended it to me as a fine way to explore a text, so long as you send the author a postcard.

28. LKPP, 33. This is what I take Nancy Fraser to be doing with her appropriation of Arendt's "social" to designate "a site of contested discourse" over questions regarding which needs ought to be publicly attended to. See *Unruly Practices* (Minneapolis: University of Minnesota Press, 1988), 169–170.

of visiting might be conceived as telling oneself the story of a situation from the plurality of its constituent perspectives.

If Arendt's differentiation of understanding from empathy seems peculiar, that is because understanding is often defined *in terms of* empathy, as the capacity to see through someone else's eyes. The difficulty with Arendt's account of visiting is that it seems that by standing as myself in someone else's position, I would be seeing their world through my own prejudices, in a parochial or ethnocentric way. Arendt suggests that there is all the difference in the world between closing your eyes to the world, claiming to see through the eyes of someone else, and attempting to visit—see with your own eyes from—someone else's position.

I think Arendt's insistence that telling yourself the story of an event from an unfamiliar standpoint involves "doing and thinking in my own identity where I am not," is the most compelling insight of the judging lectures. This precludes two common strategies of taking agreement for granted, imputing a claim to others either on the belief that any reasonable person would agree with it, or on the presumptuous claim to have identified all relevant perspectives and incorporated them into it.[29] Both of these tend toward the erasure of difference, the former by its abstraction and the latter by its empathy. Visiting makes it possible to appreciate just how different the world looks from unaccustomed vantage points, precisely because it does not assume that perfect understanding will be possible.[30] At the same time, visiting does not rule out all possibility of understanding. Her claim that stories are varied accounts of a

---

29. With respect to the former, see Michael Walzer's description of John Rawls's theory of justice as monological. Walzer writes that "it makes no difference whether [the legislators in the Original Position] talk to one another or one among them talks only to himself: one person talking is enough," *Interpretation*, 11. See also Iris Marion Young, *Justice and the Politics of Difference* (Princeton: Princeton University Press), 101–102. For a consideration of empathy and identity politics, see Terry Winant, "The Feminist Standpoint: A Matter of Language," *Hypatia* 2 (1987): 123–148.

30. There is a point of connection between Arendt and Iris Young on this distinction between understanding and empathy. Young argues that an ideal "of the transparency of subjects to one another" underlies assumptions about both "common consciousness" and liberal "reciprocity." Young, *Justice*, 230–231. Like Arendt, Young rejects both of these as tending toward the production of a "unitary" public.

shared world, unknowable in itself and yet present nonetheless as a condition of human existence, departs from the axiom of some poststructuralists that knowledges are radically incommensurable. Arendt defends the possibility of visiting on the premise that human differences are *irreducible* to one another but not *incommensurable*. Thus, although there is no reason to expect public debate to produce consensus, there is no reason to assume that differences obviate understanding and render all consensus suspect. Just as Arendt thought solidarity could be meaningfully distinguished from enforced unanimity, so, too, she believed that the imposition of norms could be differentiated from their democratic contestation. Situated impartiality is, in effect, the epistemological counterpart to acting in concert, and storytelling is one more way Arendt affirms her commitment to human plurality.

Arendt's account of situated impartial representative thinking both makes a break with her earlier writings and follows a thread from those writings in the way that she spins out the connection between storytelling and judgment. The break occurs with respect to the question of how one comes to be situated in a common public space with others, and it can be attributed to a change in Arendt's understanding of publicity. Arendt argues in the early writings that there is publicity only where plurality is acted upon; it has literally to do with the public space that "springs up between men when they act together and vanishes the moment they disperse" (HC, 200). In the Kant lectures, she makes publicity internal to the mind. The question is whether plurality loses out in this move to the mind. The image of a poet-philosopher in "anticipated communication" with imaginary others carries with it the disquieting suggestion of a return to Archimedean thinking.

Visiting: A Return to Archimedean Thinking?

It is possible that the description of judging as "visiting" will satisfy neither humanist critics of modernity nor radical critics of humanism. To the former, *situated* impartiality will sound like an oxymoron. It will seem that Arendt's account leaves no way to differentiate between principled judgment and mere opinion.[31] To the latter, it will seem that *impartiality*—situated or not—ushers in a claim to Archimedean validity through the back door. Arendt's visitor is, by her own admission, a solitary figure in an imaginary public space. I return to the first of these in the conclusion and address the second in this final section and in the following chapter.

I approach the question of whether Arendt readmits Archimedean impartiality into her conception of judging through a back door by contrasting judging against the account of thinking she develops in the first volume of *Life of the Mind*. There is a vivid illustration of Arendt's resistance to the ideal of abstract, transcendent impartiality in the metaphors she uses to express the differences between thinking and judging. The visiting metaphor depicts the activity of judging as a withdrawal to a space in the mind around which you have imaginatively arrayed several viewpoints that bear on a particular situation.[32] Although it does not take place in an actual public forum, judging is specific to a place and time, nonetheless. Thinking is, by contrast, an absolutely private activity: "While thinking I am not where I actually am; I am surrounded not by sense-objects but by images that are invisible to everybody else. It is as though I had withdrawn into some never-never land, the land of invisibles, of which I would know nothing had I not this faculty of remembering and imagining. Thinking annihilates temporal as well as spatial distances" (LM: 1, 85). She communicates this contrast between publicity and absolute privacy by describing judging as a hypothetical public space, and thinking by the abstruse metaphor of a diagonal line.

She introduces the diagonal line as a metaphor for thinking over the course of explicating a parable from Kafka about the position of the

---

31. See Riley, "Hannah Arendt." See also Peter J. Steinberger, "Hannah Arendt on Judgment," *American Journal of Political Science* 34 (1990): 803–821. Steinberger asserts that Arendt's conception of judgment "fails to answer the most important questions about judgment" because she does not provide an independent criterion by which to distinguish good judgments from bad ones, 804.

32. The fact that one does not judge by means of debating in a public forum discredits representative thinking by participatory democratic standards. Given the difficulties of convening at any one time an actual forum that is genuinely plural, an "anticipated conversation" in the imagination of a well-traveled visitor could be more representative than any single public debate. I consider to what extent Arendt's "visiting" meets the criterion of plurality in the final section of this chapter.

thinker in relationship to the past, the present, and the future. In Kafka's parable, a fighter stands in the middle of a long road, engaging in combat with two antagonists. One of these (the forces of the past) is at his back, and the other (the forces of the future) is in front of him. The fighter is the thinking ego, and its struggle is to establish a position for the present by stopping the flow of time to fix "now" as a point of reference from which thought can take its bearings. The struggle is futile "be-cause—by virtue of the mind's incarnation in a body whose internal motions can never be immobilized—time inexorably and regularly in-terrupts the immobile quiet in which the mind is active without doing anything" (206). Kafka ends up by invoking an Archimedean fantasy of the fighter jumping out of time to "the position of umpire" over the forces of history (202).

Arendt accepts Kafka's description of the thinker's relation to history as a struggle between past and future, writing that "Man lives in this in-between, and what he calls the present is a life-long fight against the dead weight of the past, driving him forward with hope, and the fear of a future (whose only certainty is death), driving him backward toward 'the quiet of the past' with nostalgia for and remembrance of the only reality he can be sure of" (205). But, consistent with her critique of Archimedean thinking, she rejects the fantasy of jumping outside time. Arendt observes that there would be no history to think about if man jumped outside of time, because without the insertion into time of be-ings whose life spans are limited and nonrenewable, "there would be no difference between past and future, but only everlasting change" (208). Just as there can be no space without human plurality, there can be no time without human natality. Even though Kafka recognizes the con-nection between natality and history, "strangely enough," he does not adjust his conception of time to account for it: "Since Kafka retains the traditional metaphor of a rectilinear temporal movement, 'he' has barely enough room to stand and whenever 'he' thinks of striking out on 'his' own 'he' falls into the dream of a region over and above the fighting-line—and what else is this dream and this region but the old dream which Western metaphysics has dreamed from Parmenides to Hegel of a timeless, spaceless, suprasensuous realm as the proper region of thought?" (BPF, 11).

In order to account for the possibility of a place to think *in* time, Arendt reconfigures the battleground from a single road to two one-way paths that run perpendicular to each other and terminate when they meet (forming an "L"). She locates the fighter not in the middle of one road but at the intersection of the two, which both run toward him. By contrast to Kafka's story, where the present is perpetually squeezed between its antagonists on a narrow lane, in Arendt's L-shaped "parallelogram of forces," the present is located at the juncture of a 90° angle. This new configuration makes it possible to draw a diagonal line that begins at the point where the past and future converge and runs outward between them:

> If Kafka's "he" were able to walk along this diagonal, in perfect equidistance from the pressing forces of past and future, he would not, as the parable demands, have jumped out of the fighting line to be above and beyond the melée. For this diagonal, though pointing to some infinity, is limited, enclosed, as it were, by the forces of past and future, and thus protected against the void; *it remains bound to and is rooted in the present*—an entirely human present though it is fully actualized only in the thinking process and lasts no longer than this process lasts. (LM:I, 209; emphasis added)

Thought-events "happen" within time, but they cannot impinge on the actions of the past and future. They are, by contrast to historical events, utterly private.

Thinking and judging are quite distinct in Arendt's work, although not in a predictable way. As evidenced by her re-telling of Kafka's parable, both are bound to human experience. Both, then, are opposed to the Archimedean ideal. The principal difference between them, illustrated by the contrasting images of line and circle, is that thinking is utterly solitary. There seems to be no question of its being partial or impartial because it is on a trajectory of its own that does not take up a position in the public space.

If Arendt denies recourse to a standpoint out of time even to the thinker, then she clearly could not hold out such a position to the judging subject, who must take a stand in a public space. Again, it is not absolute withdrawal but publicity that guarantees impartiality in Arendt's account of judging. The question is whether visiting, the metaphor by which she describes representative thinking, is adequate to the task of guaranteeing that a decision is public. This is another instance where the classic version of the social/public separation constrains plurality. Excluding social differences from the public space causes her to reproduce in her own account of representative thinking as "visiting" a model of understanding she unequivocally rejects: empathy.

As I have shown, Arendt's objection to empathy is that it is assimilationist. She takes it as a literal attempt to "be or to feel like somebody else," while visiting is hypothetically to think and to feel *as myself* in a different position (BPF, 241). But when Arendt asserts that judging is a "solitary business," she necessarily presupposes that a single person can imaginatively anticipate each one of the different perspectives that are relevant to a situation (LKPP, 43). It is this presupposition that reproduces an aspect of empathy; it effects an erasure of difference. There are, as I mentioned, important distinctions between visiting and tourism, on one hand, and visiting and assimilationism on the other. Tourists carry so much with them, literally and figuratively, that they manage to travel without ever leaving home. Assimilationists are willing to leave home behind, provided that they can appropriate the customs of a new place and play at being at home where they are not. Visiting is a temporary change of place, a liminal state that is at once exciting, disorienting, and uncomfortable because it is an encounter with the unfamiliar. That Arendt makes no mention of discomfort in her account of visiting belies her insistence that it is—as distinct from empathy—an encounter between myself and something I cannot and do not identify with.

These doubts can be brought into focus by comparing Arendt's account of visiting to María Lugones's "world-travel." Like Arendt, Lugones attempts to formulate a model of thinking that makes possible the articulation of solidarities in a pluralist society. Lugones argues that the possibility of pluralist solidarity depends on "world-travel," which she describes as an "acquired flexibility in shifting from the mainstream construction of life where she is constructed as an outsider to other constructions of life where she is more or less 'at home'."[33] The capacity for world-travel is not an automatic "consolation prize" of marginality but a learned practice like the craft of the storyteller.[34] Lugones's description of the "world-traveling" self resembles Arendt's "disclosing" self. Both are plural and inhabit plural societies. Lugones writes that the experience of world-travel "is of being a different person in different 'worlds' and yet of having memory of oneself as different without quite having the sense of there being any underlying 'I'." For Lugones, identity is not a static or inherent property of an individual. Rather, to "be" is to "animate" a partial construction of identity within a particular world that may or may not be available in all the worlds you inhabit at any given time.[35] Just as with Arendt's "self-disclosing" self, Lugones's "world-travelling" self is known by the way its words and actions appear in various worlds.

Despite the similarity of the metaphors they use to describe the concepts of identity and relationship in a pluralist society, there are pronounced differences between Arendt's and Lugones's descriptions of what this experience is like. Arendt argues that the experience of visiting involves traveling to another place so that I can begin to understand just how the world looks different to you. Lugones adds that by traveling to someone else's world, "we can understand *what it is to be them and what it is to be ourselves in their eyes*."[36] Travel to a different position changes not only my perspective on the world but it also the identities that are available to me to animate. It is not a question of deliberately changing to fit in but, rather, of becoming aware of how differently my words and actions "play" to an unfamiliar audience.

33. María Lugones, "Playfulness, 'World'-Travelling, and Loving Perception," in *Lesbian Philosophies and Cultures*, ed. Jeffner Allen (Albany: SUNY Press, 1990), 159. I am indebted to Naomi Scheman who suggested I look at Lugones's essay after hearing a much earlier version of this chapter that she invited me to present at a Philosophy Department Colloquium at the University of Minnesota in 1990.

34. Terry Winant criticizes early feminist standpoint literature for assuming that critical understanding is a "consolation prize" of oppression. See "The Feminist Standpoint," 129.

35. Lugones, "Playfulness," 170, 169.

36. Ibid., 178; italics in the original.

Two differences follow from this. First, Lugones argues that if world-travel is genuinely to come to an understanding of plurality, it must be interactive. Arendt holds open the possibility of an "anticipated communication" in the mind of a solitary storyteller who imagines what various members of a community might say in response to a particular world event. Lugones would argue that this solitary exercise makes only part of the trip; the only way to know not just how different the world looks but how different you appear to those who are different from you is to take notice of what they do say, not what you imagine they would say. Second, once travel becomes interactive, it also becomes potentially threatening. Where there is no suggestion of discomfort in Arendt's description of visiting, Lugones makes it clear that world-travel involves being ill at ease. The more remote the world to which I travel is from that in which I am at home, the more disoriented I may be there, and the less comfortable I may be with the constructions I animate in it. In short, the *Lectures* make visiting sound so easy that it is doubtful that it could be a genuine encounter with plurality.

In terms of contemporary critical theory, Arendt's various public spaces are not genuinely plural because of the distinction she makes between the public and social realms. I argued earlier that there are two accounts of this distinction in *The Human Condition*, the classic or disciplinary version and the overgrown version. Where the former constrains plurality to differences of perspective, the latter acknowledges that social location is one condition of perspective. The conceptual account of visiting that Arendt gives in the unfinished lectures is, as I have noted, a retreat from the space of speech and action she describes in *The Human Condition* to a metaphorical public in the mind of the political critic. It is also an abandonment of the overgrown public space and a retreat to the relative comfort of the disciplinary one. Although not an embrace of rationalism, because Arendt maintains her insistence that the particular standpoints a critic visits are irreducible to a common measure, it tends toward a reaffirmation of a classic liberal version of plurality; the differences without which there can be no publicity and no visiting are differences in principle, not in social location. This does not mean that Arendt's account of judgment has nothing to offer contemporary critical theory, but it does mean that any attempt to appropriate this account for present purposes must either acknowledge its own predisposition toward liberal humanism or make clear its departures from Arendt's text.

This admission is at odds with the animating concern of this study, which has been to show how Arendt breaks out of the sterile opposition between neohumanists and their critics. If, in the end, I have either to admit that Arendt (and I) are liberal humanists or to break with Arendt in order to get beyond that tradition, then I will have disappointed this objective. I think that there is a way to break with Arendt's humanism on her own terms, however. In this chapter I have concentrated on the unfinished lectures on judging in which Arendt gives an abstract, conceptual account of visiting, a kind of critical understanding that is neither particularistic nor universalist. I have argued that the questions she brings to this project are not dictated by a philosophical tradition but, rather, unresolved problems from her own writings on politics. I have acknowledged that in answering these problems conceptually Arendt takes the edge off her critique of philosophy. Not so in her writings on Jewish identity, her literary essays, and her correspondence with Karl Jaspers, however. There she takes up the same questions of the relationship between particular experience and critical understanding—but with the imagination of a storyteller, not that of a philosopher.

6   At Home in This World

∎

"Ever since I've known that you both came through the whole hellish mess unharmed, I have felt somewhat more at home in this world again" (C, 23). This sentence begins the first letter Hannah Arendt writes to Karl Jaspers after World War II, on November 18, 1945. It is a remarkable sentence that breaks a seven-year silence without melodrama or triviality. In the text that follows, she makes no attempt to recount the specific details of that "whole hellish mess," for, as she argues in her public writings from this same time, there is no human story more difficult to tell than that of totalitarianism. Its telling is the task of poets, not political scientists, historians, or even philosophers. With this greeting to Jaspers, so moving in its simplicity, Hannah Arendt is a poet.

Being at home in *this* world is a concern in the correspondence, in Arendt's writings on Jewish identity and politics, and in the connection she draws between marginality and critical understanding.[1] Arendt identifies this concern with the figure of the pariah, one who is not at home in the world by virtue of being deemed "other." That estrangement carries with it the privilege of critical vision is quite a common assumption, as is the belief that the estranged critic is a hero. As Michael Walzer has observed, there is something disingenuous about this heroic pose for, although "it is a hard business (though harder in some societies

---

1. C. S. Kessler's essay "The Politics of Jewish Identity: Arendt and Zionism" considers the relationship between Arendt's use of the term *homelessness* and Jewish politics in the Holocaust and post-Holocaust era. In *Hannah Arendt: Thinking, Judging, Freedom*, ed. Gisela T. Kaplan and Clive S. Kessler (Sydney, Australia: Allen and Unwin, 1989).

than in others) to wrench oneself loose, either emotionally or intellectually . . . it has to be said, however, that the difficulty of finding a properly detached position is compensated for by the *ease of criticism once
one is there.*"[2] As I have demonstrated, Arendt's critique of the Western
tradition is directed precisely at the cowardice of the retreat to the myth-
ical Archimedean vantage point, which she views as an attempt to "escape the haphazardness and moral irresponsibility inherent in a plurality
of agents" (HC, 220). Arendt suggests that the ideal of the rebel hero is
a pose that is impracticable for the everyday situations in which ordinary
people find themselves called upon to enact resistance and that reproduces the oppositional power relations it purports to challenge.

There is an important difference between these well-known images
and Arendt's conception of marginality. Whereas the ideal of the alienated rebel rests on the premise of an absolute opposition between insi-
dership and outsidership, Arendt's writings on German Jewish identity
put forth a conception of marginality *as distinct from* outsidership by
differentiating among pariahs, *parvenus*, and conscious pariahs. Her portrait of the conscious pariah is another instance where Arendt draws on
familiar ideas and recasts them in a unique way.

Homelessness is a theme of many of the essays Arendt wrote toward
the end of the war and in its immediate aftermath. In her almost mor-
dant "We Refugees," Arendt describes the condition of the displaced
German Jews like this: "We lost our home, which means the familiarity
of daily life. We lost our occupation, which means the confidence that
we are of some use in this world. We lost our language, which means
the naturalness of reactions, the simplicity of gestures, the unaffected
expression of feelings."[3] Homelessness is the loss of a sense of place that
is not just geographic but also moral and cultural. For Arendt, as for
Michael Walzer, home is "a dense moral culture within which [one] can
feel some sense of belonging."[4] Marginality means not being simply at
home in the world and, so, having deliberately to reflect on and construct a moral space in which to be at home by the thoughtful cultivation

2. Michael Walzer, *Interpretation and Social Criticism* (Cambridge: Harvard University
Press, 1987), 36–37; emphasis added.
3. Hannah Arendt, "We Refugees," JP, 55–56 (originally published in January 1943).
4. Walzer, *Interpretation*, 16.

of friendship. It is possibly because of the extraordinary effort that marginals put into the cultivation of that which the relatively privileged can take for granted that Arendt writes to Jaspers after the war that "I'm more than ever of the opinion that a decent human existence is possible today only on the fringes of society, where one then runs the risk of starving or being stoned to death. In these circumstances, a sense of humor is a great help"(C, 26). In the preceding chapter, I argued that what is unique about Arendt's conception of judgment is her account of the practice of "visiting." Yet, the content of this practice is vague, described only as an "anticipated communication" with an unspecified community. Where the unfinished lectures on judgment leave the nagging suspicion that "visiting" may be Archimedean impartiality in disguise, in Arendt's writings on Jewish identity and especially in her correspondence with Jaspers she insists that critical understanding and principled resistance are inspired by one's experience as a particular historical individual.

In this chapter I argue that visiting is not just warmed-over Archimedean thinking. I explore the "conscious pariah" as an exemplar of Arendt's critic "on the fringes." I begin with a close reading of Arendt's public writings on Jewish identity, and I then turn to her personal correspondence with Karl Jaspers. The writings on Jewish identity provide a conceptual vocabulary for distinguishing critical marginality from absolute outsidership. The letters continue this discussion of marginality by means of a sustained dispute between the Kantian philosopher and his Jewish student over the relationship between particular identity and principled judgment. The correspondence also demonstrates the kind of communication that visiting involves. It tells a story of two philosophers who identified with each other as pariahs and whose letters are part of their effort to find a way of being at home in the world again without relinquishing a critical perspective on the events that displaced both of them from their homeland. This extended communication with Jaspers reveals what it meant to Arendt to be a marginal or "conscious pariah" more effectively than any of her public work. Where she filters her public treatment of these themes through biographical essays on historical figures whom she considers typical pariahs, in the letters she writes as a pariah herself: she speaks from her particular experience as a German

Jewish expatriate to the one person through whom she has a connection to Germany.

Jewish Identity

Arendt uses the terms *parvenu* and *pariah* to lay out the problem of Jewish identity during the period of Jewish integration into Western European society.[5] The *parvenu*/pariah distinction constructs the problem of integration as a choice between assimilation and alienation.[6] The *parvenu* views membership as a privilege to be won on the paradoxical grounds "that, although he [ought] not behave like an 'ordinary Jew,' he be and produce something out of the ordinary, since, after all, he was a Jew" (OT, 56). The *parvenu* views membership as a problem to be solved by performing the inherently contradictory role of the individual "exception Jew"—one who is both Jew in the sense of having exotic appeal and not-Jew in the sense of honoring no cultural traditions and displaying none of the "undesirable traits," stereotypically associated with Jewishness.

In contrast, the pariah is a non-conformist who refuses the constraints of membership "to stay out of society altogether" (OT, 66). For the average Jew, who could neither rise to the demands of exceptionalism nor assume the role of the outsider as rebel hero, being a pariah meant only "an empty sense of difference which continued to be interpreted, in all its possible psychological aspects and variations from innate strangeness to social alienation" (67). In a later essay she gives a more romantic portrait of average pariahs, writing that "pariah peoples" are distinguished by an exceptional sensibility for "fraternity." But she makes it quite clear that this moral privilege of great "humanity" is not just distinct from but also *at odds* with privileged critical judgment. It "is often accompanied by so radical a loss of the world, so fearful an

---

5. Arendt delimits this as a period of about 150 years from the late eighteenth through the nineteenth centuries, OT, 56.

6. Arendt borrows the terms *pariah*, *parvenu*, and *conscious pariah* from Bernard Lazare, *Job's Dungheap*, trans. Harry L. Binsse (New York: Schocken, 1948).

atrophy of all the organs with which we respond to it—starting with the common sense with which we orient ourselves in a world common to ourselves and others and going on to the sense of beauty, or taste, with which we love the world—that in extreme cases, in which pariahdom has persisted for centuries, we can speak of real worldlessness." The *parvenu* is an assimilationist who plays at being at home among strangers, and the pariah a separatist who withdraws to the "warmth of persecuted peoples" (MDT, 13). Where *parvenus* buy respectability in an imperfect society at the cost of being able to criticize its imperfections in public, pariahs not only cede the freedom of public criticism but also, by their withdrawal from plurality, lose their capacity to "respond" to the world and with it their very faculty of judging.

Much has been made of the critique of assimilationism that Arendt puts forward by means of this contrast between the *parvenu* and the pariah. But there is a second criticism here, in Arendt's charge that the pariah is "worldless." As far as Arendt is concerned, to be an outsider is not to enjoy a privileged critical vision but, on the contrary, to be altogether incapable of public judgment. Consequently, Arendt calls into question the typical conception of the pariah/*parvenu* contrast as an opposition between alienated spectators (who are incapable of making common cause) and partisan members (who are incapable of finding fault). Arendt suggests that these two may be more alike than they are different by the fact that they are equally susceptible to parochialism, the *parvenu* on behalf of the dominant community, and the pariah on behalf of its outcasts. By reconfiguring the pariah/*parvenu* opposition as a distinction between worldlessness and being too much at home, Arendt makes room for a third possibility: homelessness.

Her account of homelessness as a condition of critical understanding emerges from the articulations within the category pariah that Arendt explores in the essay "The Jew as Pariah: A Hidden Tradition." She proposes to delineate four types of pariah existence through sketches of four exemplary figures: the "*schlemihl*" and "lord of dreams" in the poetry of Heinrich Heine, radical French Zionist Bernard Lazare, the character of the "little man" or "suspect" as portrayed by Charlie Chaplin, and "K." in Franz Kafka's novel *The Castle*. Written in 1944, this essay is frustratingly consistent with other work during this period in which Arendt uses highly unorthodox methods of analysis as if they were entirely a matter of course. One peculiarity of the essay is the list of exemplary pariahs. Arendt proposes to elucidate what she claims is an actual historical phenomenon through the "lives" of three fictional characters and one nonfictional person as if it goes without saying that their lives are of equal analytical validity.[7] This essay, composed during the same period as the writings on storytelling, rests implicitly on the "more truth than fact" thesis I discussed in Chapter Three. As with her other writings during this period, Arendt only alludes to the possibility that her use of fiction to explain a historical phenomenon could be defended, without actually making that defense. Again, my objection is not to Arendt's method but to her failure to justify it. It may be defensible to argue that fiction *is* as true as fact or even more true than what can be recognized as fact, but it certainly does not go without saying.

By using both fact and fiction as a basis for her analysis of marginality, Arendt implies that she is being truthful to the phenomenon to which the very concept of pariah refers. That is, to be a pariah is to discover that assimilation is a false promise for a Jew in a predominantly Christian society because one cannot appear there in public as a Jewish person but only as an "exception Jew." To be unable to appear as a peer among equals is to be deprived of publicity—the "presence of others who see what we see and hear what we hear assures us of the reality of the world and ourselves"—and to be consigned to an existence that is somehow unreal. In her biography of Rahel Varnhagen she describes the exception Jew as a character "without a stage-set" who is exhausted by "always having to represent oneself as something special, and having to do it all alone, in order to justify her bare existence" (RV, 217, 219). To put it in terms of the vocabulary of *The Human Condition*, what is denied Rahel is the possibility of spontaneous self-disclosure; she is, instead, consumed by the task of making up a self that is fit to present in public. One reason Arendt finds it neither noteworthy nor remarkable to explicate the concept of the pariah through stories of "real" people and "fictional" characters alike is that to be a pariah is to be not at home in the world

7. It would be similar to my proposing to delineate various concepts of womanhood in America as exemplified by the lives of Scarlett O'Hara, Fanny Lou Hamer, or Diane Keaton playing in *Annie Hall.*

and, hence, to have a kind of fictional existence on the margins of society.

Further, she claims that it is artists, not historians or social scientists, who must be theorists of social phenomena such as marginality. Arendt suggests that the sense of perpetual strangeness that is a condition of pariah existence may not be empirically observable but that it "has nevertheless loomed larger in the thinking of assimilated Jews than might be inferred from standard Jewish histories" ("JP," 100). The pariah phenomenon is real, but it takes a poetic sensibility to discern it. It is one of the "social factors, unaccounted for in political or economic history [that are] hidden under the surface of events, never perceived by the historian and recorded only by the more penetrating and passionate force of poets or novelists who are pariahs themselves" (OT, 87). The "essential kinship" of poets and pariahs is that both are superfluous, the former by the vocation of being an artist, and the latter by social discrimination that excludes pariahs from meaningful work. The public significance of the personal experience of superfluity is evident in the work of poets, writers, and artists who alone have the capabilities to bring feelings to light in a way that they can be the subject of discussion. Arendt suggests that poets and storytellers are theorists when it comes to understanding phenomena such as marginality. Thus, a fictional character might count as "historical" evidence in a study of something such as the pariah phenomenon.

Another peculiarity of this piece is that Arendt presents the four pariah types in historical order, even though this is at odds with the conceptual order implicit in her evaluation of each of them. The four types can be divided into two categories: political and anti-political. The *schlemihl* and the suspect are anti-political; K. and Lazare are political. Of these four figures, it is Lazare, the 'conscious pariah,' who exemplifies Arendt's distinctive conception of marginality.

The *schlemihl* and the suspect are escapists because they both play out a utopian conception of freedom that consists in living outside the law. Heine's pariah is a figure of childlike innocence who escapes into the "higher reality" of nature and, from the standpoint of natural freedom, mocks both the corruption of tyrants and the stupidity of those who put up with them ("JP," 104). This belief in a pre-social freedom to be reclaimed by abandoning civil society is the utopian element in Heine's vision of pariah existence. She writes, "From this standpoint [of natural freedom] . . . the pariah is always remote and unreal; whether as *schlemihl* or as 'lord of dreams' he stands outside the real world and attacks it from without" (105). Chaplin's pariah is also outside the world, not in Heine's utopian land of dreams but in the "stateless" condition of the refugee. He is an ingratiating "little man" in an arbitrary relationship to the laws and norms of the society in which he seeks refuge. Though not innocent, he is never really guilty either but perpetually under suspicion. He is "always being 'nabbed' for things he never did, yet somehow he can always slip through the toils of the law, where other men would be caught in them" (112). In conniving to evade the law, this character confirms the stereotype of the pariah as suspect, thereby legitimating it at the same time as he parodies it. To Arendt, these two types are alike in that both attempt to escape or evade the laws of corrupt societies rather than confront and transform them; consequently, they are both powerless with respect to the capacity for self-determination.

In contrast, Kafka's *The Castle* is the story of K.'s repeated attempts to stage a confrontation with the distant and inaccessible powers of the Castle in order to secure his rights as an individual. Arendt claims that the story Kafka tells of the impossibility of K.'s struggle exemplifies the "real drama of assimilation," which neither Heine nor Chaplin recognize (116). This is that Jews can neither be admitted into the community defined by Enlightenment universals *as Jews* nor escape the identity that marks them as pariahs to be accepted as men in the abstract. As she observes in the Varnhagen biography: "Reason can liberate from the prejudices of the past and it can guide the future. Unfortunately, however, it appears that it can free isolated individuals only, can direct the future only of Crusoes. The individual who has been liberated by reason is always running head-on into a world, a society, whose past in the shape of 'prejudices' has a great deal of power; he is forced to learn that past reality is also a reality" (RV, 10). Save a reconfiguration of its standards, whereby being Jewish would no longer mean being "different," principles of reason cannot secure entrance for Jews *as Jews* into the abstract "universal" human community. Arendt's brief interpretation of *The Castle* is remarkable for its clarity in spelling out her nonessentialist conception of Jewish identity and her critique of Enlightenment humanism.

The centerpiece of the interpretation is Arendt's provocative claim that this is Kafka's only novel "in which the hero is plainly a Jew."[8] This claim is remarkable because there is nothing specific in the novel to indicate that K. is a Jew; in fact, K.'s identity is one of its great ambiguities. Because the story is told in the third person, through K.'s experiences and the thoughts he has about them, there is never a portrait of K.'s appearance from the outside. Even a psychological portrait is difficult to draw because K.'s reflections on events are frequently devoid of affect. K.'s arrival to the village makes his identity a deliberate mystery. It is not clear whether he just happened upon it and decided to pose as the Land-Surveyor in order to secure a place to sleep out of the snow, whether—Land-Surveyor or not—he is a subversive who sought out this village particularly to challenge the arbitrary rule of the Castle, or whether he is the Land-Surveyor whom the Castle summoned. The phone call in which the Castle "recognizes" him as such does nothing to dispel this ambiguity, because K. does not interpret it as confirmation of his identity but rather as a sign that the rulers have taken up his challenge and may perhaps be trying to outwit him.[9]

Arendt acknowledges all of this, noting that what makes it so plain to her that K. is Jewish is not an essential property or characteristic but the conditions of his relations with the village and with the Castle. Thus, her choice of K. to exemplify Jewish identity is a deliberately paradoxical move that underscores her own refusal to define identity in terms of essential characteristics. She writes that "what characterizes him as such is not any typically Jewish trait, but the fact that he is involved in sit-

8. "JP," 115. I am indebted to Kathleen Fluegel for setting me off in this direction by her surprise at this aspect of Arendt's interpretation.
9. "K. pricked up his ears. So the Castle had recognized him as the Land-Surveyor. That was unpropitious for him, on the one hand, for it meant that the Castle was well informed about him, had estimated all the probable chances, and was taking up the challenge with a smile. On the other hand, however, it was quite propitious, for if his interpretation was right they had underestimated his strength, and he would have more freedom of action than he had dared to hope. And if they expected to cow him by their lofty superiority in recognizing him as Land-Surveyor, they were mistaken; it made his skin prickle a little, that was all." Franz Kafka, *The Castle*, trans. Willa and Edwin Muir (New York: Schocken, 1930, rpt. 1983), 7–8.

uations and perplexities distinctive of Jewish life" ("JP," 115). K.'s situation and its perplexity, according to Arendt, is that he is a stranger to the village confronted with the option of being either an " 'Official' Jew" or trying to be an ordinary man of good will (116). If he chooses to be sponsored there by the Castle, he gains entrance to the village, but at the cost of being a creature of the rulers and having nowhere to be at home; although he would not be permitted in the Castle, his exceptional status would keep him from living as one of the people. If he renounces the Castle, then he must make his way as a stranger among the people with no support at all against their parochialism and inhospitality.

Arendt takes the Castle as a symbol of the dilemma of Western European Jews during the period of assimilation. This dilemma is that it is impossible to be admitted "*as Jews* to the ranks of humanity" (100) and impossible to contest this fact. It is incontestable because there is no way to challenge the implicit rule that "the Jew might only become a man when he ceased to be a Jew," without speaking *as a Jew* (107). But to speak as a Jew is to speak from a position constructed as "different" in terms of Enlightenment humanism, which means that one's claims will be deemed self-interested and dismissed as unprincipled. Arendt's account of the problem of assimilation concurs with what Martha Minow calls the "dilemma of difference," that any claim to speak *from difference* against the abstract norms by which difference is equated with inferiority will be interpreted—in light of those norms—to confirm one's status as an outsider and inferior.[10] Whether by denying difference or calling attention to it, a group seems to validate the prejudices and reproduce the power relations that mark it as "other."

K. chooses the course of denying difference, attempting to make himself indistinguishable as a Jew by demanding that the Castle grant him the rights of any villager. Arendt argues that Kafka uses K.'s insistence that the recognition he seeks be granted him as his right, not "in the form of 'an act of favor from the Castle'," to dramatize the self-delusion of the *parvenu* strategy of Jewish exceptionalism ("JP," 117). The consequence of exceptionalism is utter loneliness, as evidenced by Kafka's

---

10. Martha Minow, *Making All the Difference: Inclusion, Exclusion, and American Law* (Ithaca: Cornell University Press, 1990), chap. 1.

portrayal of K. "as if he were alone on earth, the only Jew in the whole wide world—completely, desolately alone" (116). Arendt comments that this "lonely isolation merely reflects the constantly reiterated opinion that if only there were nothing but individual Jews, if only the Jews would not persist in banding together, assimilation would become a fairly simple process" (116). But the significance of this story goes beyond detailing the specific problem of Jewish assimilation; by having K. renounce the role of *parvenu* or exception Jew for the demand of individual rights, Arendt argues that Kafka presents this alienation as a general "problem of mankind" (117). Thus, she interprets the novel not just as the story of Jew as pariah but also as a broader critique of humanism.

From the pariah perspective, the story of K. discloses the impossibility of assimilation *in the abstract*, which is a specific problem for Jews and other outsiders by virtue of the Enlightenment opposition of universality against particularity. Enlightenment humanism turns on an implicit distinction between individuals whose identities *as members of groups* are invisible, and "others" who are visible *only* as members of groups. Being a member of a group that is invisible as a group makes it possible for one's particular qualities to stand as universal standards. But being a member of a group that is visible *only* as a group marks one as other, so that one's inclusion within the purportedly universal community is not a matter of course but conditional on dissociating oneself from any "differences" that cast suspicion on one's capacity to put the universal ahead of the particular.

A further irrationality of humanism for the pariah is that this distinction between universality and particularity is unquestionable from within. Arendt notes that in Kafka's novel, "The simplest inquiry into right and wrong is regarded as querulous disputations; the character of the regime, the power of the castle, are things which may not be questioned" ("JP," 119). Petitioning the Castle and challenging its rule serve only to confirm the suspicion that you are an outsider and to deny you a position from which to speak *on principle* against the regime. Describing this dilemma as it is depicted in the films of Charlie Chaplin, Arendt argues that Chaplin's "little man" is "always and everywhere . . . under suspicion, so that it is no good arguing rights and wrongs" (111). As K. cannot challenge authority, he must try to outwit it. The villagers, however, do not even try to outwit the Castle but accept its rule in an attitude that Arendt elsewhere calls "fatefulness" (C, 11): accepting the law as if it were not a human construction but "an inexorable natural force" to which one must submit as to fate ("JP," 112).

From the perspective of mankind, the irrationality of humanism is the discontinuity between principles defined in the abstract and imposed from an Archimedean vantage point and the specific plurality of people's historical existences. This problem is caricatured in the Castle, a faceless, disembodied, remote authority whose pronouncements have only the most arbitrary connection to the particulars of the lives on which they are imposed. The absurdity of the villagers' existence in the shadow of the Castle is that recognition is meaningless under such conditions; yet each of them desperately overinterprets any sign from the Castle for a glimmer.[11] Arendt's insistence that *The Castle* discloses a "basic human problem" suggests that she does not see Kafka's work as an allegorical attack on a perversely bureaucratic incarnation of Enlightenment ideals ("JP," 116). The regime of the Castle is not an instance of the Enlightenment gone wrong; rather, it is a storyteller's version of her own critique of the Archimedean separation of philosophy and politics that is inherent in rationalism, not accidental to it. The human problem of the Castle is also exemplary of what Arendt calls the "inhumanity" of Kant's categorical imperative that, "in its absoluteness introduces into the interhuman realm—which by its nature consists of relationships—something that runs counter to its fundamental relativity" (MTD, 27). She recognizes that the move from the abstract to the particular always entails arbitrary exclusions, whether explicitly so, as in the politics of nationalism and example of the Castle, or insidiously so, as in the moral universalism of the categorical imperative that is untenable in politics.

The story of K., seen from K.'s perspective, is a failure; he dies exhausted with his goal endlessly postponed. But this story is a success in

---

11. This absurdity reaches its height with Olga's account of the "parody of service" at the Castle. She reveals that Barnabus's position as a messenger and K.'s position as the Land-Surveyor are mutually self-referential. Where Barnabus interprets the directive to deliver an important message to the Land-Surveyor as recognition of *his* importance as a messenger, K., in turn, interprets the fact that he has been visited by an official messenger to confirm *his* importance as the Land-Surveyor. Kafka, *The Castle*, 292–296.

a way that is far more important to Arendt. Arendt claims that K.'s life inspires a few other villagers with the conviction "both that human rights are worth fighting for and that the rule of the castle . . . can be attacked" ("JP," 120). This spirit of taking responsibility to confront a regime in its injustice is what is missing from the *schlemihl* and the suspect, both of whom enjoy the "freedom and untouchability of outcasts" with the consequence that their lives are "shorn of political significance" (121). Although K.'s story is one of failure in terms of his motives and goals, Arendt claims that it is a success in the vision it inspires in others.

The difference between K. and Bernard Lazare, who is the one figure Arendt sets apart in her typology of pariahs by calling him a "conscious pariah," is that Lazare sees beyond the individual struggle for individual rights to the possibility of collective action for rights that apply to individuals *as members of groups*. Lazare was a radical French Zionist who distinguished himself as a pamphleteer on behalf of the rights of Alfred Dreyfus and as a proponent of a confederated Jewish nation based on neither a religious nor a racial identity but in a democratic cross-national and cross-class alliance against anti-Semitism.[12] According to Arendt, it is Lazare who first attempts to "bring the Jewish question openly into the arena of politics" as a choice of exile, assimilation, or political resistance ("JP," 108).

Lazare argues for a Jewish nation built on the principle of plurality, both among Jewish peoples and between Jews and other peoples. He refutes the myths of Jewish unity premised on religious and racial identity, underscores the class differences between pariah Jews segregated in ghettos and bourgeois *parvenus*, and at the same time argues that all Jews are united by their common situation in the face of anti-Semitism. Although they experience it from different positions, the effect of anti-Semitism on pariahs and *parvenus* is the same: exhaustion. Pariahs, such as K., exhaust themselves attempting to live *as Jews* among Christians,

---

12. See "Jewish Nationalism," in Lazare, *Job's Dungheap*, 54–79. Such a proposal would appeal to Arendt because it is a model of solidarity based in plurality rather than essential identity. Jeffrey C. Isaac notes that Arendt is less concerned about discussing the feasibility of Lazare's strategy than to deploy it as an alternative to the nationalist and utopian Zionism of Theodor Herzl. Jeffrey C. Isaac, "At the Margins: Jewish Identity and Politics in the Thought of Hannah Arendt," *Tikkun* 5 (1990): 86.

which involves resisting the "inevitable tendency" of all peoples "to reduce the heterogeneous elements existing among them." By contrast, the
energy of the *parvenu* is expended not in separatism but in aspiring to
a "fusion" that cannot be achieved. All of this energy can be construc-
tively expended only in concerted action to establish an independent
Jewish nation. The realization of a Jewish nation involves that Jews of
different classes, nationalities, and religious practices first acknowledge
their heterogeneity and affirm their common commitment to justice
across that heterogeneity and then that heterogeneous and scattered
groups of Jews constitute themselves as a people for the purpose of
establishing a nation in which "all men" are welcomed.[13] As Lazare envisions it, the Jewish nation would be unique not only from the perspective of the Jewish people because it would be a public space in which
they can act freely *as Jews*, but also from the perspective of humanity
because it would be a space in which heterogeneity of any kind would
not suffer constraint.

In Arendt's writing on Jewish identity there are three possible re-
sponses to social discrimination: assimilationism, separatism, and collective action. Through her descriptions about the characters who typify
each of these responses, Arendt explores the way out of the opposition
between the stance of Archimedean abstraction and that of particularism,
expressed as either skepticism or empathy. The characters in Arendt's
writings on Jewish identity—the pariah as *schlemihl* or suspect, the *parvenu*, and the conscious pariah—correspond to the various positions in
the debate about critical understanding. The "divine impudence" of the
pariah is a kind of Archimedean stance, the self-effacing accommodative
strategy of the *parvenu* a version of empathy, and the polemical activism
of the conscious pariah a kind of situated impartiality ("JP,' 105).

There is a similarity between pariah and *parvenu* types that can be
lost by an exclusive focus on the dichotomous opposition of their re-
sponses to the problem of integration: they are incapable of visiting. The
pariah, whether *schlemihl* or suspect, has to be self-centered in order to
remain an outsider. The *schlemihl* cannot sustain the "lord of dreams"
fiction except by refusing to tell the story of a situation as anything other

13. Lazare, *Job's Dungheap*, 63, 72, 106, 101.

than a personal fantasy of superiority. Not being at home in the world is the core of *schlemihl* identity, and it depends on maintaining a self-presentation as someone who is inevitably, even maliciously misunderstood by the dominant society. To put it colloquially, the *schlemihl* has a chip on his or her shoulder. Similarly, the suspect is too preoccupied to be able to imagine a situation from anything but the perspective of his or her own survival. In contrast, the assimilationist *parvenu* is consumed by the attempt to make him or herself at home in an unwelcome environment, which involves refusing to recognize differences in perspective. Describing the young Rahel, Arendt writes, "There is only one aim: always, at any given moment, to be different from what one is; never to assert oneself, but with infinite pliancy to become anything else, so long as it is not oneself" (RV, 13). It is not escapism but self-effacement, accommodation, and false politeness that make it impossible for the *parvenu* to visit. The conscious pariah, by contrast, neither turns homelessness into a badge of honor nor "insist[s] upon entering a house where [he or she] will be insulted,"[14] but rather accepts homelessness as a condition of existence and attempts to live as a marginal among marginals.[15]

Homelessness, as distinct from worldlessness, is requisite to critical understanding as Arendt describes it.[16] Being at home in the world means having a teleological conception of one's life history: "If we feel at home in this world, we can see our lives as the development of the 'product of nature,' as the unfolding and realization of what we already were" (RV, 4). In contrast, not being at home in a world means being ill at ease with what is taken for granted there, and especially to be

14. Lazare, *Job's Dungheap*, 100.

15. Jennifer Ring also emphasizes Arendt's departure in describing the conscious pariah not as a lone rebel but as an outsider who acts "*as* a member of a group of outsiders *against* the prevailing community." In "The Pariah as Hero: Hannah Arendt's Political Actor," *Political Theory* 19 (1991): 441.

16. In her essay "What Is Existenz Philosophy?" *The Partisan Review* 13 (1946): 34–56, Arendt uses the term *homelessness* to describe a distinctively modern skepticism, alienation, and solipsism. The term encompasses both critical thinking and its opposite, the loss of common sense that is a consequence of the disappearance of the public space. Over the course of writing *Origins*, she becomes more precise in her use of terms and introduces the term "worldlessness" for the political naivete of pariah peoples. For a discussion of worldlessness, see Ron H. Feldman, "Introduction," JP, 20–28.

uncomfortable with the discontinuities between the ways you wish to appear and the identities you animate in that world. Not being at home in the world is a characteristic of a conscious pariah who does not identify totally with any group or place and is none the worse for it. The distinctive quality of the "conscious pariah," relative to both the pariah and the *parvenu*, is that of being at home only in the company of conscious pariah friends. This friendship is distinct from the "fraternity" of the enclaves that pariah peoples create by "avoid[ing] disputes and try[ing] as far as possible to deal only with people with whom they cannot come into conflict." It depends not on "the excessive closeness of a brotherliness that obliterate[s] all distinctions," but on plurality that opens up space for "a discourse between thinkers" (MDT, 30). This discourse would not be intimate or comforting but would be disputational in order to foster the articulation of differences. As I have already argued, she credits Lessing with having a particular gift for writing in a way that opened such spaces. In a sentence that calls to mind Kant's enlarged mentality, she explains that "the reason that [Lessing's thought] is essentially polemical" is because it is not oriented toward contemplation, "the (Platonic) silent dialogue between me and myself" but toward "an anticipated dialogue with others" (10). This kind of disputation opens up public spaces in which it is possible to engage in "visiting."

Arendt praises public intellectuals such as Lessing and Lazare for what I would call situated impartiality. She admires Lessing for his independent thinking, which she takes to be a consequence of his refusal to declare his solidarity with a particular identity or ideology. This independence results in what she calls the "astonishing lack of 'objectivity' in Lessing's polemicism . . . his forever vigilant partiality, which has nothing whatsoever to do with subjectivity because it is always framed not in terms of the self but in terms of the *relationship of men to their world, in terms of their positions and opinions.*"[17] This character-

---

17. MDT, 29; emphasis added. Dagmar Barnouw comments that the qualities Arendt admires in Lessing are qualities for which she too is both admired and attacked, writing that "the peculiarly independent position from which Arendt spoke . . . has caused her readers to praise her brilliance but also lament her singlemindedness, even arrogance, in insisting on seeing alternative aspects of a problem, always and at any cost." *Visible Spaces: Hannah Arendt and the German-Jewish Experience* (Baltimore: Johns Hopkins University Press, 1990), x.

ization of Lessing brings to mind Arendt's description of the "enlarged mentality" in the lectures on judgment. She praises him for writing in a way that is critical without being abstract and explicitly partial but not subjective. In effect, she describes him as positioned neither inside nor outside, but as traveling "on the fringes."

Public intellectuals such as Lazare or Gotthold Lessing and storytellers are alike in that this marginality is necessary to the practice of their crafts. Recall Arendt's statement in her essay on Isak Dinesen that becoming an artist requires "a certain detachment from the heady, intoxicating business of sheer living that, perhaps, only the born artist can manage in the midst of living" (MDT, 97). Without being "in the midst of living," there would be no stories to tell, but without withdrawing periodically from its "heady intoxicating business," those stories would never find their way into words and on paper. To be a writer is to be someone who is as in love with—in the sense of being precisely attentive to and enlivened by—the solitary act of writing as with the social activity of living. The critic, like the storyteller, has to feel some connection to the world and some expectation of an audience for his or her work to be moved to write at all. But to have anything to say, this connection must be discontinuous. It cannot be an empathic identification or partisan membership.

Furthermore, as Arendt describes it, visiting is not the unique prerogative of the conscious pariah. Although storytellers, essayists, and theorists such as Hannah Arendt are visitors, the purpose of their work is not to transmit information and establish themselves as exclusive authorities but to make the experience of marginality accessible to the reader. As Walter Benjamin puts it, "it is half the art of storytelling to keep a story free from explanation as one reproduces it . . . [so that it is up to the reader] to interpret things the way he understands them, and thus the narrative achieves an amplitude that information lacks."[18] The "amplitude" of a story consists in its bringing to light more truth than fact. By truth, I do not mean that stories provide an accurate representation of the world. Rather, as Arendt claims in an essay on Kafka, a

18. Walter Benjamin, *Illuminations*, ed. Hannah Arendt, trans. Harry Zohn (New York: Schocken Books, 1969), 89.

well-crafted story is a "blueprint" that can "sometimes in a page, or even in a single phrase, expose the naked structure of happenings."[19] A story can make explicit the assumptions that determine the standards and practices of a particular regime but are so essential to its foundation and structure that they are never stated and, hence, not visible to outsiders *or* insiders but only to visitors.

This essay on Kafka is Arendt's most detailed account of the way in which the writings of a marginal makes the practice of visiting, and hence critical understanding, accessible to its audience. Kafka's stories force the reader to the fringe by building a fictional world in which the familiar is re-presented in strange, dreamlike, and even nightmarish terms. The stories stand in relation to reality as a blueprint to a house, "compared with a real house, of course, a blueprint is a very unreal affair; but without it the house could not have come into being, nor could one recognize the foundation and structures that make it a real house." That they are blueprints means that the stories "are in a sense the product of thinking rather than of mere sensational experience."[20] In other words, Kafka is not a storyteller for what might be termed the vicarious reader. You cannot inhabit the characters for the same reason that you cannot step imaginatively into a blueprint: it is not a portrait or a painting that attempts to provide the illusion of three dimensions but a schema. Just as you cannot imagine living in a blueprint, you are not invited to make yourself at home in Kafka's stories but rather to use the stories to make yourself *less* at home in the familiar world.

Arendt argues that the critical power of Kafka's storytelling is that it brings to light *as nightmarish or perverse* the assumptions that make the standards and practices of a regime seem normal and natural, thereby making it possible to call into question what otherwise passes for "reality" in that regime. That she claims that it is only pariah writers—not historians or storytellers—who can do this makes an important insight about the critical analysis of power. Like Foucault, Arendt suggests that a unique character of force in modern societies is that in many instances it is inscribed in the very structures of society. In *The Castle*, for example,

---

19. Hannah Arendt, "Franz Kafka: A Revaluation," *Partisan Review* 11 (Fall 1944): 419.
20. Ibid., 419, 418–419.

Olga tells K. that she bears Frieda no ill will for spreading gossip that ends up ostracizing the Barnabus family from the village, explaining that Frieda acted "not in the least from enmity to us, simply from a sense of duty, which anybody would have felt in the same circumstances."[21] Kafka's villagers enact the power of the castle without its being explicitly exercised over them and without their experiencing it as subjection. Arendt's remarks on Kafka suggest a partial connection to Michel Foucault's analysis of the "micro-physics of power."[22] The Archimedean conception of power as mastery is inadequate to the task of analyzing micro-power, because such power no longer needs an external fulcrum from which to dominate subjects. Consequently, techniques of critical social analysis that are calibrated only to detect force as leverage will overlook many instances where force is being exercised in and through subjects; as long as it does not appear as *leverage*, it will not be recognized as *force*.

It is precisely because power can function coercively without being explicitly exercised as force that its critical analysis cannot proceed from the perspective of either the insider or the outsider but must work at the fringes. It is to visitors who are in a society but not at home there that its "reality" appears to be just a particular set of prevailing conventions and to whom its common sense may plainly be nonsense. Further, visitors who are conscious pariahs, that is, whose audience is not just the dominant society but a community of resisters, may be able to imagine alternatives to its conventions.

Arendt's claim that storytellers, poets, and public intellectuals such as Lessing or Lazare typify the "conscious pariah" suggests a way out of the insider/outsider dichotomy. The problem with this dichotomy is that it leaves no room for critical understanding. The *parvenu* or insider has no interest in critique but assimilates to prevailing standards by accepting as legitimate the challenge to "live up" to them. The pariah, on the other hand, refuses those standards on the grounds that they do not recognize the kinds of achievements by which he or she would like to be known. The problem is that if the pariah is identified in opposition

21. Kafka, *The Castle*, 269.
22. Michel Foucault, *Discipline and Punish*, trans. Alan Sheridan (New York: Vintage Books, 1979), 26.

against the *parvenu* as a lone outsider, then the pariah's claim to be not only different from the dominant community but also superior to it can neither be justified nor acted upon. The contradiction in conceiving the pariah as a lone hero is that the pariah is described simultaneously as an outsider to what passes for common sense and as a critic who possesses a special capacity for judging, which means having a uniquely developed common sense. When the pariah is described as a lone re-sister, this contradiction is unresolvable and the claim to common sense cannot be defended: there can be no thought at all—let alone judg-ment—beyond all common sense. The pariah is no more capable of acting alone than of thinking alone. As in the example of K., the lone pariah dies exhausted.

One conclusion to which Arendt's writings on pariahs point is that no one who claims to be a critic by virtue of being an outsider can be telling the truth. The fact is that to be genuinely outside and isolated is to be unseen and unheard in public and so to be utterly without power. It is simply arrogant for someone who is a recognized critic to defend his or her claim to that perspective on the grounds that he or she is absolutely different and alone. The distinction between pariahs and "conscious pariahs" is that where the former romanticize outsidership, the latter acknowledge that they could neither see nor speak critically and certainly not write without the company of other conscious pariahs. It is to the friendship of other pariahs, not to isolation, that the conscious pariah owes a special capacity for judgment.

In the preceding chapter, I noted a disquieting resemblance between the model of judging that Arendt introduces with the image of the sol-itary poet-philosopher engaging in a representative thinking that is in-different to social factors and the ideal of Archimedean impartiality. I acknowledged that Arendt's reaffirmation of the need for a disciplinary separation between the public and social realms for the purposes of judging reproduces an aspect of liberal humanism that I have said she transforms. In this chapter so far I have used Arendt's writings on Jewish identity to argue that the exemplar of the "conscious pariah" offers a way out of the dichotomy between the abstract universal "outsider" stance of liberal humanism and the blind partisanship that follows from radical skepticism toward the possibility of critical distance. That way out is inhabiting the fringes, which involves neither a lone rebellion against the world in a posture of disdain nor parochial solidarity with one's so-called people. Rather, it is a commitment to resistance enacted in concert with a community of resisters. Arendt's correspondence with her mentor Karl Jaspers continues this debate over the impossibility of resolving basic human problems of existence when they are framed in terms of an opposition between universalism and particularism. In the letters of Jaspers and Arendt, the dilemma of spectatorship and membership comes alive. Jaspers repeatedly cautions Arendt against relinquishing an abstract universalist pespective—which he identifies first with her German heritage and later with Enlightenment philosophy— and Arendt responds by affirming her friendship to Jaspers, which testifies to her "ambiguous connection" to both of these.[23] Through their pariah friendship she accepts her German heritage *in light of* its irreconcilability with the fact that she is also a Jew: it tells a story of visiting that both counters and complements the lectures on judging.

The Arendt-Jaspers Correspondence

The correspondence is a conversation between two thinkers, who, with the rise of the Nazi regime and in its aftermath, cannot simply be at home in the world as German humanists. Their letters bring the abstract question of the relationship between particular identity and principled critique to life. For the Jewish expatriate living in the United States and for the Enlightenment philosopher teaching in Basel, the problem of marginality is sufficient fuel for a nearly life-long engagement in correspondence. This correspondence documents an exemplary pariah friendship. Marginality is a vital point of connection between both of them in their identity as German exiles. But, as Arendt attempts to explain to Jaspers before and after the war, the discontinuity that is a condition of her existence as a *German Jew* is quite different from the alienation he experiences as an exiled German. The question of the possibility of German-Jewish identity is something about which Arendt and

23. This phrase, again, is by Walzer, *Interpretation*, 37.

Jaspers never come to see eye to eye; yet, it is nonetheless at the center of their conversations and their friendship.

The story that this correspondence tells gives dramatic specificity to the terms natality, plurality, and visiting. It is a story of new beginnings for Arendt and Jaspers, who both find a way back into the world after their displacement by the war through each other's company. Many of the letters are about visiting, planning literally for Arendt's many trips to Switzerland, and figuratively exchanging differences and reflecting on that exchange. Jaspers assures Arendt of the importance he attaches to their "testing" of their beliefs against each other: "Now, as you know, when I read you or listen to you, I'm immediately prompted to talk with you, which is to say, argue with you. I always want to put my finger on the forces present in an intellectual product, just as I do with the things that come into my own head. If we try to remain purely objective, we will have trouble getting hold of the 'demons' that get hold of us. . . . I know you enjoy this kind of discussion and are of one mind with me in it" (C, 208). Theirs is not an all-encompassing connection based in a kinship wrought by denying differences; instead, it is a shared space that is opened by the articulation and specific recognition of those differences.

Before the war, their conversations are mediated through their different projects: his book on Max Weber and her lecture on the themes of the *Habilitation* project she proposes on the life of Rahel Varnhagen. Jaspers has reservations about the fact that Arendt uses Varnhagen's life to examine German-Jewish identity, which she constructs as a unique existential problem of homelessness. He questions whether it is philosophically coherent to define as an existential condition a problem that she claims is specific to being Jewish under particular historical circumstances. He warns her that an existential condition "can no longer be taken altogether seriously if it is *grounded* in terms of the fate of the Jews instead of being rooted in itself." She responds that the lecture is an attempt at a preliminary discussion of "fatefulness," which is not, as Jaspers takes it, the same thing as fate but rather a "possibility of existence" that "arises from the very fact of 'foundationlessness' and can occur *only* in a separation from Judaism" (C, 10–11). It appears from this response that she was trying to describe both the experience of not being at home in the world that she takes to be a given condition of being an assimilated Jew and to connect it to a nonfoundationalist way of thinking.[24] Jaspers objects to Arendt's suggestion that the particular and, to him, secondary characteristic of Jewishness could define an existential condition.

If Jaspers questions the validity of Arendt's focusing on the particular situation of assimilated Jews in Berlin to raise questions of philosophical—that is, universal—significance, Arendt, in turn, criticizes Jaspers for presuming that the particular historical phenomenon of the German nation exemplifies the triumph of Enlightenment humanism. Arendt expresses reservations about Jaspers' study of Max Weber for identifying Germany and the German character with the Enlightenment values of scholarship and philosophy. She is particularly bothered by the introduction and the title—"Max Weber: The German Essence in Political Thought, in Scholarship and in Philosophy"—which she tells him put her off by suggesting that these humanist universals are "something like basic qualities of the German character." Positioning herself as a "conscious pariah," she tells him quite forthrightly that the "title and introduction made it difficult for me from the start to comment on the book." She explains that "as a Jew" she can identify with German cultural pride but states "I do not feel myself unquestioningly identical with it. For me, Germany means my mother tongue, philosophy, and literature. I can and must stand by all that." But she adds, "I am obliged to keep my distance . . . when I read Max Weber's wonderful sentence where he says that to put Germany back on her feet he would form an alliance with the devil himself" (6, 16). This letter, written in Berlin on New Year's Day, 1933, when it was clear to Arendt that Germany was making a pact with the devil, is remarkably understated. She is trying, with the utmost tact, to effect the very separation that Jaspers himself would later insist on, between the German nation and German culture and philosophy.

Given that Arendt is so careful to state that she *does* identify herself

24. Dagmar Barnouw perceptively notes that Arendt employs in her response "obfuscating self-defensive academic language" that is "uncharacteristically opaque" and in striking contrast to the honesty with which she voices her disagreements in later letters to Jaspers. Barnouw, *Visible Spaces*, 33.

as a German but that as a Jew this identification can only be partial and somewhat contradictory, it is interesting that Jaspers interprets her subtle distinction as an assertion of separatism, writing, "I find it odd that you as a Jew want to set yourself apart from what is German" (17). He attempts to convince her that given what she accepts of its language and culture, she *is* German and that "all you need add is historical-political destiny, and there is no difference left at all" (18). He also tells her that he wrote the book to instruct "Our nationalistic youth . . . of the demands on themselves that are inherent in being German while at the same time acknowledging their need to feel pride in being German" (17). In effect, he intends Max Weber to stand as an "ethical" counterweight to German militarism. Finally, he assures her that the "destiny" of Germany is not to take Europe by force but to participate as one nation in a unified European community. To achieve this, he asserts that "the devil with whom we will inevitably have to make our pact is the egoistic, bourgeois anxiety of the French; for the empire of what is German, an empire that would have to reach from Holland to Austria, from Scandinavia to Switzerland *is an impossibility* and would still be too small in today's world anyhow" (18; emphasis added). Once again, he wants her to assume what he constructs as an Archimedean spectatorial vantage point in German reason to quiet her fears about German nationalism. She resists again, arguing that there is all the difference in the world between the German language and culture in which she can participate and the manifestly dangerous present course of Germany's historical-political destiny: "I know only too well how late and how fragmentary the Jews' participation in that destiny has been, how much by chance they entered into what was then a foreign history" (18–19). It is only barely ironic that this philosopher would have found it so hard to imagine that German nationalism looked threatening to this Jewish woman in 1933.

This question of the possibility and necessity of taking a spectator's vantage point persists between them even after the war, though on slightly altered terms. After the war, Jaspers shares Arendt's homelessness, because the "historical-political destiny" of Nazi Germany had betrayed the traditions by which he identified himself as a German. For Jaspers, German identity is no longer a vantage point for universal humanism; the war has changed his relationship to that country by its mockery of his vision of its participation in a Europe united in accordance with the values of the Enlightenment. Now his concern is not that Arendt separates herself from what is "German" but from the Enlightenment tradition. He expresses this in his assessment of the completed Varnhagen biography, nearly twenty years after this early conversation. He judges the work to be "unfair to Rahel and the Enlightenment" because Arendt has chosen to tell the story of Rahel's life as a Jew, which is "only the outward guise and only the point of departure" for the "unconditional aspect of Rahel."[25] Just as earlier he had cautioned Arendt against adhering too closely to her particularity, attempting to separate herself as a Jew at the expense of her identity as a German, he now criticizes her for fastening on Rahel the Jew at the expense of Rahel the person and for diminishing her humanity by it. He tells her, "Your book can make one feel that if a person is a Jew he cannot really live his life to the full" (C, 194). The letter concludes with a suggestion that is almost insulting, though Jaspers doesn't mean it to be and there is no hint in Arendt's response that she took offense at it. He remarks that Arendt "wrote this book before Heinrich Blücher came into your life" and suggests that if she were to rewrite it now, "she could reduce Rahel's Jewishness to one element in [her] presentation and let the greatness of her soul stand in the foreground" (195). Jaspers' intimation that Arendt's marriage enables her to "live . . . life to the full" in spite of her Jewishness is not only sexist, it borders on one of the misconceptions Arendt attributes to Rahel, the belief "that Judaism was an unfortunate personal quality" that could be overcome by marriage (RV, 220).

Arendt resists Jaspers' attempt to rewrite Rahel's story in universalist terms, telling him frankly that "The picture of Rahel that you put up against mine is in all its essential features the one drawn by Varnhagen. You know what I think of Varnhagen" (C, 198). She reaffirms her commitment to the theme that was most disturbing to him—that one cannot live life to the full as a Jew—claiming that it "is of course a central point" that she would still make. She writes, "I still believe today that

25. C, 195, 194. As Barnouw notes, this response makes "a neo-Platonic split between the real, true, essential Rahel and her Jewish 'Kleid,' the dress, the surface of her existence" (61).

under the conditions of social assimilation and political emancipation the Jews could not 'live' " (198). Contrary to Jaspers' romanticizing humanism, Arendt's marriage to Blücher did nothing to erase for her either the fact of her Jewish identity or her sense that Jewishness is not simply an "unfortunate" accident attached to a more fundamental human essence.[26] But she is unwilling to undertake any dramatic restructuring of the book because, she tells Jaspers, questions of German Zionism, Jewish assimilation, and its relation to Enlightenment humanism are "no longer important to me" (201). The only change she would make if she retold Rahel's story from her present position—not as a Jewish woman happily married to Heinrich Blücher but as the leading theorist of totalitarianism—would be to make it clear that the kind of social discrimination that Rahel confronted had "hardly anything to do" with the unprecedented and distinctly political phenomenon of totalitarianism (197).

Arendt's letter to Jaspers on his seventieth birthday makes an eloquent closing statement to this long conversation about the relationship between universality, particular identity, and critical understanding. In it, Arendt describes herself as a marginal by virtue of her relationship with Jaspers, which gives her a connection to Germany that she would not want to eradicate. She writes:

> I want to thank you for the early years in Heidelberg when you were my teacher, the only one I have ever been able to recognize as such; and for the happiness and relief I found in seeing that one can be educated in freedom. I have never forgotten since then that the world and Germany, whatever else they may be, are the world in which you live and the country that produced you. (206)

The theme that Arendt sustains throughout this discussion with Jaspers is that she conceives of her identity as partial and discontinuous, no

---

26. Writing to Jaspers in 1949 about her marriage to Blücher, Arendt asserted: "Thanks to my husband, I have learned to think politically and see historically; and . . . I have refused to abandon the Jewish question as the focal point of my historical and political thinking" (C, 31).

matter how often he presses her to resolve the parts into an integrated whole. In this letter to Jaspers, Arendt acknowledges their connection *as Germans*. She neither distances herself from her German identity, nor attempts to resolve it by some transcendental synthesis. Rather, acknowledging that she is German through her friendship to Jaspers permits her to *recognize* her German-ness without *reconciling* it with the fact that she is also Jewish.

This letter both embraces and extends the conception of the multiple and contradictory self that contemporary critics of humanism offer as resistance to the integrated autonomous individual. The correspondence dramatizes this debate in that Arendt resists Jaspers' attempts to get her to resolve the contradiction she perceives between participating in both German and Jewish histories and traditions. She affirms that it is precisely the discontinuities of her own multiple identities that make her a marginal and justify her claim to critical understanding. But she carries this connection between multiplicity and criticism forward by arguing that it is her friendship with Jaspers that gives these divergent and partial identities a space in which to visit and test each other. It is not fragmentation per se but disputation that accounts for the possibility of critical understanding. The visits by which Arendt and Jaspers sustain their pariah friendship become a literal model of the conception of enlarged thinking that Arendt describes in her lectures on Kant as "training the imagination to go visiting."

So far I have used the letters to tell the story of Arendt's separation from Germany, Jaspers, and the framework of Enlightenment philosophy by focusing on her commitment to making herself understood in distinction from this tradition. But separation stories are not only about difference but also about connection. I want now to explore the intersection of visiting and pariah friendship. The visiting theme is both literally and metaphorically a topic of Arendt's and Jaspers' conversations. In many of the early letters Arendt reports on her attempts to secure financing for trips to see Karl and Gertrude Jaspers in Basel, negotiates with them the timing of her visits, and verifies the arrival of the many packages of food she sent them after the war—a very practical way in which she visited them with her concerns for their health and safety.

Further, visiting, in the metaphorical sense of opening a space in the mind, is a connecting thread throughout their correspondence.

Just how deeply personal is the conception of judgment that Arendt communicates so imperfectly in her public writings becomes clear from her correspondence with Jaspers. In that first eloquent letter she writes after the war, Arendt explains that she has held him with her in conversation in her mind throughout her exile: "What I want to tell you after not being able to write for more than twelve years now is this. I may have thought or done some things in those years that will put you off, but there is hardly anything I've done that I didn't do without thinking how I would tell you about it or justify it to you" (23). The connection she describes here is premised on the articulation of difference in friendship. Arendt does not claim to have acted with the goal of pleasing Jaspers, which would be a denial of difference, or to rebel against him, which would be a pose. Rather, she describes making herself accountable to him by testing her actions against the response she imagined he would make.

Jaspers' immediate answer to this letter is to invite Arendt to return home to Germany—figuratively—by writing an essay for *Die Wandlung*.[27] Although, of course, he wants her to write what she pleases, he suggests that she might perhaps "write something on what truly unites us across all the barriers between us—and by us I mean Americans and Europeans, including Germans?" (C, 26). Given that they had disagreed before the war on precisely this question of the relationship between the particular "barriers" that separate people and the putative universal traditions that unite them, this suggestion seems quite odd. Once again, Jaspers wants her to adopt the perspective of Kant's world-citizen, and once again, Arendt responds by reminding him that she is a Jew. Why would Jaspers think she would find this kind of thinking more acceptable after World War II than she had before it when the Nazi regime had proved so grotesquely the importance of her particular identity as a Jew? Even though in the body of this letter Jaspers asks for a rather tra-

---

27. This was a monthly magazine edited by Dolf Sternberger and published in Heidelberg in 1945–49. Jaspers was on the editorial board. Lotte Kohler and Hans Saner, "Notes," C, 694.

ditional humanist statement of universality, in the postscript he recognizes Arendt's comment about their differences. He proclaims his own willingness to "visit" Arendt, not with a literal trip but by listening to her account of the thoughts or actions that she felt would have put him off. His response quite explicitly opens the space in-between that Arendt describes in the judgment writings. In a postscript he tells her: "You wrote: 'I may have thought or done some things in those years that will put you off. . . . I thank you for trusting me. . . . How happy I would be to hear these "things that will put me off," to be together with you and respond to them. —I know in advance that they would make me re-examine my views and—whatever else they may be—would deepen my respect for you" (26). However obvious or ordinary his words may seem, it is significant that he attempts neither to make light of their differences nor to dismiss them. He does not promise to agree with her but to listen to her with an openness to changing his own position. In effect, he offers to use her stories to stand hypothetically as himself in her position, imagining how he might think differently if it were so.

Arendt takes him up on this promise in her response to his request. Entering into the space he opened, she reminds him that they disagree on these questions of identity and universality, "Do you remember our last talks together in Berlin, in 1933? I did not find some of your arguments convincing, but on a human and personal level you were so utterly convincing that for many years I was, so to speak, more sure of you than I was of myself" (28). If Jaspers' request was reminiscent of the position he argued in their early exchanges about the Varnhagen and Weber projects, Arendt's answer also seems to pick up that conversation where they left off. She tells him that it is "not an easy thing for me to contribute to a German journal" and warns him that it may not be an easy thing for him to publish what she would produce:

> It seems to me that none of us can return (and writing is surely a form of return) merely because people again seem prepared to recognize Jews as Germans or something else. We can re-. turn only if we are welcome as Jews. That would mean that I would gladly write something if I can write as a Jew on some aspect of the Jewish question. And quite apart from other

problems—objections you might raise to my text, for instance—I don't know if you would be able to print something
of that nature under the present difficult circumstances. (31–
32)

As before the war, Arendt communicates a sense of connection, affirming that she does not want to remain in exile from Germany or Europe.
Yet, she also takes care to assert her particular Jewish identity against
the generality of the categories Jaspers proposes and to make its recognition a condition of her return.

Jaspers' response to this letter is most interesting for his recognition
of Arendt's claim to speak and write as a Jew. He accepts for publication
the manuscript she sent him and honors her request that it be accompanied by a note stating that her "point of view is entirely that of a
Jew." His assessment of the reason for and importance of such a note
is consistent with Arendt's "visiting," although of course Jaspers does
not identify it as such. With respect to including the note he explains:
"The German reader will show how he reacts. For *us* [the editors], however, this is not a 'political' or 'tactical' move. The point has to be made
with absolute certainty and as a matter of course."[28] In effect, Jaspers
constructs the publication of Arendt's article in Germany as an invitation
to the "German reader" to visit with the exiled Jew. He has understood
Arendt's claim that she cannot return to Germany except as a Jew and
that she must write about the possibility of Jewish-German understanding from this position in the world, not from a transcendent standpoint.

This exchange is a perfect illustration of the difference that I have
argued exists between the Arendtian and Kantian conceptions of common sense. It is not by imputing her tastes to Jaspers or by securing his
assent to them that Arendt makes herself at home again in the world.
Rather, it is the "testing" of her thinking against someone who respects
her that gives her a place from which to judge (LKPP, 42). As she tells
him, his criticisms are a "great delight" because "when you debate me

---

28. C, 35. The manuscript she sent was "Organisierte Schuld," which was published in the
United States as "Organized Guilt and Universal Responsibility," *Jewish Frontier* (January 1945): 19–23.

like this, coming from outside, as it were, it seems as if I had solid ground under my feet, as if I were back in the world again" (C, 55). Not empathy or agreement, but critical engagement over "difficult" questions gives her a means by which to locate herself in the world.

The clarity of expression in this private communication to Jaspers surpasses almost any of her public attempts to explain the "anticipated communication" that she describes as requisite to judging. It seems to me in keeping with her claim that judgment is "connected with particulars" that I find greater insight into its practice in the correspondence than in the incomplete and abstract third volume of *Life of the Mind* (LKPP, 44). The letters are an account of judgment in particular through the story of her friendship with Jaspers. This friendship may be one of those stories Arendt describes as containing "as in a nutshell" an experience that she attempted to translate into the more abstract language of theory with the metaphor of training the imagination to go visiting.

Visiting does not simply recapitulate Enlightenment humanism. As is evident from her interpretation of the predicament of Kafka's K., Arendt took humanism to confront its "others" with the paradox of assimilation—extending an invitation to them *as humans* to enter an abstract universal community but barring their way *as Jews*. By contrast, visiting meets differences as a storyteller might, seeking to render them with ever more precision and specificity. Like other contemporary theorists, Arendt argues that it is not the rational detachment of humanism but discontinuity that makes critical judgment possible. In turn, she situates discontinuity in a richly detailed historical and political context by her discussions of Heine, Kafka, Herzl, and others. These portraits lend historical specificity to the conscious pariah, the critic who occupies a position of ambiguous connection to the people or society he or she is called upon to judge.

The correspondence dramatizes visiting and ties it together with the questions of identity and political judgment that are a pervasive theme in Arendt's work. Against Jaspers' wish to assert the primacy of abstract humanist ideals over particular identity, Arendt affirms the fact that she is a Jew. Yet, together with that, she affirms that she is a German, a discontinuous aspect of her identity to which her friendship with Jaspers is proof. The pariah perspective that Arendt defends in her theoretical work, describes in her literary writings, and assumes in her friendship with Jaspers consists in speaking out of the contradiction among these aspects of her historical position. Their friendship provides one space in which she can bring these into conversation with each other.

7 Beyond the Civic Public: Partisanship for the World

▌█

Hannah Arendt once remarked that living in the "dark times" after the Holocaust had "shattered" the "pillars" of Western religious and secular truths was like "standing in the midst of a veritable rubble heap." She regarded this condition as both a political crisis and a possible new beginning. It was a crisis because political communities depend on such pillars to secure temporal laws in the timeless principles of morality, thereby according them a permanence beyond their limited historical ascendancy. But it was also a new beginning because it held out the promise of "a new kind of thinking that needs no pillars and props, no standards and traditions to move freely without crutches over unfamiliar terrain" (MDT, 10). Arendt's rubble heap is one more metaphor for the fragmentation of an age in which it is no longer possible to affirm a relationship between law and morality by appealing to divine authorship or natural right. That these pillars lay in rubble necessitates that human beings identify themselves as members of communities and justify the principles and practices of those communities without reference to an independent normative framework.

What to do with this rubble heap is a central point of contention for neohumanist critics of modernity and poststructuralist critics of humanism. The neohumanist approaches the pile with the caution of an archaeologist who believes that if she works carefully and scientifically, she can retrieve enough of the pieces to reconstruct the pillars and thereby restore the public space. Seyla Benhabib, for example, characterizes the task of contemporary critical theory as one of reforming the "project of modernity" from within its legacy of "moral and political universalism, committed to the now seemingly 'old-fashioned' and suspect ideals of universal respect for each person *in virtue of their humanity*," and the various democratic ideals that follow from this first premise.[1]

Poststructuralist critics of humanism argue that such caution and reverence are not just unwarranted but undesirable because emancipatory promise resides not in moral universalism but in fragmentation and discontinuity. Because no attempt to reestablish a public space can be other than an exercise of power, including some and excluding others, the ideal of publicity must cede to sheer discursive plurality. The task of critical theory is still to open up political spaces, not by means of mutual understanding but by taking any decision that purports to effect a consensual settlement and focusing attention on what it displaces. To the neohumanist, the poststructuralist is about as welcome on the rubble pile as an ill-mannered tourist at an archaeological site, rummaging through the ruins for an eye-catching fragment that would make an arresting conversation piece.

There are problems with both positions. The poststructuralist affirmation of discursive plurality threatens a breakdown of communication and fragmentation of public space. How is adjudication possible where we find a diversity of opinion *together with* diverse forms of communication? Absent some neutral criterion or common standard in accordance with which each of the speakers in a conversation can defend his or her preferred alternative, how can any political decision be public, that is, reasoned and nonarbitrary? The sheer celebration of differences, without regard to the social inequalities by which they are often conditioned, is little more than liberal pluralism. Yet, to adjudicate political conflicts in accordance with purportedly neutral ideals—the general interest or the better argument, for example—is to reduce a diversity of both positions and voices to a standard denominator and thereby to compromise plurality.

I have argued that Hannah Arendt makes a distinctive contribution

---

1. Seyla Benhabib, *Situating the Self: Gender, Community, and Postmodernism in Contemporary Ethics* (New York: Routledge, 1992), 2; emphasis added.

to this debate by virtue of the tension she sustains between plurality and publicity. She takes up a provocative position on the rubble heap because she is at once a neohumanist who takes herself to be engaged in a political project initiated by Immanuel Kant and a critic of humanism who rejects practical reason as a model for political rationality. The projects of the two most prominent neohumanist critics of modernity, John Rawls and Jürgen Habermas, begin with an attempt to politicize Kantian practical reason by reconstructing it through the hypotheticals of the original position and the ideal speech situation, respectively.[2] Where Rawls posits the veil of ignorance as a device to ensure generalizability, Habermas argues that the conditions of generality are implicit in the very structures of communication, in the possibility of reaching consensus by rational argument. In contrast to the original position, in which rational agreement need not entail direct speech, Habermasian communicative ethics aims to specify procedures of public debate by which one could legitimately claim to have reached an intersubjective consensus on general norms.[3]

By contrast, Hannah Arendt argues that it is a mistake to look to the *Critique of Practical Reason* for a model of generalizable reasoning that can serve the needs of public life, because it is not a political philosophy but a moral philosophy. As I have argued, the difficulty she identifies is that the categorical imperative is a cognitive device that postulates duty as a moral absolute and so "runs counter to [the] fundamental relativity" (MDT, 27) of the public realm. Arendt is not dismissing either morality or the possibility of a principled politics. Rather, she is making a distinction between moral imperatives and political principles. Moral imperatives imposed on politics close off the "interspaces between men" that are conditions of the possibility of open disagreement in that realm (31).

Even if Arendt conceded the success of Rawls's and Habermas's at-

---

2. Rawls suggests "that we think of the original position as the point of view from which noumenal selves see the world." John Rawls, *A Theory of Justice* (Cambridge: Harvard University Press, 1971), 255. David M. Rasmussen characterizes communicative ethics as an attempt "to reconstruct Kant's 'Categorical Imperative' as an intersubjectively valid norm." In *Reading Habermas* (Cambridge: Basil Blackwell, 1990), 60, n. 18.

3. Jürgen Habermas, *The Philosophical Discourse of Modernity*, trans. Frederick G. Lawrence (Cambridge: MIT Press, 1990), chap. 11.

tempts to reconstruct practical reason in political (i.e., humane) terms, she would still reject as utopian the attempt to restore the pillars of public order on the premise of the rational or reasonable individual that both these theories presuppose. In her writings on the Holocaust, Arendt makes it clear that the fundamental premises of humanism, the norms of respect and reciprocity, are no longer available because totalitarian domination committed a crime against the very notion of humanity by which they are secured. That crime was to reveal that human rationality is not a faculty or property that is somehow essentially *in* all human beings and constitutive of human individuality but a possibility that is contingent on the legal and social instantiations of plurality and publicity. Totalitarian domination made those conditions visible by systematically dismantling them, through arbitrary arrest, deportation, and institutionalized torture.[4] In other words, what totalitarianism accomplished was to shatter the single most important "pillar" of Western humanism: the reasonable individual. The problem is not just to guarantee value pluralism within a context of shared assumptions about what it means to be reasonable but also to make communication possible once that context has been irreparably ruptured.

Arendt takes it as her task not to reconstruct moral and political universalism but to recover a fragment of that tradition that was unappreciated in its time and use it to strike up a new conversation. This fragment is the understanding of taste in Kant's *Critique of Judgement* that, according to Arendt, details a model of rationality that is appropriate to the conditions of political action. As I have noted, it is common to interpret Arendt's turn to the *Critique of Judgement* as a retreat from a concern for public life into the "embrace" of Kantian rationalism.[5] By failing to take seriously the significance of Arendt's turn to taste as her model of political rationality, this interpretation misses the subtlety of Arendt's neo-humanist critique of humanism. It also obscures what is most provocative about Arendt's position in contemporary critical debates, which is that she can be allied neither with the neo-humanist

---

4. As I argued in Chapter 4, the first of these destroys responsibility, the next destroys identity, and the last reduces action to behavior.
5. Benjamin R. Barber, *The Conquest of Politics* (Princeton: Princeton University Press, 1988), 198. See also Ronald Beiner, "Interpretive Essay," in LKPP, 89–156.

project to reconstruct moral and political universalism nor with the poststructuralist assertion that the relationship between law and reason is always arbitrary.

Even though Arendt rejects Kantian practical reason as a model of political rationality, she does not regard politics as an agonistic struggle for power whose outcomes are ethically arbitrary. On the contrary, she proposes the public or "representative" (BPF, 241) thinking of Kant's taste, which she characterizes as training "one's imagination to go visiting" (LKPP, 43), as a model of rationality that does not violate human plurality. Visiting involves imagining the story of an event from a plurality of contesting positions not to reconcile them in a general statement of principle but to arrive at a public interpretation of the event's meaning. Such a judgment is only provisional, and defending it does not involve proving it is right.

This practice shares with poststructuralism a commitment to disputation. It stops short of radical skepticism, however, in that Arendt believes that a kind of mutual understanding is possible even in light of differences. There is a similarity to the project of communicative ethics as Seyla Benhabib describes it: an attempt not primarily to reach consensus on a general interest but to specify by reasoned argument a "suppressed generalizable interest by which to uncover the under-representation, the exclusion and silencing of *certain kinds* of interests."[6] But where Benhabib, like Habermas, relies on the faculty of practical reason to generate a new "yardstick" for politics, Arendt abandons the project to define a general interest as utopian. She turns to Kant's *Critique of Judgement* for a model of public reasonableness that does not rely on yardsticks.[7] I suggest that if in Benhabib's account the "sup-

---

6. Benhabib, *Situating the Self*, 48.
7. Seyla Benhabib also attaches importance to Arendt's reading of Kant's *Critique of Judgement* as a way to press communicative ethics toward a greater recognition of plurality. For Benhabib, however, Arendt's "representative thinking" is an aspect of practical reason; it is the means by which to contextualize general moral principles. She criticizes Arendt for claiming that the faculty of judgment is "specifically political rather than moral," attributing this error to Arendt's "rather narrow conception of the moral domain." See "Judgment and the Moral Foundations of Politics in Hannah Arendt's Thought," in ibid., 133. By contrast, I argue that Arendt's separation of the political and the moral, and her attempt to account for the possibility of contextual political thinking

pressed generalizable interest" is what makes public justification possible, in Arendt's account storytelling serves this function.

Arendt's is no traditional account of storytelling. It does not function to illustrate how "we" do things, to insulate traditional customs from critical scrutiny, or to enforce homogeneity. Rather, its purpose is to activate the visiting imagination and foster publicity in Arendt's distinctive sense of a decision that is tested against a plurality of divergent perspectives that it purports neither to transcend nor to reconcile. It is the distinctiveness of this conception of publicity that I attempt to capture within the paradox of "situated impartiality."

I suggest this paradox as a way out of the twofold problem of experiential critical understanding: to find a way to speak critically from experience without the dogmatic parochialism that asserts *my* experience as an unquestionable ground of *my* authority, and to find a way to hold various claims to experience open to question without the reluctant skepticism that postpones decision making to the point where it becomes politically paralyzing. Resolving this problem means accounting for the possibility of judgment without invoking a critical standpoint that is secured either by affirming abstract, timeless values or by asserting an affiliation with a particular oppressed group. I have argued that the conception of critical understanding implicit in Hannah Arendt's offhand remarks about storytelling offers a way out of the stalemate between dogmatic claims to a critical standpoint and radical skepticism.

To account for the possibility of critical understanding from experience, storytelling must answer a question posed by Iris Young: "How is it possible for norms to be both socially based and measures of society?"[8] In other words, what makes "visiting" critical? Simply affirming that questions of political judgment generate a plurality of competing interpretations is not enough. In order to act in concert, those who assert these various interpretations must have some way to adjudicate among them that does not reduce their common "*inter-est*" to a single common denominator. Visiting is a suggestive metaphor for Kant's "enlarged

---

in the absence of agreement about general moral principles, is the innovative alternative that Arendt poses to neohumanist accounts of practical reason.

8. Iris Young, *Justice and the Politics of Difference* (Princeton: Princeton University Press, 1990), 5.

mentality," but Arendt never quite specifies what it is that makes this practice impartial. I have introduced the paradox "situated impartiality" to characterize it as an alternative to the typical abstract model of impartial adjudication, but I have neither justified its use nor explained what a situated impartial process of adjudication would entail.

This problem takes me out of Arendt's texts to engage works of contemporary democratic and feminist political theory. Consequently, I shift from *explicating* Arendt's ideas in light of current problems to pursuing what Michael Oakeshott would call the "intimations" of her thought.[9] These I take to involve pressing a concept such as visiting beyond the limits of the positions she actually took.

Situated impartiality is a model of detachment for political actors who must adjudicate conflict from within the public realm, no matter how pluralist and conflictual. It is, then, a model for judging without appealing to either moral or strategic imperatives. As such, it is a nonfoundationalist conception of validity that involves a shift from grounding decisions (by an appeal to truth, right, or tradition) to defending them publicly. Most important, the criterion for adequate public defense of a decision need not be that the defense satisfies a general interest—either suppressed or consensually secured. Rather, I suggest a procedural model, whereby publicity entails locating a decision *in its context of dispute* by recording dissenting positions as part of the decision. That is to say, dissenting perspectives would be positioned in the figurative public space of a particular conflict by thinking through alternative ways of diagnosing a situation, formulating the problem, and devising its solution. The point of this hypothetical exercise is to ensure that public decisions are inclusive and representative but to do it in a way that differs from the way inclusivity is typically achieved.

When political or administrative decision-making processes are inclusive, they usually take inclusivity to involve securing participation by representatives from each group whose interests can be said to be relevant to a particular decision. In a question about land use, for example, the decision-making body will include state and local government officials, technical experts, advocates for the proposed land use, and citizens

9. Michael Oakeshott, *Rationalism in Politics* (1962; New York: Methuen, 1981), 125.

who are members of the surrounding community. The decision-making process will involve deliberation within this body in accordance with established criteria, such as a statewide plan for economic growth or hazardous waste management, as well as one or more hearings or meetings in affected communities so that those not empowered to make the decision can nonetheless have a voice in deliberations. This model assumes that inclusivity is satisfied as long as the various parties to a decision are accorded a "hearing." As such, it centers debate on the question of whether a particular solution should be ratified or blocked, leaving the problem or situation at hand to be defined *implicitly* by the proposed solution.[10]

In this model of inclusivity, what goes without saying or being heard is what Hannah Arendt would call the "innumerable perspectives and aspects" on which "the reality of the public realm relies" (HC, 57). In other words, this model of representation does not practice "representative thinking": decentering a debate from the feasibility and efficacy of a particular solution to "visit" the plurality of locations from which the situation itself might be differently interpreted (BPF, 241). If the various participants to the debate are to take action, however, they must have some way of adjudicating among these perspectives. If that action is to be public, the process of adjudication would have to come to a decision *without* reducing the plurality of perspectives to a "common measurement or denominator" (HC, 57). This would involve resisting the conciliatory move to pass off any settlement as the expression of an impartial general principle. Publicity, as I define it, entails *concluding* a decision without *resolving* it. It involves making explicit both whom a particular interpretive framework excludes and whom it includes and how a shift

---

10. For example, as Robert W. Lake and I have argued, the fact that hazardous waste management legislation provides for participation in facility *siting* decisions frames the waste management problem "as a *locational* problem for the state rather than a *production* problem for industry." The construction of waste management as a siting problem precludes an interrogation of basic assumptions such as (1) products that generate hazardous wastes will continue to be produced; (2) waste is an inevitable outcome of their production; (3) it is up to the state, not industry, to assume responsibility for the undesirable effects of industrial production. See R. W. Lake and L. Disch, "Structural Constraints and Pluralist Contradictions in Hazardous Waste Regulation," *Environment and Planning–A*, 24 (1992): 671, 678–679.

in interpretive criteria might reconfigure the boundaries. Inclusivity is defined not just as "hearing" the dissent but as recording it as part of the decision, so that it can be cited as a precedent for future dissent.

On this account, the publicity of a decision turns on securing the participation of a plurality of groups and on inscribing plurality into the final record of a decision. Just what it would mean, in practice, to record a decision in a manner consistent with publicity would vary according to context. The judicial opinion is one model, specific to a relatively unrepresentative institution. Plurality is inscribed in court decisions by the fact that in the case of a close or contentious vote, justices can write concurring and dissenting opinions in which they put forward rival *interpretations* of a case. Plurality consists both in the diversity of opinions and in the fact that the arguments of each justice are accorded respect, regardless of whether he or she was in the majority or the minority. A dissenting opinion is not dismissed as wrong simply because it did not prevail in a particular instance: it can be cited as precedent for future challenges to the decision. This respect for the decision-makers, manifest in the treatment of any decision as a precedent for future affirmation of the status quo and for future opposition, is crucial to inscribing plurality into the final record of a decision.

A 1993 Supreme Court decision illustrates how court opinions can be said to be public. *Shaw v. Reno*, the particular case I discuss, is also interesting because the conflict among the justices can be described (if read with attention to epistemology as well as to doctrine) as a conflict about impartiality. The doctrinal issue at stake was whether an oddly-shaped legislative district constituted racial gerrymandering.[11] The rival styles of ar-

---

11. 61 LW 4818 (1993). The plan, which was challenged by five white voters, facilitated the election of black representatives to the Congress "for the first time since Reconstruction" (61 LW at 4831). The Court ruled it unconstitutional on the grounds that the redistricting was "so extremely irregular on its face that it rationally can be viewed only as an effort to segregate the races for purposes of voting, without regard for traditional districting principles and without sufficiently compelling justification." The majority chose to categorize the reapportionment plan as a racial classification; as such, it fell within the purview of the Equal Protection Clause of the Fourteenth Amendment where it would be presumed unconstitutional unless the state could show a "compelling interest" that could not be met without invoking race (61 LW at 4822 & 4825).

gument that the justices used to interpret the districting plan dramatize
some of the differences between abstract and situated impartial reasoning.

The district was proposed as part of a North Carolina reapportionment plan in response to a constitutional mandate to enhance blacks'
voting power in that state. As such, the plan posed what Martha Minow
calls a "dilemma of difference." A question of justice arose because race
difference had been underscored in order, paradoxically, to foster the
eradication of inequities that originated in that very difference. Such
dilemmas emerge because although a focus on differences such as race,
ethnicity, or gender may further stigmatize, "refusing to acknowledge
these differences may make them continue to matter in a world constructed with some groups, but not others, in mind. The problems of
inequality can be exacerbated both by treating members of minority
groups the same as members of the majority and by treating the two
groups differently."[12] With her attention to how differences play out in
a particular public context, Minow's dilemmas call, in my terms, for
situated impartial reasoning. The majority in *Shaw v. Reno* chose to
overlook the complexities of such dilemmas and to construct the opinion
around the classic liberal aspiration toward a justice that is "color-
blind." Justice O'Connor asserted that race-conscious districting should
be considered an invidious "racial classification" that "reinforce[s] the
belief, held by too many for too much of our history, that individuals
should be *judged* by the color of their skin." Further, she argued that
race-conscious districting, whether to disenfranchise blacks or to em-
power them, is an unqualified harm that "may balkanize us into
competing racial factions; it threatens to carry us further from the goal
of a political system in which race no longer matters—a goal that the
Fourteenth and Fifteenth Amendments embody, and to which the nation
continues to aspire."[13] This is an abstract impartial argument that assumes that all the contestants to the North Carolina dispute are equal
and that, consequently, racially neutral districting will foster equality
between the races.

12. Martha Minow, *Making All the Difference* (Ithaca: Cornell University Press, 1990), 20.
13. 61 LW at 4822, 4836; emphasis added, 4826.

Where the majority identified justice with color-blindness, the dissenters asserted that blacks are "an identifiable group of voters" in North Carolina and, further, that they are disadvantaged by an "unequal distribution of electoral power" in that state. The dissenters assumed that if race is a determining factor for inequalities with respect to electoral power, then impartiality necessarily consists in taking historical and present race-based power differences into account.[14] Exemplifying situated impartiality, Justice Souter wrote that, "electoral districting calls for decisions that nearly always require some consideration of race for legitimate reasons *where there is a racially mixed population.*"[15] Similarly, Justice Stevens wrote:

> The duty to govern impartially is abused when a group with power over the electoral process defines electoral boundaries solely to enhance its own political strength at the expense of any weaker group. That duty, however, is not violated when the majority acts to facilitate the election of a member of a group that *lacks such power* because it remains underrepresented in the state legislature—whether that group is defined by political affiliation, by common economic interests, or by religious, ethnic, or racial characteristics.[16]

In contrast to O'Connor's abstract appeal to the principle of color-blindness in a context where differences of color *do* make a difference, the arguments of Souter and Stevens evidence situated impartial thinking in two ways. They situate the principles of rights and equality in the

---

14. 61 LW at 4832. The doctrinal dispute between the majority and the dissent turned on the question of whether the case presented a cognizable claim under the Fourteenth Amendment. The dissenters' concern was to refute the majority's application of the Fourteenth Amendment to this case by discrediting the underlying assumption that taking account of race for the purpose of districting is equivalent to "judging" individuals by the color of their skin. Districting is distinct from other instances of classification because, in a heterogeneous society, the end goal of equitable representation makes it appropriate and necessary to take into account group characteristics (ethnicity, religion, race) that would be unconstitutional in other policymaking contexts.
15. 61 LW at 4832; emphasis added.
16. 61 LW at 4832; emphasis added.

context of existing power relations. They also make explicit the consequences their arguments will have for perpetuating or for transforming existing racially patterned inequities in the distribution of electoral power.

By raising the judicial opinion as an example of publicity and by examing this particular decision, I do not mean to recommend the Court as a public institution in the sense I have in mind. The Supreme Court is an appointed body whose claim to legitimacy rests on a pretense to be above the conflict of partisan interests. Further, the core idea of publicity, modeled after Arendt's conception of judgment, is visiting. The Supreme Court is an institution that exercises tight control over the "visitors" it will receive and also discredits the practice of visiting in its claim to nonpartisanship. I have used the Court only to suggest *some* ways in which the principle of situated impartiality might inform a public decision-making process.

I have argued so far that situated impartiality informs publicity in two ways. It prescribes disputation as the way to arrive at a decision, and it requires that any decision be justified not as a resolution of conflict but as a position in a specific political context. At the moment of concluding a decision, then, it would be necessary to provide a hearing for and a record of the positions the decision affirms and also of those that it "remainders."[17] Such a record would not just tally dissenters but would also give an account of how they diagnosed the situation and formulated the problem differently. Further, in transcribing such a record, it would be important to hold open for emendation not just the opposing positions that are attributed to those who dissent from it but also the as-

17. This term is from Bernard Williams, cited in Bonnie Honig, *Political Theory and the Displacement of Politics* (Ithaca: Cornell University Press, 1993). To "remainder" someone is to assert a purportedly general principle or policy that generates rogues, misfits, deviants, and criminals by its disingenuous neutrality. Honig argues that it is a propensity of liberal democracies to "dissolve" their remainders, making them seem accidental to a system rather than admitting they are necessary to it and produced by it (127). She calls for a politics that uses its "remainders" to proliferate spaces of resistance against its authority. "Remaindering" calls to mind the practice whereby booksellers put their mark-downs on a sale table, making the fact of their devaluation graphically evident. This is part of what I have in mind in requiring that a decision be located in its context of dispute; in Honig's terms, situated impartiality is one way for a group or a system to get its remainders on the table.

senting positions that are attributed to its supporters. The purpose of this second requirement is to check claims to a false mandate. Locating a decision in its context of dispute limits its power in two ways. It ensures that the majority does not discredit dissenters by reconstructing their opposition for polemical purposes, and it ensures as well that the majority cannot assume a self-congratulatory pose that imputes unanimity to its allies. The record, then, is an account of how they reasoned, not just a statement of what they decided to do.

To locate a decision in its context of dispute by committing to record the arguments of both supporters and opponents is to institutionalize openness by providing for the fullest possible expression of dissent *after* a decision is taken. This seems a matter of course, but, as Benjamin Barber has argued, liberal pluralism typically provides institutional mechanisms for citizens' dissent prior to decision making and tends to silence it afterward. According to Barber, electoral politics, because it limits the participation of the average citizen to voting, makes it "impossible for losers and dissenters to voice their postelectoral regrets *in a public place where it will be heard*." Even the more active citizens who participate in policymaking through lobby groups are constrained by the "rational choice" presumption "that [dissenting] views should be aired only before the decision is made and that such self-expression has no rational function afterwards."[18] The need for compromise in a liberal democracy also works to silence dissent, as proponents of the most radical change are eliminated over the process of coalition-building so as not to endanger its broad base of support.[19] Barber argues for institu-

---

18. Benjamin R. Barber, *Strong Democracy: Participatory Politics for a New Age* (Berkeley: University of California Press, 1984), 192; emphasis added, 193.

19. For example, Alexander Cockburn has recently argued that the 1993 Clinton administration policy on logging in old-growth forests incorporated the resistance of environmental advocacy groups into a compromise that is nothing less than a sellout of their position. The policy permits 40 percent of old-growth timber to be cut down and makes no guarantees to preserve the remaining 60 percent. In spite of this, the policy has been touted by the administration as a victory for the environment and proof of the radical environmental advocacy of Bruce Babbitt, Secretary of the Interior. Cockburn characterizes the decision-making process, its packaging as a victory for these groups, and their capitulation as "the classic posture of liberalism before power: exaggeration of the enemy's strength, belittling of one's own, preference for compromise

tional mechanisms for expressing and recording dissent after the fact, "not to change the decision this time, for it has been taken, but to bear witness to another point of view (and thereby to keep the issue on the public agenda)."[20] Leaving a record of both dispute and consensus opens historical justification as a strategy for reformers as well as traditionalists. It is one way to take the practice of visiting out of the imaginary space of the theorist's mind and move it into the public space of democratic institutions.

Publicity, as I describe it, conforms to many of the assumptions of liberal pluralism. Like pluralism, it is a procedural standard that defines fairness in terms of the inclusivity and heterogeneity of a decision-making process. But as critics of the pluralist model have argued, because interest group competition is the mechanism through which fair decision making is institutionalized, there is no "public" in pluralism. Further, the vast disparities of informational and financial resources that prevail in this society make interest group competition neither inclusive nor heterogeneous; rather, some groups are systematically blocked from mobilizing and participating in decisions that affect them. To be public in the sense I describe, liberal pluralism would have to introduce substantive democratic reforms.[21]

---

rather than the protracted anxiety of struggle and possible defeat." See "Beat the Devil," *The Nation*, August 23/30 (1993), 199.

20. Barber, *Strong Democracy*, 192.

21. One way would be to provide resources for mobilizing and empowering a diverse range of relevant publics. There are instances in liberal pluralism where this need is recognized. In hazardous waste siting statutes, for example, there is a gesture toward publicity in the fact that many states provide funds for a local community group to hire an independent consultant to assess the need for a proposed facility and the feasibility of the proposed site, and to prepare an alternate environmental impact statement. The funding makes it possible for local interest groups to mobilize and to contest a siting decision from a position of power that is based in rival technical knowledge. Without this power, public participation in a siting process can be little more than symbolic. Siting hardly meets the standard of public decision making, however. As Robert Lake and I have argued, these processes actually constrain democratic participation. The channeling of resistance into interest group bargaining with respect to a particular site displaces an interrogation of basic policy assumptions, thereby fostering the perception of the state as a neutral arbiter among equal social groups. In this instance, publicity would be furthered by the proliferation of mobilized publics so as to enlarge the geographical arena of conflict beyond that of the purportedly general state versus partic-

One important difference between situated impartial plurality and liberal pluralism is that the latter is justified solely on its claim to being public where the former aspires to be both public and "power-charged." I take this second requirement from Donna Haraway's concept of "situated knowledges," which puts forth the ideal of "embodied objectivity," achieved not by ascending to a disinterested, abstract stance but by "critical positioning."[22] The strategy Haraway offers for critical positioning is conversation, ordinarily a conventional metaphor for liberal pluralism to which Haraway gives a socialist twist. Democratic theorists frequently invoke conversation to suggest a politics of egalitarian, noncoercive, deliberative interaction against the competitive bargaining of interest group liberalism.[23] Where the bargaining model defines politics in terms of conflict and economic interest, advocates of democratic conversation claim that political participation has a transformative effect on self-interested citizens, making them "more public-spirited, more tolerant, more knowledgeable, more attentive to the interests of others, and more probing of their own interests."[24] Although its proponents do not assume that conversation can do away with conflict altogether, the expectation of consensus does tend to suppress social (i.e., class, gender, ethnic) differences and, in turn, the power differentials that follow from them.[25] Haraway counters with a model of conversation that is a "power-charged social relation" that takes place *in the midst of* relations of inequality.[26] I suggest that under such conditions, a decision could still be public even if it did not treat all those affected by it equally, or even fairly. Under such conditions, the publicity would consist in spelling out

ularistic local interest and to raise the question of the state's structural imperative to legitimate capital accumulation. See Lake and Disch, "Structural Constraints."

22. Donna Haraway, "Situated Knowledges: The Science Question in Feminism and the Privilege of Partial Perspective," *Feminist Studies* 14 (1988): 581, 586.

23. See Barber's discussion of "strong democratic talk," *Strong Democracy*, chap. 8. See also the distinction between "adversary" and "unitary" democracy in Jane Mansbridge, *Beyond Adversary Democracy* (Chicago: University of Chicago Press, 1983).

24. Mark Warren, "Democratic Theory and Self-Transformation," *American Political Science Review* 86 (1992): 8–23, 8.

25. Mansbridge acknowledges this and argues that groups need to shift from consensual to adversarial decision mechanisms in the event of conflicting interests. Mansbridge, *Beyond Adversary Democracy*, 32–33.

26. Haraway, "Situated Knowledge," 593.

precisely how the decision empowers some at the cost of the disempowerment of others.

Something like situated impartiality is a point of connection between the work of feminist theorists such as Donna Haraway and political theorists who have argued that Archimedean thinking is incompatible with democratic politics. For example, Iris Young has suggested publicity as an answer to the problem of adjudicating conflicts in the absence "of a philosopher-king with access to transcendent normative verities."[27] Similarly, Benjamin Barber proposes "public choices" as a political alternative to philosophic truths and defines them as "choices informed by an extension of perspective and by the reformulation of private interests in the setting of potential public goals."[28] Barber's publicity, insofar as it requires "an extension of perspective," coincides with that aspect of situated impartiality I have borrowed from Arendt's visiting. But there is an inextricable moral dimension to Barber's formula in his insistence that a decision cannot be public unless it results in a "reformulation" of private interest. Public choices, for Barber, are necessarily civic-minded. In place of this moral dimension, I suggest that publicity can characterize a decision regardless of whether it promotes a general "public good." That is to say, it can be public even if it is not civic-minded, provided there is an institutional record of the positions it affirms and those it discounts.[29]

The conception of publicity I propose reconfigures what Iris Young calls the model of the "civic public."[30] As I define it, a public decision need satisfy only the procedural requirement I have adapted from Arendt's visiting: that there be some institutionally recognized account of

27. Young, *Justice*, 92.
28. Barber, *Strong Democracy*, 128.
29. I make this substitution not because I object to civic-mindedness but because I am persuaded by critics of liberalism in the United States who argue that given the country's vast economic, political, and social disparities, civic-mindedness is more often a facade that suppresses dissent than an egalitarian public principle. I do not mean to suggest that Barber does not recognize these disparities, or that he deploys civic-mindedness to function in this way.
30. Young argues that the civic public is an "Enlightenment ideal of the public realm of politics as attaining the universality of a general will that leaves difference, particularity, and the body behind in the private realms of family and civil society." Young, *Justice*, 97. This civic ideal rests, in turn, on the moral ideal of impartial reasoning.

the decision that makes explicit who has been included in a public and who has been excluded from it by a prevailing articulation of *inter-est*. This is a procedural means for concluding a decision on principle *without securing its inclusions and exclusions against questioning*. Defined in this way, publicity is necessary but in no way sufficient to democratic decision making—there is no guarantee that the principles that will inspire any particular collective to act will satisfy the Western liberal norms of equality and liberty. Although it is an unconventional attitude, treating publicity and democracy as *distinct* aspects of an action offers the possible advantage of sustaining openness even among those whose differences are irreconcilable. The debate remains open because there is no pretense that the inspiring principle of the action with which it concluded was either impartial or generally valid. Further, the refusal to cover over or discredit dissent accords a greater measure of respect to the dissenters than does a patronizing or self-aggrandizing gesture of inclusivity.

In short, "situated impartiality" is a conception of validity that underlies a process of public decision making in an adversarial public. Such a public must begin from the assumption that parties to most decisions are *not* equal with respect to social power, that they may *not* share a common cultural or normative framework, that no *single* decision can reconcile their differences. What accounts for the guarantee of impartiality in such a situation is twofold. First, practicing something like Arendt's "visiting" would be necessary to understand just how different are the concerns, interests, and understandings—the locations—of various parties to a dispute. Second, a public decision would not pretend to resolve these differences by claiming to represent a consensus or to articulate a general interest on which consensus could be reached in a hypothetical decision-making situation. Instead, it would make explicit how a particular decision *plays into* existing power relations. Situated impartiality requires that a decision-making process be held accountable not just to *perspectival* differences but also to *social* differences conditioned by ethnicity, class, gender, and so on.

I propose this conception of publicity to make a connection with what Hannah Arendt calls "partisanship for the world" (MDT, 8), which is her answer to the problem of the pillars that I raised at the outset of this chapter. She recommends that we not seek to restore these pillars or make souvenirs of the rubble but that we pick up the pieces, turn them in our hands, and tell stories about what we think they mean or might have meant to us. This kind of storytelling does not help us to sort the pieces, to categorize them, to determine what they really are. But it is an activity of value nonetheless, because it is talking that is

> concerned with the common world, which remains "inhu-man" in a very literal sense unless it is constantly talked about by human beings. For the world is not humane just because it is made by human beings, and it does not become human just because the human voice sounds in it, but only when it has become the object of discourse. However much we are affected by the things of the world, however deeply they may stir and stimulate us, they become human for us only when we can discuss them with our fellows. . . . We humanize what is going on in the world and in ourselves only by speaking of it, and in the course of speaking of it we learn to be human. (MDT, 25)

This image of a place where people are engaged in constant disputation over the import of worldly objects and events is in striking contrast to that of being "surrounded by an empty space" in Berlin, 1933.[31] Both images describe the relationship of the critical intellectual to the world. Whether describing the space emptied by German intellectuals who failed to denounce fascism, or the fragmented publics of the postwar era, the striking thing is that Arendt situates the critical intellectual in the world, not above it. Ultimately, Arendt's answer to the problem of the pillars is to fill the rubble pile with actors, opposed and allied, engaging in an explicitly partisan and comparative practice: "taking sides for the world's sake, understanding and judging everything in terms of its position in the world at any given time" (MDT, 7–8).

31. Young-Bruehl, *Hannah Arendt*, 108, cited in Chapter 1.

Index

■